How to Do Things Right

As comprising:

BOOK ONE
How to Do Some Particular
Things Particularly;
OR,
The Revelations of a Fussy Man

BOOK TWO
How to Retire at Forty-One;
OR,
*Life among the Routines and Pursuits
and Other Problems*

BOOK THREE
How to Be Good;
OR,
*The Somewhat Tricky Business of Attaining Moral
Virtue in a Society That's Not Just Corrupt but
Corrupting, Without Being Completely Out-of-It*

How to Do Things Right

THE REVELATIONS OF A FUSSY MAN

*Three incomparable books of wit, charm,
and wisdom finally available in one volume,
as revised, edited, and enhanced by the author*

L. Rust Hills

D·R·G

DAVID R. GODINE, PUBLISHER
Boston

First published in this form in 1993 by
DAVID R. GODINE, PUBLISHER, INC.
Horticultural Hall
300 Massachusetts Avenue
Boston, Massachusetts 02115

LIBRARY OF CONGRESS CATALOGING-IN-PUBLICATION DATA
Hills, L. Rust.
How to do things right : the memoirs of a fussy man : three
incomparable books of wit, charm, and wisdom finally available in
one volume / as revised, edited and enhanced by L. Rust Hills.
p.   cm.
Contents: How to do some particular things particularly — How to
retire at forty-one — How to be good.
1. Conduct of life.   2. Hills, L. Rust.   I. Hills, L. Rust. How
to do some particular things particularly.   II. Hills, L. Rust. How
to retire at forty-one.   III. Hills, L. Rust. How to be good.
IV. Title.
BJ1581.2.H548   1993   93-15086
170'.44—dc20   CIP

ISBN 0-87923-968-9 (HC)
ISBN 0-87923-969-7 (SC)

First printing
Printed in the United States of America

Contents

BOOK TWO

How to Retire at Forty-One
or,
Life Among the Routines and Pursuits and Other Problems

BOOK THREE

How to Be Good
or,
The Somewhat Tricky Business of Attaining Moral
Virtue in a Society That's Not Just Corrupt but Corrupting,
Without Being Completely Out-of-It

CHAPTER FIVE: *An Intricate Ethics*

✍ **Book One** ✍

How to Do Some Particular Things Particularly

OR,

The Revelations of a Fussy Man

"Nobody," ~~said reasonably,~~
He ~~whimpered,~~
"Could call me
A fussy man;
I *only* want
A little bit
Of butter for
My bread!"

—A. A. MILNE
"The King's Breakfast"

Two Introductory Revelations

IF YOU are interested in doing something right (for a change), my revelations will surely help you. You'll find all the answers here, no matter what questions are bothering you: whether it be how to save your marriage, what to do about America's industrial growth, how you can be absolutely certain your alarm will go off in the morning, or how to counteract the chaos and immorality of modern life. All the answers to such specific questions (and many, many more) are given on a step-by-step basis. And the principles by which you can solve virtually any other question are clearly set forth.

Now it may seem to some of you as you first get into this that the answers are harder than the questions, that the solutions in fact turn out to be far worse than the problems ever even thought of being. But that's because you don't yet understand the problems-and-solutions relationship. Anyone interested in doing something right, *really right,* is necessarily going to be much more intrigued by a problem than he is by a solution. If you are only interested in a so-lution—just any old simple solution—then the best thing to do is not even *think* about the problem. Most problems just go away—*poof!*—if you stop thinking about them.

Difference in degree of interest-in-the-problem creates the fun-damental division of all mankind: between those who believe in *get-ting things done,* on the one hand, and those who believe in *doing things right,* on the other. Most of the complex problems we've got in this country today are the result of slap-dash, "can-do" men at-tempting to solve once-simple problems in careless ways that left a mess, left vicious half-solved problems, like wounded lions, in all our streets. Simple solutions and easy ways seem very seductive, but when you go to repair something for the third or fourth time, you realize it would have been truly easier to have done the job carefully in the first place. "The right way is the hard way" sounds like an LCT (one of Life's Cruel Truths), but a reasonable man wouldn't have it otherwise. For the hard way to be the wrong way too would be completely unfair; it's bad enough the way it is.

Say the reporters are asking the press secretary about a specific problem. "Oh yes," he assures them, "we're doing something about that." What "something" means here is *any*thing, for the emphasis is really on the *doing;* and whatever it is they're doing will eventually shape their conception of what the problem was. The solution will determine the problem, instead of the right way around. How much better if the spokesman were to say: "We're becoming fascinated by that problem, as a matter of fact, and we're watching it develop so as to determine the steps necessary to solve it forever."

Problems have their pride, you know, as well as a strong sense of self-preservation, and they quite naturally resist yielding up their existence to an inferior solution. But when a problem is confronted with a solution that demonstrates full appreciation and entire comprehension—matches it intricacy for intricacy, complexity for complexity, even absurdity for absurdity—then it gives way utterly to this flattery and understanding.

Since the "perfect" solution to a problem, the *exact* match-up, is unlikely to occur to anyone, a certain amount of overkill in problem-solving is quite obviously necessary. Thus what I present in this book (proudly) is a sequence of apparently complicated solutions to apparently simple problems. The fact that they may not work either is completely irrelevant. It's *a whole new approach!* It shows that what we must do to make our problems succumb to us is first comprehend them, then appreciate them, and finally actually delight in them.

So, as my First Revelation, I say unto you, verily: Learn to *love* thy problems as thy self.

In a paranoid mood I feel that all these Revelations about How to Do Things Right were maybe sent to me as another of God's jokes, like the one He kept playing on Moses. You remember how He sent down the Ten Commandments and then made the Israelites keep forgetting them; then He'd get after Moses about it, and Moses would tighten the people up for a while; then they'd start forgetting again. The Commandments are pretty good rules, easy to understand; and ten is a nice round number, easy to remember. How come people can't do a few simple things like that, the way they ought to?

The answer, of course, is that human life is by nature chaotic and that any attempt to impose order on it is as absurd as Hitler's mustache. That's the *answer.* But as I've said, questions are far more intriguing than answers; the fun is in acting *as if* human problems could be solved.

The irony is, that within this admittedly essential wrongness that's implicit in any futility, we *are* right—God, Moses, and me. Things *would* be better if people did things right. The trouble is that the sloppy people just go ahead and get things done, in their half-assed way, then take strength from that and go on and do something else, while we careful people hang around deploring all the mess. I believe (and common sense demands you do too) that seven eighths of what's done nowadays (*eight* eighths in the case of some professions—developers, geneticists, etc.) is not just not worth doing but would be better off left *und*one. It's clear to me, therefore, that a careful person who may do very little, but does it right, stands in a State of Grace substantially higher than all those others who do a lot of things badly. But *they're* the ones who get to do it all! The poor tidy fellow who believes "No job is ever done until the tools are put away" keeps finding he has to clean up the workbench that someone else has left a mess, before he can even start. So he's standing there in his State of Grace, doing a slow burn.

Thus it cometh about that many fussy people are either pretty angry or very lonely, and sometimes both. It appears we are more cursed than blessed by our rage for order. An orderly person is usually either feared or laughed at. And since to be feared is surely the worst thing there is, I come to my Second Revelation: We must study harder to be laughed at.

❦

How to Eat an Ice-Cream Cone

BEFORE YOU even get the cone, you have to do a lot of planning about it. We'll assume that you lost the argument in the car and that the family has decided to break the automobile journey and stop at an ice-cream stand for cones. Get things straight with them right from the start. Tell them that there will be an imaginary circle six feet away from the car, and that no one—man, woman, or especially child—will be allowed to cross the line and reenter the car until his ice-cream cone has been entirely consumed and he has cleaned himself up. Emphasize: Automobiles and ice-cream cones don't mix. Explain: Melted ice cream, children, is a fluid that is eternally sticky. One drop of it on a car-door handle spreads to the seat covers, to trousers, and thence to hands, and then to the steering wheel, the gear shift, the rear-view mirror, all the knobs of the dashboard—spreads everywhere and lasts forever, spreads from a nice old car like this, which might have to be abandoned because of stickiness, right into a nasty new car, in secret ways that even scientists don't understand. If necessary, even make a joke: "The family that eats ice-cream cones together, sticks together." Then let their mother explain the joke and tell them you don't mean half of what you say, and no, we won't be getting a new car.

Blessed are the children who always eat the same flavor of ice cream or always know beforehand what kind they will want. Such good children should be quarantined from those who say "I want to wait and see what flavors there are." It's hard to just listen, while a beautiful young child who has always been perfectly happy with a plain vanilla ice-cream cone is subverted by a young schoolmate who has been invited along for the weekend, a pleasant and polite child, perhaps, but spoiled by permissive parents and flawed by an overactive imagination. This schoolmate has a flair for contingency planning: "Well, I'll have banana, if they have banana, but if they don't have banana, then I'll have peach, if it's fresh peach, and if they don't have banana or fresh peach, I'll see what else they have that's like that, like maybe fresh strawberry or something, and if they don't have that or anything like that that's good, I'll just have chocolate marshmallow chip or chocolate ripple or something like that." Then—turning to one's own once simple and innocent child, now already corrupt and thinking fast—the schoolmate invites a similar rigmarole: "What kind are *you* going to have?"

I'm a great believer in contingency planning. But none of this is realistic. Few adults, and even fewer children, are able to make up their mind beforehand what kind of ice-cream cone they'll want. It would be nice if they could be all lined up in front of the man who's making up the cones and just snap smartly, when their turn came, "Strawberry, please," "Vanilla, please," "Chocolate, please." But of course it never happens like that. There is always a great discussion, a great jostling and craning of necks and leaning over the counter to see down into the tubs of ice cream, and much consultation—

"What kind are *you* having?"—back and forth, as if that should make any difference.

Humans are incorrigibly restless and dissatisfied, always in search of new experiences and sensations, seldom content with the familiar. It is this, I think, that accounts for others wanting to have a taste of your cone, and wanting you to have a taste of theirs. "Do have a taste of this fresh peach, it's delicious," my wife used to say to me, very much (I suppose) the way Eve wanted Adam to taste her delicious apple. An insinuating look of calculating curiosity would film my wife's eyes—the same look those beautiful, scary women in those depraved Italian films give a man they're interested in. "How's *yours?*" she would say. For this reason, I always order chocolate chip now. Down through the years, all those close enough to me to feel entitled to ask for a taste of my cone—namely wife and children— have learned what chocolate chip tastes like, so they have no legitimate reason to ask me for a taste. As for tasting other people's cones, never do it. The reasoning here is that if it tastes good, you'll wish you'd had it; if it tastes bad, you'll have had a taste of something that tastes bad; if it doesn't taste either good or bad, then you won't have missed anything. Of course no person in his right mind ever *would* want to taste anyone else's cone, but it is useful to have good, logical reasons for hating the thought of it.

Another important thing. Never let the man hand you the cones of others. Make him hand each one to each kid individually. That way you won't get disconcerting tastes of butter pecan and black raspberry on your own chocolate chip. And insist that he tell you how much it all costs and settle with him *before* he hands you your own cone. Make sure everyone has got paper napkins and everything *before* he hands you your own cone. Get *everything* straight before he hands you your own cone.

Then, when the moment finally comes, reach out and take it from him. Strange, magical, *dangerous* moment! Consider what it is that you are about to be handed: It is a huge irregular mass of ice cream, faintly domed at the top from the metal scoop that dug it out and then insecurely perched it on the uneven top edge of a hollow inverted cone made out of the most brittle and fragile of materials. Clumps of ice cream hang over the side, very loosely attached to the main body. There is always much more ice cream than the cone could hold, even if the ice cream were tamped down into the cone,

7 ≈

which of course it isn't. And the essence of ice cream is that it melts. It doesn't just stay there teetering in this irregular, top-heavy mass, it also *melts*. And it melts fast. And it doesn't just melt, it melts into a stickiness that cannot be wiped off. The only thing one person could hand to another that might possibly be more dangerous is a live hand grenade on which the pin had been pulled five seconds earlier. And of course if anybody offered you that, you could say, "Oh. Uh, well—no thanks."

Ice-cream men handle cones routinely, and are inured. They are like professionals who are used to handling sticks of TNT, their movements quick and skillful. An ice-cream man may attempt to pass a cone to you casually, almost carelessly. Never accept a cone on this basis! Keep your hand at your side, overcoming the instinct by which everyone's hand goes out—almost automatically—whenever he is proffered something delicious and expected. The ice-cream man will look up at you, startled, questioning. Lock his eyes with your own, and *then,* slowly, calmly, and above all, deliberately, take the cone from him.

Grasp the cone firmly but gently between thumb and forefinger, two thirds of the way up. Then dart swiftly away to an open area, away from the jostling crowd at the stand. Then take up the classic ice-cream-cone-eating stance: feet from one to two feet apart, body bent forward from the waist at a twenty-five-degree angle, right elbow well up, right forearm horizontal, at a level with your collarbone and about twelve inches from it. But don't start eating yet! Check first to see what emergency repairs may be necessary.

Immediate action is sometimes needed on three fronts at once. Frequently the ice cream will be mounted on the cone in a way that is perilously lopsided. This requires immediate corrective action to move it back into balance—a slight pressure downward with the teeth and lips to seat the ice cream more firmly in and on the cone—but not so hard, of course, as to break the cone. On other occasions, gobs of ice cream will be hanging loosely from the main body, about to fall to the ground (bad) or onto one's hand (far, far worse). This requires instant action too: snapping at the gobs with the split-second timing of a frog in a swarm of flies. But sometimes trickles of ice cream will already (already!) be running down the cone toward one's fingers, and one must quickly raise the cone, tilting one's face skyward, and lick with an upward motion to push the trickles away from the fingers and (as much as possible) into the mouth.

Which to do first? Every ice-cream cone is like every other ice-cream cone in that it has the potential to present all three problems, but each ice-cream cone is paradoxically unique in that it will present the problems in a different order of emergency, and hence require a different order of solutions. And it is (thank God!) an unusual ice-cream cone that will present all three problems in *exactly* the same degree of emergency. It is necessary to make an instantaneous judgment as to which of the basic three emergencies—lopsided mount, dangling gobs, already running trickles—presents the most immediate danger and then *act!* Otherwise the whole thing will be a mess before you've even tasted it.

In trying to make wise and correct decisions about the ice-cream cone in your hand, you should always try to keep your ultimate objective in mind. The first objective is to get the cone under control. Secondarily, one will want to eat the cone calmly and with pleasure. Real pleasure, of course, lies not simply in enjoying the taste of the ice-cream cone, but in eating it *right*, which is where the ultimate objective comes in.

Let us assume that you have darted to your open space and made your necessary emergency repairs. The cone is still dangerous, of course—still, so to speak, "live." But you can now proceed with it in an orderly fashion. First revolve the cone through the full 360 degrees, turning the cone by moving the thumb away from you and the forefinger toward you, so the cone moves counterclockwise. Snap at the loose gobs of ice cream as you do this. Then, with the cone still "wound," which will require the wrist to be bent at the full right angle toward you, apply pressure with the mouth and tongue to accomplish overall realignment, straightening and settling the whole mess. Then, unwinding the cone back through the full 360 degrees, remove any trickles of ice cream. Now, have a look at the cone. Some supplementary repairs may be necessary, but the cone is now defused.

At this point, you can risk a glance around you to see how badly the others are doing with their cones. Then, shaking your head with good-natured contempt for the mess they're making, you can settle down to eating yours. This is done by eating the ice cream off the top, at each bite pressing down cautiously, so that the ice cream settles farther and farther into the cone, being very careful not to break the cone.

If these procedures are followed correctly, you should shortly arrive at the ideal, your ultimate objective, the way an ice-cream cone is always pictured as being, but never actually is when it is handed to you. The ice cream should now form a small dome whose large circumference exactly coincides with the large circumference of the cone itself: a small skullcap that fits exactly on top of a larger, inverted dunce cap.

Like the artist, who makes order out of chaos, you have taken an unnatural, abhorrent, irregular, chaotic form like this: and from it you have sculpted an ordered, ideal shape that might be envied by Praxiteles or even Euclid:

Now at last you can begin to take little nibbles of the cone itself, being very careful not to crack it. Revolve the cone so that its rim remains level as it descends, while you eat both ice cream and cone. Because it is in the geometrical nature of things, the inverted cone shape, as you keep nibbling the top off it, still remains a cone *shape;* and because you are constantly reforming with your tongue the little dome of ice cream on top, it follows in logic—and in actual practice, if you are skillful and careful—that as you eat the cone on down it continues to look exactly the same, so that at the very end you will hold between your thumb and forefinger a tiny, idealized replica of an ice-cream cone, a harmless thing perhaps an inch high.

Then, while the others are licking their sticky fingers, preparatory to wiping them on their clothes, or going back to the ice-cream stand for more paper napkins to try to clean themselves up—*then* you can hold the miniature cone up for everyone to see, and pop it gently into your mouth.

❦

How to Be Kindly

A FUSSY MAN is at a disadvantage in his family not because of his vices, but because of his virtues. Kindliness is generally reckoned to be the foremost familial virtue, and it seems to be in some sort of psychological-philosophical conflict with fussiness. Occasionally in literature you'll find some figure who combines the two—I think of Aunt Betsy Trotwell in *David Copperfield* and what's her name, Aunt Sally or Aunt Polly, in *Huck Finn*—but I suppose it scarcely needs pointing out that each of these is an *aunt*, not the man of the house, and their kindliness is concealed anyway under what used to be known as "a gruff exterior," something no one goes for these days.

Sloppiness and kindliness, however, seem to go hand-in-hand, to have one of those awful "natural" affinities, like sloth and melancholy. Your tidiness, they'll tell you, is just a manifestation of your hostility toward others. But if we take an orderly approach to this matter, I think we can out-fox them.

We will assume, to begin with, that there are two kinds of kindliness: innate and acquired. And thus there are two ways to be kindly: naturally kindly and—uh—the opposite. Now it is clear that the second kind of kindliness is far superior to the first kind. There is very little credit in being innately kindly: if that's just the way you are, it wouldn't be *right* for you to get any credit for it. But a person who *forces* himself to be kindly deserves all the credit in the world. A new, learned, acquired virtue is always far shinier and better than a dull old natural one.

The first step toward becoming kindly is to *appear* kindly. You should smile sweetly a lot, more or less all the time, but especially when the children spill or anything like that. Practice your sweet smile when you're alone, in the bathroom mirror, say; and if you're sure you're alone, practice saying soothing and reassuring things like "There, there," or "Oh, don't worry about *that*," or "That's *per*fectly all right," or "How could you help it? It certainly wasn't *your* fault!" Actually, I suppose it might not be a bad idea to leave the bathroom door slightly ajar, so the family can overhear you practicing saying kind things like these—that way they'll realize how hard you're trying to be able to put up with the things they do.

What's important is to learn to say kind things so they sound really natural. If, when your dinner comes to the table, you are going to try to say something enthusiastic like, "What have I done to deserve this!?" then you've got to get the tone and emphasis exactly right or you'll be misunderstood. Apparently that's where a lot of being kindly is, in the inflection rather than the words. They tell me, for instance, that saying "How could *you* help it?" actually has something of an *un*kindly tone. At any rate, you have to be constantly on guard: people, children especially, are always on the alert for any note of sarcasm in your voice. You know how suspicious children always are.

Everyone knows that the way you act sooner or later becomes the way you are. If you *act* kindly long enough, surely you'll really *become* kindly. Those I love tell me it's harder than that, but I'm convinced that it can be done. Besides, even if you can't actually manage to become kindly, people may sort of let down their guard and begin thinking of you that way. Then when you *do* get angry, they feel they've done something so terrible that they've made even kindly-you lose your temper; then they feel awful about it, and you've got them where you want them.

❦

How to Organize a Family Picnic (and Keep It That Way)

Power and the Picnic

GUESTS USUALLY have a better time at a family picnic than anyone else – they have few expectations about how it should all be, no ideas of their own to get thwarted, no burdensome sense of responsibility for the picnic's success or failure. What appears to be the power vacuum of the chaotic family picnic is in fact usually the opposite: not lack of leadership, but too much; not too few leaders, but the inability of a single one to assume control. Many members of the family have their own ideas about how the picnic should be run – sometimes it seems all of them do. And because it's a family that's involved, not an army or a business or anything like that, there's no way to establish discipline, and you can't fire them or demote them. They're all family members and feel they have their rights. They're all in a position to dispute your decisions every step of the way – *every step of the way*, from whether or not to take a particular beach blanket in the first place, to whereabouts on the beach is the best place to put it down. Since there's no such thing as unquestioned leadership on a family picnic, if you do become the organizer you'll have the pleasure (or the consolation) of knowing that your leadership qualities are being supremely tested, forged in the white-hot furnace of family contention, tempered by the easygoing way you have to act.

You will also have to go on most all the picnics yourself. "We couldn't *do* it without you," they may say after a while. This sense of your own indispensability will be one of your few rewards.

So if you can, then you must. If you have the necessary skills as dietician, auto packer, boatsman, games organizer, diplomat, weather forecaster, and so on, then you owe it to your family to take on this task, as men who run for the presidency are recognizing their obligation to the nation. Take *absolute* control, if you can. Remember this—although it may sound totalitarian to you—that the more you can keep the others in the role of guests, the more likely they are to enjoy the picnic.

The Prepare Committee

I sometimes dream of a bureaucratic solution to the picnic problem—a special committee for Picnic Recruiting, Exhorting, Provisioning, Authorizing, Regulating, and Expediting—the PREPARE Committee, I call it in my imagination. It is a sort of Planning and Operations Board comprised of the more sensible and effective members of the family without regard to their actual age and rank, or even their niceness. This informal committee, because of its absolute efficiency, would gradually gain absolute control of all aspects of family picnic planning, cutting across all the normal lines of authority and control. One member of the committee would be in charge of coordinating Provisions; another for coordinating Transportation; another could be on Communications and Scheduling; and so on. Because they had all the information, everyone would have to come to them for decisions. All such questions as "What can *we* bring?" and "Will you have room for the three of us in the sailboat?" and "When and where shall we meet you?" would thus be referred to the appropriate PREPARE Committee member for an immediate and accurate answer.

All of this is daydreaming, of course. No one would want to be on the PREPARE Committee if all it meant were a lot of draggy work; and if it turned out for some reason to have any power or to be fun, every member of the family would want some role in it, which would put you back where you started.

One has to be more realistic: the best ideas are the ones you have to abandon first, if you're working with people.

Six Trusty Serving Men

Unfortunately, instead of the PREPARE Committee, you have only your Six Trusty Serving Men to help you organize your happy family picnic. You remember them, I'm sure, from your happy childhood:

> I have six trusty serving men;
> They taught me all I knew.
> Their names are *what* and *why* and *when*
> And *where* and *how* and *who*.

They'll help you decide who will come on your family picnic, where to go, how to get there, what to take, when to go and come back, and maybe even shed some light on why you're going.

Why

The point of a family picnic is that you're doing this thing *together*. More and more nowadays the generations are separated; the urbanization, bureaucratization, and industrialization of America are destroying the family as a value-providing institution; everyone goes his separate way; it is an *atomized* society we live in. The point of a family picnic is to bring the family together to have a picnic together.

Who

The rationale of the family picnic thus determines the personnel of the family picnic: in theory, everyone has to come, or else be made to feel slightly guilty about not going. All the generations must be there, too. It's only in television advertisements for soft drinks and beer that all the people at a picnic are the same age. God never yet made a family where everyone was the same age.

A picnic would be really kind of pointless without the littlest kind of children to watch playing in the sand and worry about. A picnic needs adolescents to raise the achievement level in touch football and so one can worry about them swimming out too far. It needs middle-aged people to overexert so people can worry about that. And it needs older people to do most of the worrying, although they can be worried about too, by the others. Worrying about others is an important aspect of the happy family picnic.

Where

A family picnic, you know, is not just a backyard barbecue—you have to *go* somewhere, and not just to someone else's backyard; that's just an outdoor party. Every family has at least two places they picnic more or less regularly, one near and one far—and the farther one is always better. If there are more than two places, then the best one is always farthest away of them all. This appears to be one of Life's Cruel Truths, but it really can be more easily understood: for no family in its right mind would travel *farther* to picnic in a *worse* place, and especially not farth*est* to picnic in *the* worst place. A happy family picnic will seldom if ever go anyplace new—the hazards are too great, the expectations too varied. Tried and true places are the best, even if people are a bit sick of them. Tradition and continuity are also important aspects of the family picnic.

How

As to "how to go," this is arguable mainly on the basis of who gets to go in which car or boat with whom. For many young children this may represent their first experience with DCG—the Dyscohesion of Companionable Groups. A child will often complain about the car or boat he's assigned to, saying he'd rather be in one of the other ones with his cousins rather than his siblings, or with his siblings rather than his cousins, or whatever. What's required here is a simple matter of education: the child has just not lived long enough to understand how things are. Explain to him that this *is* one of Life's Cruel Truths—that *no one* ever wants to ride with the people he has to ride with; the fun people are *always* in the other boat. That's in the nature of things, tell him, an LCT. When you get older and get to go to dinner parties, child, the people you want to talk with are always seated at the other end of the table, where all the laughing is. One of the main reasons we *have* family picnics, child, is so that you can learn about life. Education of the young in the ways of adults is a prime aspect of family picnics.

The "TF," or Transferral Factor

"How to go" also provides the Transferral Factor, which is a major determinant, in turn, of "what to take." Often one of your picnickers will want to bring along something "extra." Don't let a child persuade you with the line, "I promise I'll carry it myself"; make it clear to him that if he's carrying *that*, then he won't be able to carry something that's necessary. Point out that the act of taking this one other thing seems easy now, but it must be multiplied by the Transferral Factor. The TF varies from picnic to picnic, depending on how you go. It can perhaps be as low as four: taking whatever it is from the house to the car, *one*; from the car to the picnic, *two*; from the picnic back to the car, *three*; from the car back into the house, *four*. But a TF of four is the absolute minimum. In some cases the TF can be quite frightening. If it's a question of transferring all the stuff from the house to the car to a dock to a dinghy, and from the dinghy into a big boat, then from the big boat back into the dinghy and from the dinghy to the landing place, then carrying it all to the picnic site— plus doing it all back the other way—you get a TF of fourteen.

And with a TF that high, you must be very stern about the "what."

What

While everybody knows that a lot has to be taken on a family picnic, few realize just *what* a lot. I've often wanted to mimeograph up a Family Picnic Comprehensive Master Checklist to make sure nothing would be forgotten, but I know something would be forgotten anyway. Just to begin with, there are Frisbees, beach balls, footballs, whiffle balls (and whiffle bats); snorkels, flippers, and masks; huge hats, for the shade; sweaters for all, in case it gets chilly; slickers, in case of rain or spray; a change of clothing for the children on the way home; a different bottle or tube of a different brand or kind of suntan lotion for each and every family tanner; mustard; sneakers or flip-flops for the hot sand; shovels and pails for the littlest; bathing suits and bathing caps, of course; rubber rafts and surfboards and truck-tire inner tubes; beach mats, beach towels, beach chairs, beach umbrellas, beach blankets, beach bags, and L.L. Bean carryalls; something to read; sunglasses; life jackets for the safety of the little ones and life jackets for all for the sake of the Coast Guard; knives and forks and spoons and paper cups and paper plates; charcoal, hibachi, and charcoal-lighter fluid, or else wood, kindling, and newspaper, for the beaches are picked clean of driftwood by midsummer; and matches; also lots of cigarettes, enough for the people who forget to bring an extra pack; a bottle opener; combs; and lots and lots of other stuff I've forgotten. For instance, I think I've forgotten the food. And I've also forgotten—perhaps deliberately but it would be disaster if we didn't bring it—the most cumbersome thing of all, the most recent inevitability of the family picnic: a giant styrofoam chest, light in itself, but heavy beyond credence with ice and slopping water and beer and soda pop, with a shifty center of gravity and a double handle excruciating after six steps on the sand. Even the gone-but-not-forgotten (and certainly-not-lamented) Scotch Cooler seems lighter than this in memory.

When

Planning a family picnic a week or so in advance is good for the anticipation of the event, so that family members won't make other plans, but it is bad because one can never be sure what the weather will be. Ideally you should have such an avid family picnic organizational cadre set up that no advance planning would be necessary. "It looks like a beautiful day . . . ," you ought to be able to say in a certain alerting tone at breakfast. There's a sudden, dramatic hush at the table; everyone looks at you expectantly, hopefully. "So, let's go on a picnic," you say, releasing the tension with a smile. Instantly they go into action: one person leaps to phone the prearranged list of family picnic members; two others are off in the car to the grocery store with the preprepared shopping list; others as preassigned, put on the hard-boiled eggs, do the breakfast dishes, get out the ice, pack the always-ready fried chicken from the freezer, get out the baskets and blankets and so on; the whole family swinging into motion like a well-oiled machine. You should be ready to leave within an hour if you want, two at the most; but the decision still has to be made as to exactly when.

Establishing the ETD

Before you can decide what time to go on a picnic, you need to know what time you want to get back home. The secret of good planning is looking ahead and then calculating backward. Say you want to be home at 4:45 P.M. You know it takes fifteen minutes to put everything away when you get home, half an hour to get back from the picnic place, and another fifteen minutes to pick up all the stuff at the picnic place and pack it neatly for the return journey—a total of one hour. So you want to leave the picnic place for home at 3:45 P.M. Suppose you want two hours to have your picnic and enjoy it or whatever you plan to do with it. Thus you should arrive at the picnic place at 1:45. That's your ETA. To find your Estimated Time of Departure, subtract forty-five more minutes (how long it takes you to get from home to the picnic place and get unpacked). Thus ETD is 1 P.M., or 1300 hours. And if anyone objects that thirteen hundred is just when you ought to have lunch, make it clear that it's all been worked out scientifically and stop eggbeating.

The Countdown

For an ETD of 1300, you'll want to begin your countdown at noon. Call out loudly to the whole household: "Sixty minutes to ETD." For the first half hour call out the time remaining in five-minute intervals: "Fifty-five minutes to ETD," "Fifty minutes," and so on. For the first twenty-five minutes of the remaining half hour, call it out each each minute: "Thirty minutes to ETD," "Twenty-nine minutes to ETD," and so on, down to "Five minutes to ETD."

For most of the second half hour, probably, and certainly for what follows, it is best to get a child to hold the watch and do the calling, as loudly and enthusiastically as possible. These final moments should be scary for everyone—leader and led alike. The leader has planned well: he knows the picnic preparers and packers are not as likely to turn on the child as on himself. But there's always the possibility of revolt at this key moment, or—even worse—the workers may just ignore the countdown. So if he sees they're pretty far behind, the leader may adjust the countdown to the situation, telling the child to put it on hold for a few minutes. "E T D minus three minutes and *holding!*" shouts the child every once in a while. Then, for the last few minutes, down to one-minute-to-go, the child should call out every five seconds: "Two minutes and fifty-five seconds remaining to E T D!" "Two minutes and *fifty* seconds!" and so on, down to "*One minute to* E T D!" This should be the really scary moment. From this point on, the child simply calls out the seconds remaining.

At the beginning of this final phase of the countdown, or perhaps a bit earlier if it is getting too tense in the house, one takes one's position behind the steering wheel of the car, getting ready to start sounding the horn at the moment for blastoff. Meanwhile, the child follows the others around the kitchen or wherever they are, packing and preparing things as fast as they can. It certainly should speed them up to have a child shouting: "Twenty-eight seconds," "Twenty-seven seconds," and so on.

Final Moments

At the car, you are checking over what is being brought out of the house to go on the picnic: trying to tell what's been forgotten; trying to see if too much is being bought, in violation of the proscriptions of the Transferral Factor.

It is often in these final moments that your family-picnic leadership qualities are most crucially tried. You will learn now whether the training and discipline you've established will hold up under this climactic pressure, whether your methods of preparation and organization are going to pay off.

That's because it's a good idea at this point, if you're truly devoted to organizational efficiency and if you've got the outstanding leadership qualities required for this exercise, to take the family through an operational dry run. After everything has been packed, and the whole family is sitting there in the car all ready and waiting to go on the picnic, get them all to get out of the car again, *as if* they had arrived at the picnic place, each of them taking that which is assigned to him to carry, so as to demonstrate to you that they can indeed handle in one load, one "trip," everything that needs to be transferred. If there is anything left over that they are not able to manage, patiently repeat the ten or fourteen stages of the Transferral Factor to them, and engage them in a calm discussion as to what part of the excess they as a group feel is least necessary to the happiness of the picnic. This is the time to use the democratic approach. The overload should then be returned to the house before departing and put carefully back where it belongs, preferably by the individual family member who was responsible for bringing it out in the first place.

This additional procedure may perhaps delay a specific departure or two until it is established as routine. It may at first be necessary to follow the faulted family members into the house and spend valuable moments persuading them that they really do want to go on the picnic, that it will be fine when we get there, that it wouldn't be any fun without them, and so on. This shouldn't be necessary, but people are funny. They want someone to organize a family picnic for them, but then they don't want it *kept* that way.

How to Set an Alarm Clock

IF YOU think it's such a simple thing to set an alarm clock, then how come your alarm clock doesn't always go off?

A psychoanalyst would tell you it's because you don't want to get up—but I have a better explanation.

Imagine a plaza in the shape of a five-pointed star. Five men are to meet there early one morning, to go fishing or something, and they all arrive late, but simultaneously. Hurrying together in the middle, they all say apologetically in one breath (they are all out of breath): "My *alarm* didn't go off!"

"I forgot to set the clock to the right time," says man number one.

"I forgot to set when it should go off," says number two.

"I forgot to wind the clock itself," says number three.

"I forgot to wind the alarm part," says number four.

"I forgot to pull out the little knob," says number five.

They all look at one another in amazement: there are *five* things to remember when setting an alarm clock!

It's a wonder anyone's alarm clock ever goes off at all! Things are really always much more complicated than we think, even the simplest things. It isn't that we make them complicated; they *are* complicated.

Just remember the magic number "five" whenever you have to set an alarm clock. Most people, once they know there are five things to do, can figure out what the five things are—and it doesn't much matter what order they're done in. Just remember there are five things to do, and do them. Then check them, if you want. Say to yourself, "Now there were five things to do, have I done them?" Check them each over in your mind to make sure you've done them. Then look to see that each of the five has been done. Watch out that in handling the clock so much you don't inadvertently push in the little knob—the supercareful are always vulnerable to Life's Little Ironies. Check the knob, and then you'd better check the other four things again. It's nice to be certain, of course, and it hardly seems possible to check an alarm clock too many times; but don't stay up too late doing this if you have to be up early. Go to sleep secure in the knowledge that with system and care the complications of life *can* be mastered, and that your alarm will probably go off in the morning.

However . . . However, it is *modern* life we have to contend with. You don't get progress without problems, you know. The whole thrust of technology is to make conveniences more convenient, and these new conveniences can't always be solved in the old ways. You get the old alarm clock problem solved, and then they invent new, *more* convenient alarm clocks. First, the electric alarm clock. Second, the kind of alarm clock where when you wind the clock, you are winding the alarm at the same time.

It would seem the easiest solution to these new conveniences simply to avoid them, but it's getting harder and harder to buy an old-fashioned alarm clock. I saw an ad in *The New Yorker*—

The Clock That Turns Back
The Clock to *1910*

Pure Americana. The classic 1910 Big Ben alarm clock, handcrafted in a working, nickel-plated edition. Best gift idea of the last half century for collectors, connoisseurs and con-firmed nostalgia buffs. A limited edition, at leading stores. $40.

Forty dollars?!—they used to cost a buck. Only the very rich can afford to deny progress. The rest of us have to accommodate to innovation, which means trying to outwit it.

And this isn't simply a matter of adjusting our old systems. It's not really a system anyway when you have to remember that while on an old-fashioned alarm clock there are indeed five things to do, there are on an electric clock only three—

1. Set the time;
2. Set when it's to go off;
3. Pull out the little knob—

and on the double-wind kind there are four things to do—

1, 2, 3, as above;
4. Wind the combined time and alarm.

A magic number is no longer a magic number when sometimes it's five, sometimes four, and sometimes three. The magic's gone right out of it.

What's needed to outwit innovation is what created it in the first place: imagination. You've got to *imagine* that you're doing all five of the magic things.

With the electric alarm clock, here's how you do it. You first set the time, *one*. If the time is already correct, as it almost always is with an electric clock, you can move the hands all the way through the twelve-hour cycle so that you feel as if you set it; or, if this seems self-indulgent to you, you can wiggle the minute hand back and forth five minutes or so each way, and then leave it set correctly. Next you set the alarm, *two*. Then you first imagine yourself winding the clock, *three*. Then you imagine yourself winding the alarm, *four*. If it helps, you can say to yourself, as you're sitting on the side of the bed, holding the clock in your hands, looking at the face of it, listening to it hum, "Now I'm winding the time part, *three;* now I'm winding the alarm part, *four*." Then you pull out the little knob, *five*. Then you check it over, of course: "Did I remember to imagine I was winding the time? Did I remember to imagine I was winding the alarm?" and so on. Try to think of it tick-tocking coldly and mechanically as you do this; try to ignore the lifelike purring and unnaturally *warm* feeling an electric clock always has.

With the double-wind kind of alarm clock, where there is only one of those floppy little keys in the back, one which winds both the time and the alarm, the problem is a little more difficult. I bought one of these by mistake–thinking I was lucky to find a non-electric–and how wrong I was! It nearly beat me, as you'll soon see. You could do the same kind of imaginary winding that you do with the electric, but that's not terribly sensible, is it? The plain fact is, the clock actually does need winding–and imagining you're winding it as you actually *are* winding it must be ruled out as a solution. Similarly, you can't say to yourself as you're doing the necessary winding, "Now I'm winding the alarm part, *three*," and then expect yourself to turn around and just sit there holding the clock, *not* winding it, and say to yourself, "Now I'm *imagining* I'm winding the time part, *four*." Both these solutions abuse the imagination rather than use it.

Far better, clearly far more logical and more sensible, is to wind the little floppy key *halfway* tight, for *three*, and then wind it the *rest* of the way, for *four*. But this system can be used only after you've had some experience handling your clock, for there is this very great hazard in it: that you may through some bad chance wind it up tight on *three* and then not have enough wind left in it to wind for *four*.

You follow what I'm saying, don't you? You see what this danger is? All the drama of what follows depends on your understanding how it could come about and what it would mean to wind the wretched thing tight on *three* (the alarm part) and have nothing left to wind for *four* (the time part).

I admit I got quite upset when that happened to me. My wife said I went into a rage, but then she's always thinking I'm going into a rage. Actually, as I tried to tell her, it was more sorrow, or despair, that I felt, not anger at all. When I recovered, I sat on the edge of the bed thinking of all the great inventors of the world who have brought us all these nasty conveniences, and of how they had beaten me. Thomas Edison, Alexander Graham Bell, Whosit Marconi, Robert Bruce, and all the rest–men of fantastic ingenuity, energy, and imagination. How could I have thought to match my solutions to their conveniences–me with my puny mind? I had stupidly wound the bloody wretched thing tight on *three*, now had no wind left for *four*. What could I do? What would they have done, faced with failure? They would have started all over again!

That's when the solution came to me: the alarm part of the clock and the time part of the clock, I deduced, must both be on the same spring if you use just one key to wind both! Immediately I set about verifying my intuition experimentally. I set the alarm for just a moment or two ahead of what time it was now, and then waited. A scary moment or two it was, too, sitting there with the thing right in my hands, waiting for it to go off. Fear of the unexpected, the thrill of the imminence of the hitherto unknown—I was experiencing all the excitement of the innovators, the explorers, and the inventors, but I was still right where I wanted to be, sitting on my own bed, working against them.

It seemed a lifetime until it finally happened, and when it did, the alarm sounded enormously loud and urgent. My wife, who had started to go back to sleep, jumped a mile, then groaned in amazement when she saw what I was doing. Nevertheless, I let the alarm run down, which took a long time because it had to unwind the time part too, of course. Then I started all over again. This time when I wound it back up I counted the number of turns of the floppy winding key—nine, it was—then made the necessary calculations, to divide nine by two, in my head. Then I set the clock to go off in a minute or two again, and waited again. It was not nearly so scary for me this time, but apparently even more disturbing to my wife. Then I let the alarm run all the way down again. Then I reset the time and the alarm, and—relishing the moment—I carefully wound the floppy key four and a half times for the alarm part. "*Three,*" I whispered, then saw she was awake watching me, and I might as well have spoken out loud. Finally, I wound the floppy key four and a half more times for the time part, pleased that I felt it wind up tight. "*Four!*" I cried in triumph.

Then I went to sleep, certain that everything was as it ought to be, with the clock at least. And my satisfaction with this achievement was so great that it scarcely bothered me when I discovered, late the next morning, that I'd forgotten to pull out the little knob, *five.*

❦

How to Make and Eat Milk Toast

I won't attempt to disguise the fact that milk toast is simply toast— buttered, sprinkled with sugar, eaten with warmed milk in a bowl. Admittedly, milk toast is an undeceptively simple dish; but, as is true of all Life's Activities (with no exception I can think of), it is important that a thing be done *right* for full enjoyment to occur.

You will need the following: a table and chair, a small cereal bowl, a matching plate to go underneath it (this is needed, no matter how informal you want to be—I'll explain it later), a soup spoon, a thin-necked milk jug, a saucepan, a stove, perhaps a toaster (more about toasting in a minute), a napkin (a paper napkin will do, but a cloth one is a pleasure in itself), a sugar bowl and sugar spoon, and (of course) sugar, milk, bread, and butter.

The slices of bread should be toasted (three slices are required, for just the right amount of milk toast). I myself do not favor a pop-up toaster: it fails to dry the bread sufficiently, because the heat is applied simultaneously on both sides. Also, it reduces the challenge and difficulty involved in *getting things right,* since the toaster works automatically on a timer principle, or a temperature principle, or however it is supposed to work, and doesn't, not very well anyway. Instead, consider using the broiler of your stove, which will toast bread nicely—especially an electric stove, which applies a very even heat. Here you get to watch the toast constantly, bending or squatting if necessary to peer into the broiler, or perhaps drawing up a kitchen chair to be comfortable. Besides requiring that you turn the toast over, the broiler has the added advantage of doing three pieces of toast at once, which few toasters are able to do. Incidentally, if you *are* using the toaster, do the single slice of bread first, as there will then be only one to cool off while the other two are toasting. Not a thing many people think of, but a helpful hint nevertheless; and when it comes to milk toast, one doesn't get as much helpful advice as has become customary in other areas of life—investment consulting, marriage counseling, and so on. Up to now, making milk toast has been pretty much a you-do-it-on-your-own matter.

For instance, no one ever tells you not to ever butter the toast ahead of time, although to my knowledge prebuttered toast is seen only in the coffeeshops of out-of-town hotels. Spread the butter carefully, on just one piece of toast at a time; then put it on the cereal bowl, resting it on the rim so that the four corners stick out evenly over the round edge.

Now, carefully remove the lid from the sugar bowl, placing it to one side, and then lift out from three quarters of a teaspoon to a level teaspoonful of sugar. Do not under any circumstances take out a rounded or (God forbid!) heaping teaspoonful, as some grains are bound to spill on the trip from the sugar bowl to the milk toast bowl, no matter how careful one is. Heaping teaspoonfuls are an anathema anyway! It is repugnant to imagine the sort of impatient mentality that conceived of the heaping teaspoonful in the first place.

A piece of toast may be considered, for all useful intents and purposes, square. The rounded, "upper" edge can be left out of consideration, really—although I cannot deny myself the indulgence of mentioning that I myself find it nice to have the piece of toast arranged on the bowl so that the rounded edge is away from me—just as I like to have the pointed part of a piece of pie facing toward me. It's very satisfying to arrange the toast that way, perhaps even using two hands, and then lean back and contemplate it.

One mustn't enjoy anticipation for too long, for meanwhile the milk is cooling. The problem now is to sprinkle the sugar onto the piece of toast *evenly*. Certainly no one wants all the sugar to be in the middle of his piece of milk toast, with little or none at all on the crusty corners. And yet, how difficult it is to get it right! When you go to sprinkle the corners, some of the sugar is bound to tumble over the sides and even outside the bowl. It is for this reason that there must be a plate under the bowl. (I mentioned earlier that I would give the reason!)

But plate or no plate, the sprinkling of the sugar is a difficult business. To do it, one rapidly agitates the spoon from side to side, causing the grains to fly off onto whatever is being sprinkled. What a risk, and so unlike the fastidious care involved in spreading. (In fact, sprinkling and spreading are at the opposite poles of human behavior.)

Of course, instead of sprinkling the sugar on the toast, one *could* place it there carefully, tilting the spoon and edging it off. I find this has the practical disadvantage of getting too much sugar on the toast, and the emotional disadvantage of making the tilter look a bit obsessed in the eyes of his family. It's not really proper for children to have to watch while their father, a wild gleam in his eye, fusses to get the sugar grains exactly right on his milk toast.

But few sights in this world can be so pleasing as a piece of toast sitting on the bowl, evenly sprinkled with sugar, all waiting and ready to receive warm milk. The milk should be heated carefully in a saucepan on the stove until it is as hot as it can be without boiling. It is hard to know just how much milk to prepare for three slices of toast. Depending on my mood, I heat as little as seven eighths of a cupful or as much as a cupful and one eighth. Somewhere in there is just right.

At any rate, the heated milk should be carefully poured from the saucepan into a thin-necked jug or pitcher that has been preheated with hot water to take the chill off it. This jug or pitcher is thin-necked so as to expose only a small area of the milk to the cooling air. Also – and this is perhaps the single nasty thing about milk toast – there is a scum that sometimes forms on hot milk. It's perhaps just as well to speak of it as little as possible. Suffice to say that the thinner-necked the jug is, the less surface there will be for this unpleasant layer to form on.

Pouring the milk onto the toast is as perilous as sprinkling on the sugar. It is not as difficult, but the consequences of careless action are much more dire. Sprinkle the sugar carelessly and you have a few grains of displaced sugar. Pour the milk too abruptly, and it bounces off the toast and over the side of the bowl and you've got a puddle of milk in the plate or (God forbid) on the table. Should this ever happen, I suppose that what one would do is take the whole mess to the kitchen sink and start all over again – for by the time you'd wiped everything up, the original piece of toast would be too soggy to eat. Perhaps you'd decide to have something else to eat. Or go out. Fortunately, I've never experienced this, although I suppose I will someday. I think about it every time I lift the milk jug to pour.

A gentle tipping of the pitcher, and we will be ready to eat our milk toast. After about a third of the pitcher's contents have been poured on, the toast will soften in the middle and sink slowly into the bowl.

Milk toast should be eaten with great relish, otherwise there isn't much point in it. With the edge of the soup spoon, cut pieces out of the middle, trying to get an equal amount of butter and sugar on each spoonful of milk and toast you eat. The four crusts should curl up somewhat out of the milk, so they will remain crisp longest and should be eaten last. When that piece of toast is finished, the milk in the bowl should be finished too, so that all will be fresh and in readiness for the next piece of toast. With a little experience this can be easily managed, and by the time the third piece is eaten, the pitcher should be dry.

Easy, isn't it? As I made clear at the very outset, making and eating milk toast is one of the simplest things in the world to do. Compare it with some other of Life's Activities—making oyster stew, for instance, or preparing for a family picnic, or arranging a liaison. Everything is monstrously complicated these days, *except for milk toast.* Indeed, it is milk toast's very simplicity that makes it so attractive; it is one of the few things that can be done really right.

From time to time, though, my enjoyment in milk toast is a bit soured by the realization that it is such a solitary pleasure. Sometimes in my imagination I am part of a huge farm-family all eating milk toast at once. I envision a long toast rack that runs the whole length of the table, and three sugar bowls (to minimize passing), and a giant milk jug within the reach of each person. How jolly it would be! An old-fashioned family, all carefully eating milk toast together, and no one spilling!

How to Tip

TIPPING IS troublesome for many of us Americans for a lot of good reasons—worthy reasons, worthy-of-*us* reasons. Tipping seems to belong to an old-world, out-of-date, class-conscious society that we as a nation long ago said we didn't want any part of. It seems a noblesse oblige sort of an act that doesn't come naturally, because most of us don't consider ourselves noblesse enough to *be* obliged. We tend to believe that a person should be paid a day's pay for a day's work and not have to touch his cap or kowtow to anyone.

We're not comfortable with the idea of others' cleaning up after us, fetching and carrying our stuff. We're independent, self-reliant, and proud of it. And when we ourselves are helpful to others, we certainly don't expect to be *tipped* for it.

And yet, when this total stranger comes up to you at the check-in desk in the hotel lobby—a pimply sourball of a young man, say, or some grouchy, stooped-over older guy wearing some kind of not-quite-military uniform—and he takes your key and stacks your bags, your briefcase, even the stuff you *wanted* to carry yourself, onto one of those wheeled luggage racks and guides you up to your room, grumbling away to himself about God knows what, when you get to the room, you don't just say, "Hey, well, *thanks;* nice of you to show me up here, to give me a hand with the bags and all. I'll do the same for you sometime when *you* come to *my* city." Instead you have to tip him. It's how he makes his money. It's "expected." It doesn't *feel* right, but it's the right thing to do. It's one of those rare cases where what *is* right *feels* wrong. And there's a lot about tipping that's like that.

For instance, overtipping is one of those self-created problems that probably wouldn't be a problem at all if you didn't worry about it yourself. Who cares, after all, if you overtip? Not the cabdrivers, waiters, captains, bellboys on the receiving end—that's for sure. Five or ten dollars held discreetly in your palm when you shake hands with the captain (not the owner, for God's sake!) as you leave, fifty cents extra rounding off the fare for a cabby, all done here and there and now and then as you move through life—spreads the sunshine, so to speak, and it's fine with everyone, if you can afford it.

Undertipping is a bit more of a problem—also self-created, but in a different way. It does seem awful sometimes how expensive cab fares and hotel rooms and, especially, good restaurants have gotten to be. A hundred bucks for lunch!? And then to have to add *another* twenty bucks for a tip?! It adds heartsickness to heartburn. But it's part of the essence of an expensive restaurant that one tips generously. After all, tipping isn't done on an ability-to-pay basis, and you've got to come across properly or else feel chintzy.

It's true that bad service can turn an occasion that's meant to be a jovial, celebratory indulgence into a nightmare. Hunger makes even the most even-tempered of us irritable, but it isn't only the preprandial irascibility that causes the trouble; it's also the resentment that comes from feeling you're not getting what you're paying for. If it's implied as part of the unwritten contract that you'll give a good tip for the service, then it should also be part of the deal that the service is good. If you feel they've broken their part of the contract, you're going to break yours and stiff the waiter.

There are two problems with this plan. One is that when you finally get the meal and eat it, you begin to feel better, the service usually improves, and the waiter may be full of apologies. So you relent and tip him anyway, and then you feel you haven't stood by your convictions. The other problem with stiffing is that slow service is very seldom just the waiter's fault. Who knows what all the trouble was—too many people came in at once, the kitchen was slow, who knows—almost any waiter would rather give prompt service than have the customers waving and snarling at him.

Since tips are scarcely ever withheld in restaurants, even for bad service, there's a basic formula that isn't deviated from all that much. Fifteen percent is average for an average meal out. For the kind of service that enhances a meal, in an establishment that's really doing its stuff right, you'd go the full 20 percent, plus maybe some extra bucks to the captain with thanks and compliments and congratulations to the owner for making all this possible.

But, remember, however "right" any system might be, and however right it might *feel*, there's no "justice" in any rule of tipping. Tipping usually comes after the fact, so it can't affect the occasion: you're not going to sharpen up all the waiters or cabdrivers across the country; you're not going to impose any universal value system for service. On the other hand, any system you can arrange in your own life ought to be encouraged, and long ago I decided on a system of dividing the bill by six and leaving that amount as a tip, rounding it off one way or the other, as circumstances indicate, to make it come out even mathematically. I do this more or less everywhere. It comes out to 16.66666 percent, and no one falls all over me with gratitude for it—but I can live with that. At least I don't have to pass judgment on the conduct of my fellowman every time I take a cab or eat a meal out.

How to Wash and Wax Your Car

I'M ENTIRELY in sympathy, but not agreement, with those who feel that all that's involved in properly washing and waxing a car is beginning with the rear left fender. Would that life were so simple! But it's not. One has to proceed by careful steps.

It's not until Step Five—not until then, and only then—that you begin to wash the car, beginning with the exact middle of the top and working down. This is so that dirty water won't run down onto parts you've already washed. Always use a counterclockwise motion, clockwise being for clocks, not cars.

Step Four is to procure the necessary equipment and personnel.

You really must have water and wax if you're going to wash and wax your car properly. As well as the garden hose, you need a sponge or chamois and perhaps a bucket of soapy water. Simply wetting your car will make it look shiny, but it isn't clean: you'd see when it dried. You need old khakis and sneakers you don't mind getting wet. Plus you need at least one kid, to watch and to want to help and to run to turn the hose on and off, and a dog to run back and forth with the kid.

Step Three is to make sure it's Saturday morning (the generally approved time slot for this activity), which is not always as easy as it seems. Failing that, you need a baseball game on the car radio which is really hard to do at certain times of the year. (Tapes of games don't count, and if that's the way your mind works, you don't deserve to wash your car.)

Step One and Step Two are the most difficult of all. Step One is to make sure your car is dirty. Step Two is to feel like washing your car. Seldom do Step One and Step Two go together. You can't wash your car properly if you don't feel like doing it. Washing and waxing the family car is one of those great American activities, like celebrating the Fourth of July, and you can't really celebrate anything satisfactorily without enjoying it. If all you want is a clean car, drive down to Johnny's Car Wash and run her through. Nor can you properly wash your car unless it's dirty. If all you want to do is waste your time, you shouldn't involve your automobile in your restlessness. A car that's washed all the time when it doesn't need it gets very nervous, and rightly so.

❦

How to Give a Dinner Party

EVERYBODY DOES everything wrong nowadays. Even if it's just a simple matter of getting together for dinner with a couple of other couples, they do it all wrong, meeting for some perverse reason at a restaurant, where they get bad service from rude waiters and have to shout at one another over the chatter of diners at adjoining tables. Dinner for a party of six in a restaurant, with drinks and dessert, costs a fortune; and no matter how the bill is finally settled up (an awkward business at best), everyone feels he's gotten gypped—including, probably, the waiter. It's far more civilized to invite friends to dine with you at home, providing good food and wine, and good talk, in a quiet and intimate setting.

There don't, however, seem to be all that many dinner parties anymore. What did away with the *big* dinner party in this country was the end of the servant class; what did away with the small dinner party was the end of the wife class. Now it's almost as if people have forgotten *how* to give a dinner party.

Fortunately, one of us here has a long memory and can give you step-by-step guidance on how to bring back the dinner party—single-handed, if need be. Somebody's got to get this particularly gracious social ball rolling again, and it might as well be you. If Herself is dubious about launching into all that's entailed, tell her you'll do the whole thing yourself, and all she has to do is simply attend—as a specially welcome guest. She can scarcely object to that.

Set an actual date for your dinner party, so that you'll be committed to doing it and can't back out. But make it far enough ahead so the people you want will be available, and do the inviting by phone so you can adjust to the couples' schedules as necessary. Start out with dinner for six—two couples plus the host and hostess. One of the couples can be old friends of yours if you want, but both shouldn't be: A dinner party should be just slightly formal, with people on their best behavior, making something of an effort to be charming and interesting. With nothing but old friends, the comfortable familiarity breeds a certain amount of boredom, and everybody lets down; some, not me, might say it's like the difference between a date and marriage. But don't, on the other hand, invite some stand-up, fantastically fascinating person who will dominate the evening. The successful dinner party is an ensemble event, not a role for a star. See Figure One.

The main dish should be something you can prepare in the morning, say, or the day before, and then just put into the oven, timed to be done at serving time, or else something that improves with reheating. I'm not talking about canned-tuna-and-packaged-noodle casserole with crushed cornflakes on top (that was another cause of the death of the old dinner party), but rather something that's good, or at least fairly good. Get a French cookbook and read around in it, then make maybe some sort of small, modified cassoulet or a

FIGURE ONE : INCONGRUOUS GUEST ASSEMBLY
(NOTE: One guest should not dominate.)

pot-au-feu or a *boeuf Bourguignon*. Certain things you should *not* have: for instance, don't have steaks or chops or anything broiled, or anything sautéed or fried either; they all smoke up the kitchen and have to be done at the last minute, when you want to be out having drinks with your guests, the picture of cool and calm, enjoying yourself.

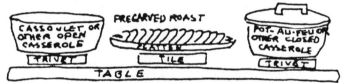

FIGURE TWO: THREE SUITABLE MAIN DISHES
(NOTE: Do not serve more than one per dinner.)

Unless you feel you can handle it easily, I wouldn't bother with any first course. Most so-called appetizers are really appetite deadeners. And even salad, whether served before the main dish (California style) or after (French style), may be more distracting than it's worth. Instead, put your energy into some good homemade dessert, like a fruit pie or a cobbler or some sort of pudding. Look up desserts—try an American cookbook this time—for an old favorite; the more nurserylike the dessert, the more your guests will appreciate that it's not store bought.

So read the recipes, make out a menu, make a list of all that's needed. Don't count on anything being on hand. Go out and do the shopping; don't forget the list. Get two loaves of the best French bread you can find, get some unsalted butter to spread on it, and get some good red wine (never white for a dinner party, except outdoors for a seafood supper in the summer, maybe).

The dining area doesn't too much matter; it's the lighting that counts. At a dinner party, all you want to see is the table and the other faces. The dining room, the terrace garden, the view of the ocean, or whatever, should become part of the background.

Candlelight is the traditional way of creating this desired effect, but it has to be done right. If it's done wrong, guests are always trying to look around the candles to see one another. The trouble is the height of the candles. Kindly refer to Figure Three.

FIGURE THREE: Candlelight shown at wrong height interrupting guests' views of one another's eyes.

The candlelight either has to be higher — very long candles in very tall holders. Or the candlelight must be lower — stubby candles that reflect a light somewhat upward, and that people can look over, to see one another's reactions as they say all those astonishing things they'll be saying at your party.

You know how to set the table, I'm sure: napkin and forks to the left of the plate, napkin on the outside, then forks as you'd use them for various courses, from the outside on in; knives and spoons on the right, knives inside, cutting edge facing in toward the plate; wineglass on the right, directly above the tip of the knife; butter plate or salad plate, if you want to bother with them, go on the left in roughly the same position. Kindly refer to Figure Four.

It's pleasant and reassuring for the guests to find the table all set and ready when they arrive; it's also one more thing that doesn't have to be done later. Your table should look nice—not fussy or fancy, but handsome, like a well-appointed restaurant table. A tablecloth, if you've got one, adds to the festive appearance, but just go bare-table otherwise; doilies and place mats are tacky at dinner.

The secret to making this all go smoothly, so that you don't look like a total idiot racing around, is to have as much as possible ready beforehand. For instance, make up a dessert tray way ahead: dessert plates with forks or spoons, and your pie or whatever; coffee cups and saucers and spoons and a sugar bowl and a small pitcher of milk. Have the coffee maker all ready, so you can just switch it on later. Uncork the wine, to let it breathe and to have it all ready: for six people, three bottles, one for each end of the table and one for the sideboard. Set out half of a quarter-pound stick of butter for each end of the table, and a loaf of bread for each end. Salt and pepper shakers for each end. There should be no need for passing anything, once the food itself is on the plates. Guests should be able to just reach out for what they want, without interrupting the flow of fascinating conversation with requests for this or that.

Serve drinks before dinner, away from the eating table. Have an ice bucket, or ordinary bowl, full of ice, with glasses ready, and try to have on hand the beverage each of your guests prefers. Have a bottle of white wine open in the ice bucket, in case someone wants an aperitif instead of whiskey. People who ask for a soft drink are usually willing to have either the club soda you have on hand for the Scotch and bourbon drinkers or the quinine you have for the gin and vodka types.

FIGURE FIVE : PRESENTING DRINKS
(NOTE: To avoid bread balls, do not let drinks run on too long.)

If people arrive on time and/or more or less at the same time, drinks shouldn't go on forever. You're all set to serve dinner at any time. Another thing that killed the old dinner-party scene, besides tuna-fish casserole and the women's movement, was the way the hostesses—because in those days young wives were either inept, re-sentful, or fun-loving (or all three)—delayed putting out the food for three or four hours, until all the guests were so smashed they later thought they'd had a memorable evening, even though they couldn't remember a thing about it—except, faintly, throwing bread balls. Well, those days are gone. Your party will be far more refined. Now-adays two drinks before dinner is considered enough.

So, now seat your guests properly. None of this "Oh-just-sit-wherever-you-want" stuff. A dinner party is a completely nonsexist affair, but you should nevertheless seat sexes separately to keep two men from talking to each other about something that interests them but not the other guests. The same with women, sadly, for sometimes they seem interested in things men aren't, although it's hard to imag-ine what they could be.

You sit at the end of the table that is closest to the kitchen, for all the getting up you'll be doing. Herself sits at the other end, with a gentleman on either side, arranged so that the couples do not sit side by side. Diagrammatically, as shown in Figure Six.

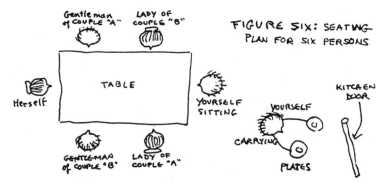

FIGURE SIX: SEATING PLAN FOR SIX PERSONS

(NOTE: An eight-person dinner party presents an entirely different dynamic—for instance, it is far more difficult to maintain a general conversation—and you can let couples sit together if they want to; but if the men and women are still to be alternated, you have to have the same sex at each end.)

Bring the food to the table, instigate the passing and serving of it, pour the wine (never fill a wineglass more than half full) for the ladies at your end, and encourage one of the gentlemen at the other end to do the honors there. If you feel like it, raise your glass in a little toast, even if it's just what I call the Jake Barnes toast ("To absent members").

There may be some well-brought-ups among your guests who remember not to eat until the hostess has picked up her fork, so tell Herself there's only this one thing you expect her to do, and that's to start eating so everyone else can begin—watch your tone of voice as you say it, of course.

As people commence eating, you can begin to direct the conversation. It's not that you want to dominate it—nothing like that—and it's not even that you want to control it; it's just that you're taking responsibility for it, the way you've taking responsibility for everything else at your dinner party. You're making sure that your guests don't get uncomfortably lodged on some inconsequential point of difference, or bogged in silly wordplay, or stuck in individual talk.

Lead the party as a group to discuss some interesting or consequential or amusing matter. Introduce, in turn, a subject that you know each of your guests has expertise in or special information about. Be sure not to let anyone run on too long. Try to lighten the tone if anyone begins to get angry; the days of shouting and pounding the dinner table went out with the Vietnam War. These skills are what hostesses were considered brilliant for in the old days, and it's how they created those famous salons. And remember, no bread balls.

When the main course is over, don't let anyone get up to help you clear the table. Any helper in the kitchen will only distract you. If people start getting up from the table, the whole closed-circle sense of the party will be spoiled. Tell your guests that, and say you won't let them get up, even to go to the bathroom. And don't let them scrape and stack the plates at the table; that looks awful and calls attention to whatever guests might not have finished. You don't want anyone to have to apologize for not eating your food.

When the table's cleared, set out the third bottle of wine and move the dessert tray over to the table. It would be permissible, I guess, to ask one of your lady guests to dish out the dessert for you, and the other one to pour out the coffee. But why not do it yourself? You've come this far alone, you might as well go all the way.

After dessert and coffee, allow the dinner party to dissolve as it will. Let people pour their own extra glass of wine, creating their own headaches; don't *you* do it. No liqueurs, no after-dinner highballs.

Presumably everyone will make noises about wanting to help clean up in the kitchen, but don't let them do it. You don't want to have to clean up anyone else's kitchen in future reciprocity.

A modern gentleman knows how to load his dishwasher better than anyone else, and he is very reluctant to trust the job to another. When everything's cleaned up, push the "energy saver" and "pots and pans" buttons so you can listen to the gentle scrubbing and whooshing sounds the machine makes as you fall off to sleep—not only exhausted from the work and a little dizzy from the wine but also actually quite pleasantly well fed; thanks to no one but yourself, of course, but still.

Perhaps Herself will wake up as you come to bed. "That was fun," she says. "Let's do it again."

This is a good time to take advantage. "Maybe you'll do it next time?" you say. If she does, and the other couples do the same, you have at least five dinner parties to go to before it's your turn again. Five pleasant evenings in which, through the magic of role reversal, you will go from being harried host to honored guest. And now after all this, don't tell me you're too tired to go out and be a charming guest, you just want to stay home and watch television; that's another thing that did away with the dinner party.

Number of chairs you will need for a six-person dinner party. Plus a table, of course.

How to Refold a Road Map

THIS IS quintessentially something that must be done right, or 'tis better never to have done it at all. Don't let careless people refold your road maps! A carelessly refolded road map bulges, assumes a nonconformist height and/or width. Also, it fails to show forthrightly what it's a map of—e.g., Idaho—because its cover is buried in there somewhere in the false folds. It's better to let the road maps accumulate unfolded in the backseat until you can get around to refolding them yourself.

Then, when the right time comes—usually when the journey's almost over, when you're all nearly there—then, pull over into a roadside rest area, one that has picnic tables. Take the accumulated unrefolded road maps from the car and spread them carefully on the picnic table. Smooth them out. Study each map carefully to determine the folding intentions of the original manufacturer.

In their continuing quest for the ultimate, best way to fold a road map, the manufacturers have evolved a variety of interim methods: a sort of vertical accordion pleat, the horizontal accordion pleat, combinations of both these with conventional half fold and double fold, and so on. I'm sure they have a technical nomenclature for their methods. But before the map was even printed, they knew how it was going to be folded! These men know what they're doing! You have simply got to respect their professionalism in this area and refold your road map exactly as it was originally folded.

You may have to inspect the road map carefully to determine which is the original crease. Use a flashlight at the picnic table, if necessary, if it's getting late and the family is gathered around you, watching anxiously. Don't hurry. Be careful. Explain it all to the young ones—the theory, the practice, the inevitability of the second fold after the first fold, the beauty of the conception.

Then, with a neat, flat stack of perfectly refolded matching road maps and a sense that for once at last you've measured up to another's expectations of you, you can continue complacently to your journey's end.

How to Cut Down on Smoking and Drinking Quite So Much

THE TROUBLE with most advice you get about smoking and drinking is that it comes from the wrong people. It's people who have somehow managed to quit smoking entirely who are only too willing to tell you how they did it and how you ought to too. It's the alcoholics who couldn't handle booze at all who are always trying to tell you you have to give it up entirely. Their solution is worse than your problem. You don't want to *stop* smoking and drinking, you just want to stop smoking and drinking *so much.*

Cutting down is a good idea, then, because it's the best way of assuring that you won't have to stop. No drinker wants to have to give up drinking. And smokers feel the same way. Lung cancer is a terrible thing (my father died of it), and early death from emphysema or heart trouble doesn't sound too good either, but a life without cigarettes for your average smoker would appear to be the way the unexamined life was for the Greeks: not worth living.

Some smokers say the only reason to *eat* is how good a cigarette tastes afterward. People who drink can't imagine having a cup of coffee without a cigarette. Life is (I have been known to say) a Three-Legged Stool, supported by Booze, Coffee, and Smokes, which interdepend essentially. Kick away any leg of the stool and the whole old corpus comes crashing to the kitchen floor.

One good thing about drinking (besides how it makes you feel) is that it is legal and socially acceptable more or less everywhere. In this, it is just about unique—except for sex, which is different—among all the euphoria-producing things, but there's an underestimated aspect to smoking, too, one that's very singular in this dislocated modern society where we're all made restless and anxious by a lot of hidden desires and aimless longings. Longing for a cigarette is one of the least aimless longings there is. Cigarettes create their own recognizable desire *and* the means of fulfilling it.

Several years ago I was bitten three times by two wasps (different pairs of them, of course) about six months apart, each time with a fantastically worse reaction. The third time I nearly died. I thought I'd had a heart attack. Coming finally out of the anaphylactic shock or whatever it's called—believe me, it's like coming back from the dead—well, *coming* back from the dead, the first thing I wanted was my sense of humor back and when I saw I'd got that the next thing I wanted, the *first* thing I wanted after I saw I was alive, was a cigarette. Dr. Haliday, who had rushed over to give me the adrenaline shot that brought me back (since gone to the grave himself), had given up smoking about six months before, but he breathed a great sigh and had a cigarette with me. Some people, if they died of *lung cancer* and then somehow managed to come back to life, what they'd want first is a cigarette.

They couldn't imagine taking a break in their work—for coffee or just for a rest—if they couldn't have a cigarette. There's no point in stopping at all, no point in even *doing* a job, much less doing it *right*, unless when you're through you can reward yourself with a cigarette.

But the "reward" idea is one of our main troubles with smoking and drinking. When the work's going well you think you "deserve" to smoke as much as you want. After a long hard day of good work at the office you deserve to unwind with a few drinks. After a long hard week, you feel you deserve to get drunk on Friday night. All that's true: you *do* deserve it. But ultimately so much self-rewarding becomes self-punishing. Feeling lousy all weekend is the reward you get for your hard week's work. It doesn't seem fair, I know; and if I were God I'd make it that people would never get hangovers unless they didn't deserve to get drunk. I would do that for you, but I can't.

It also may be that you drink and smoke so much because you like it: you like the feeling that a drink, or a lot of drinks, gives you; and while you may not exactly *like* the feeling a cigarette gives you, you sure as hell *don't* like the feeling you get when you haven't had one for an hour or two; also, you may actually like the taste of tobacco and liquor. But the real reason you drink and smoke so much is that you still have the idea, formed somewhere way back when, that smoking and drinking too much is really a very romantic thing to do. It seems very grown-up to you if you are young, and it seems very youthful to you if you are old.

In his autobiography, Lincoln Steffens describes his romance with drinking:

> Once, for example, as I staggered (a little more than I had to) away from the bar, I overheard one man say to another: "Those boys can carry some liquor, can't they?"
>
> That was great. But better still was the other loafer's reply: "Yes," he said, "but it's tough to see young men setting out on the downgrade to hell that way."

The romantic idea that one has a brilliant future somehow being ruined by drinking is natural to a college sophomore, but it ought to be abandoned in maturity. The trouble is it remains in the subconscious, sneakily invidious, so that even the ugly hangover becomes glamorous. When I was young and seldom got hangovers, or not bad ones, I'd often pretend to be in a very bad way "the morning after." It made for a lot of companionable talk in college about "the hair of the dog" and getting "a quick one." Drugs—which come complete with that great language about "turning on" and "highs" and "freaking out" and "coming down" and so on—must seem equivalently dangerous and romantic. Years and years later, when stupid pride in a hangover was replaced by sensible shame on a number of occasions, when for various reasons I tried to conceal how my hands were trembling, I remember even then having that invidious secret sense of how romantic it was that I was in such a bad way and actually trying to conceal it.

It's in our earliest, most impressionable youth that we learn how romantic it is to be dissolute. I remember how we used to hang around Lou Berry's stationery store in Williston Park endlessly discussing Wilbur Slaymacher, a stunted unattractive kid we all admired because all he ever had for breakfast was a Coke and a coffin nail. Once you have come to the realization that Wilbur Slaymacher, "setting out on the downgrade to hell that way," as Lincoln Steffens puts it, despite the key fact that there was nothing else to recommend him at all, is nevertheless *a genuinely romantic figure*, once you grasp that, in late childhood or early adolescence, it is something (a lesson learned, or something) that you never ever get over. It is with you the rest of your life, this misconception.

Oh, let me tell you this example of how romantic smoking and drinking can seem to be. When I came home from Europe determined to straighten myself out, I went to *Esquire* looking for a job, and there in this big Madison Avenue office were Frederick A. Birmingham, The Editor, and Leonard Wallace Robinson, The Managing Editor, and they were talking dirty and kidding around with Imie Camelli, The Secretary, and were real slick and smooth, but easy about it somehow; and then FAB said he had an eleven-thirty appointment with his dentist and then a lunch date with George Frazier or Leslie Saalberg or someone elegant like that, and he and Len got to joking about how when you had a martini after having novocaine you could only feel one side of the glass and when you ate the olive you could only taste half of it. It doesn't seem very funny now, but God did it seem marvelous then. I had no job, no apartment, dwindling money, my father was dying of you-know-what and my mother was a real problem, there was a heat wave, I had poison ivy, terrible athlete's foot, bleeding gums from trenchmouth, had just gotten divorced, and for the first (and probably last) time in my life I thought New York City was great. Maybe it was the idea of an expense-account lunch. But I think what seemed so romantic and great was having to have your martinis at lunch even though your mouth was shot full of novocaine.

It's no use trying to point out the horrors of smoking, even to young people today. All you do is contribute to the creation of more Wilbur Slaymacher figures. Danger is romantic, and at that age sickness and death seem very far away. The more horrible the facts and statistics that come out about smoking, the more attractive it seems to be to a certain kind of normal irrational adolescent mentality—that is, most of the kids and virtually all of the adults I know.

One of the ways to cut down is to work a kind of jujitsu on this crazy secret conviction. Get it in your mind that cutting down is really *just* as romantic. Instead of confessing (really boasting) about how much you drink and smoke, confess-boast about how much you *used* to drink and smoke. "Boy, I *had* to cut down," you can say. "I was slowly killing myself."

The actual methods you use to cut down aren't as important as getting your mind right about it. The basic idea is that you limit yourself in certain specific arbitrary ways. You can set a limit on how many you'll smoke each day—say ten or fifteen or even thirty—and count them out each morning into the elegant silver case you got from your grandfather or a junk store.

The system gets thrown off when someone disastrously bums a cigarette from you, but then there's joy when someone offers you one of his, an extra you don't have to count.

A scheme that worked awhile for me was writing down a *reason* for every cigarette I had: "work break," "before lunch," "after lunch," "need to reconsider what done so far," and so on. When I found myself writing down ten reasons *in advance* one afternoon so that I could just go ahead and smoke whenever I wanted, I gave the system up.

All these systems eventually break down: that may be in the nature of using system as a process of personal reform. You're interested in the system for a while; then you get impatient with it. The thing to do then is switch to another. I'll admit a system isn't much of a *system* when you're switching from one to another all the time. But it's what you have to do, all you *can* do.

I had one hell of a system once for cutting down on drinking so much. I was sharing a big summer house with a lot of city people, and I came to realize I'd been getting bombed every night. I was there all the time; the others would come up just weekends or on their vacations. Anyway, I devised this incredibly clever system: the idea was, I'd plan ahead just exactly what I would do drinking-wise for each and every day of a four-day cycle. On what became known as A First Day, I wouldn't drink at all—nothing, not a single drink. This was to prove I wasn't an alcoholic and could do without it. On the next day, A Second Day, I would have one drink before dinner and one drink after dinner—that's all, no more, no matter how often they told me I was a no-fun person. This was to prove I could drink abstemiously, if that isn't a contradiction in terms. On A Third Day, I'd allow myself to drink what I called "moderately." This was to prove I could drink moderately. And on A Fourth Day, it was allout, anything goes, as much as I wanted. This was to prove I was still a fun person. Then it would be A First Day again. And so on.

Well, the system really did sort of work for a while, but there were difficulties with it, as I guess you must have imagined there would be. On A First Day, after A Fourth Day debauch, is of course just when you need a drink most, at least one drink, if not just one drink before dinner then at least one drink just before bed. On A First Day I'd be irascible all day and go to bed early and not be able to sleep. A Second Day was all right, nothing to get excited about, but the way sensible people live regularly, I guess. A Third Day was always a problem, because my idea of "moderately" kept changing as the evening wore on. A Fourth Day, of course, was just the normal disaster.

One of the main problems of the system was the four-day cycle when everyone else was more or less on a seven-day week. I can't for the life of me now remember how I decided on four days or why on earth I didn't change when I saw it wasn't working. If my Fourth Day were to come, say, on the others' Tuesday, there wouldn't be anyone to drink with me; it was awful having A Fourth Day go to waste like that. Then, others couldn't keep track of what day mine was. They'd prolong the cocktail hour unconscionably on A Second Day that happened to be their Friday night. Or I'd be moderately having a couple of drinks on A Third Day, maybe weaving a little as I told a long-winded story, maybe making myself one more at the same time, and I'd overhear one of the householders ask another, "Say, is this A Fourth Day, or what?"

Toward the end, I began switching my days around to accommodate, like a good householder, so *my* good days would coincide with *their* good days. Thus on A Second Day Saturday night, I'd decide during cocktails to have my Second Day tomorrow and my Third Day today; then later in the evening I'd decide to make today my Fourth Day and have my Third Day tomorrow and have my Second Day after that. But things tended to get confused, and of course the First and Second Days got kind of lost, and pretty soon every day was A Fourth Day again. It's really hard to organize systems when you're sharing with others.

But good planning is still really the central secret in cutting down. Good planning features (or *would* feature, if one could ever work things out right) each cigarette and each drink as a pleasant event occurring routinely in the course of a well-ordered day. You would have your first cigarette with your second cup of coffee after you've finished your breakfast. You would have your second when you took your coffee break. Then if you take a glass of sherry before lunch you have another cigarette then. And so on, through a prescheduled, *ordered* day.

So there should be a sense of occasion for having your drinks. I don't for heaven's sake mean a party or anything like that. There's nothing worse than a party for making you forget you're having your drink! No, I mean like a particular time of day to have it, or them. If you're only having two or three you'll want to make them good big strong ones with some punch to them, so you'll *know* you're having them. Nice brown drinks. Certainly you'll want one, or two, before dinner. Maybe you'll want one before lunch, or a glass of wine with lunch (counts one half); and maybe you like to take a nice scotch on the rocks upstairs to bed with you? That's fine, as long as it's not a TUD—although for some, the TUD is the best drink of the day. "TUD" is an acronym for that Totally Unnecessary Drink, the so-called nightcap, as used in fond phrasing like this: "I think I'll just make this last little Tuddy to take up with me to Lily White's party."

A good way of creating a proper sense of occasion about drinks is to have a different kind of drink for each of the different occasions. I mean, if you go through life never having anything but Johnnie Walker Red Label and water, the only difference between your drinks is the time of day you have them. My parents always had, every night before dinner, either a martini or a manhattan. "Which did we have last night?" one of them would say, and then, "Well, let's have the other, then," or "Oh, let's have it again tonight anyway." A manhattan is a much underrated drink: it *is* kind of sticky and you certainly wouldn't want it every night or even every other night; but it is a cheerful drink, and if it is cold and bleak (the weather, I mean) and you wish you had an open fire, a manhattan is good, perhaps because the cherry in it has some of the same bright warm color. Martinis give you a headache, as everyone knows; but made in a good expensive restaurant there is nothing like them.

Anyway, my theory is that if you enjoy each of your drinks you won't want so many of them. What gets you drunk is thinking that subsequent drinks are going to pick you up the way the first one did, but of course it doesn't work that way.

Drinking to a schedule presents some of the same hazards and delights as smoking a definite, limited number of cigarettes each day. You have to get everything all set and ready so that you realize both that you're having your drink and also that you're appreciating it. Sometimes you forget, or get busy doing something else, or you're talking with somebody and you forget you're having your drink, and you just drink it down, and then you've drunk it and didn't even realize you were having it, much less appreciate it, and that makes you feel as if you'd been cheated out of it, so you want to have another right away to make up for it, and that's bad.

It may really be that routines, schedules, systems, and the general imposition of order on one's self and one's life are ultimately no match for the tendencies toward indulgence, excess, and chaos that are abroad in the land and apparently inherent within. But you do see, don't you, that all the things I've been telling you hang together? An ordered system-schedule *ought* to work, God knows. It takes fully into account your first realization about smoking and drinking—that you feel you "deserve" a drink or smoke as a "reward." And the method accounts for—in fact, utilizes—your second realization—that you think smoking and drinking are romantic—for this is a truly grown-up way to drink and smoke. And your third realization—that the ordered, scheduled life ultimately provides more pleasure (I realize you haven't really *realized* this yet)—will be manifest in the relish with which you appreciate each cigarette and each drink as it becomes available to you in the time scheme you set up. Awful as the waiting is, it's better than giving them up. Needless to say *considerable* anticipation can develop by the time to have the next cigarette or drink comes around.

Say, what *time* is it getting to be?!

❦

How to Do Four Dumb Tricks
with a Package of Camels

ANOTHER REASON for smoking Camels, besides because they satisfy, never change, are available most everywhere, are romantically-dangerously unfiltered, and taste best, is that there are four dumb tricks you can do with the package that amuse children and other simple-minded amiable people.

You need a certain amount of equipment. First and foremost you need a package of Camels, like this:

Second, you will need a small mirror. Third, a dime. And fourth, a child or reasonable facsimile.

Dumb Trick Number One

Show the front of the package, which shows the camel standing there in the desert. Ask the child: "If a sandstorm came up, where would you go?"

Child: "Into the pyramid?"

You: "No."

Child: "Up the palm tree?"

You: "No, that wouldn't protect you from a sandstorm."

Child (finally): "I give up."

You turn the package over and say, "To this city on the other side."

Dumb Trick Number Two

Show the front of the package again and give the child the dime. Say: "Cover the four legs of the camel with the dime." The child tries, the dime won't quite cover them all.

Child: "Can I use two nickels? Is that the trick?"

You: "No, it has to be a dime."

Child: "Well, can I use *one* nickel?"

You: "No. I just said it has to be a dime. The whole point of it is to try to do it with a dime."

Child: "Well, a dime won't cover all four legs."

You: "Do you give up?"

Child: "Let me try some more. There must be some trick to it."

You: "Of course there's a trick to it. That's the point. I told you I'd show you four dumb tricks to do with a package of Camels."

Child: "Well, I give up."

You take the dime and cover the *fore*feet of the camel.

Child: "You said to cover all four legs!"

You: "I said '*the* forelegs.' These *are* the forelegs, the two front legs."

Child: "Oh, I get it. That's dumb, though. What's the next one?"

Dumb Trick Number Three

You: "Find the Arabic writing on the Camel package."

Child takes package and looks all over it.

You (encouragingly): "There must be some. It's Turkish tobacco."

Child: "Well, where is it? I don't see any Arabic writing. What's it look like?"

You: "Do you give up?"

Child: "Is it on the pyramid or on one of the towers on the back?"

You: "No, there isn't any there. You don't see any there, do you?"

Child: "No. But maybe it's there, very small or something." Child looks at the mirror. "Maybe if I had a magnifying glass . . . What's the mirror for?"

You: "Never mind the mirror. Do you give up?"

Child: "I guess so."

You take the mirror and hold it so that the edge of the package that says "CHOICE QUALITY" in big letters is reflected in it, holding your finger over it so that the child sees only the reflection. For some reason known only to God and maybe a few physicists, the "CHOICE" is reflected perfectly well, but the "QUALITY" goes completely to pieces and looks very Arabic, thus:

CHOICE ÓПɅГI⅃⅄

Child: "That does look like Arabic. But why does the 'CHOICE' stay the same way?"

You: "It's very mysterious. Only a few physicists understand it."

Child: "That's better than the other ones anyway. What's the next one?"

You: "The *last* one, not the next one."

Dumb Trick Number Four

This is the worst and dumbest one of all. You say to the child: "Find the date '1914' on the package." The child looks and looks and looks. The child has been tricked three times now and really wants to guess this one.

Child: "It's really there?"

You: "Yes."

Child: "It's really *there?* I mean, it's not outside the package or something?"

You: "What do you mean by that?"

Child: "I don't know. It's really *on* the package, *written* there, the date '1914'?"

You (in a hedging tone): "Yes, more or less. The date '1914' is written there on the package."

Child (looking at the mirror): "Is it backward or anything?"

You: "Well, it may be backward and it may not. Anyway, you don't need the mirror."

Child: "What do you mean it's backward and I don't need the mirror?"

You: "I didn't say it *was* backward."

Child: "Well, *is* it backward?"

You: "I'm not saying any more. Do you give up?"

Child (musing): "It's *on* the package and it *may* be backward. It's some kind of trick, isn't it?"

You: "Of course it's a trick. These are all tricks."
Child: "But it's *there?*"
You: "Yes, for heaven's sake. Do you give up?"

Now it's important on this one that the child does give up, really gives up, is even finally put in the position of begging you to show him, because it's an especially dumb trick and he's going to be disappointed when he's shown the "1914." On the back of the package, left over for some reason from some copywriter's bright idea twenty or thirty years ago when most cigarette makers gave out gift coupons is this message:

> Don't look for premiums or
> coupons, as the cost of
> the tobaccos blended in
> CAMEL Cigarettes pro-
> hibits the use of them.

And upside-down and backward, of course, the "hibi" in "prohibits" reads "1914"—sort of.

Child: "Ugh."
You: "I know three more, but I won't show you."

How to Avoid Family Arguments

FAMILY ARGUMENTS can be between parents and children, between brothers and sisters, between husbands and wives, as well as between any of the above with any other of the above and/or anyone who happens to wander into the field of fire, like an adopted cousin, a close nephew, a live-in grandparent, or even (or rather especially) any in-law foolish enough to marry his way into this mess. Family arguments can range from routine ritualistic bickering to all-out screaming and name calling. What all these kinds of family arguing have in common is that (unlike arguing with a stranger, say) they seem to be recurrent.

All that's needed to stop family arguments of any sort is a FAT. FAT is an acronym for Family Arguing Time, a period set aside for family members to air grievances, settle differences, and generally argue away to their hearts' content. The rule is, though, that no one can argue *except* during the period allotted. At first, perhaps, as much as an hour a day might have to be set aside for this activity. Then later (as people lost interest in it, or came to dread it, or whatever) a half-hour daily might suffice. Then a weekly arguing session; eventually perhaps only one every year or so. FAT can work wonders with even the most quarrelsome family.

Ten Years Later

Mom: "Aren't we ever going to have one of those FATs again?"

Dad: "Why, is something bothering you? Are you annoyed about something?"

Mom: "No, of course not." (*Then, rather wistfully*): "I can't even remember what being annoyed felt like."

How to Daydream

DAYDREAMING IS something you've got to do on your own to a very substantial extent. I mean, I'm interested in telling you how to do things right, but it wouldn't *be* right, would it, if I told you what to daydream, and then you just went ahead and daydreamed that, out of ineptitude or sheer laziness? The whole point of daydreaming is to have it be about what you want, and it's a waste of time, anyway. If you start daydreaming about what someone else wants, you'll *really* be wasting your time. Still, I *can* show you *how* it's done.

You should develop some special overall method, then work up specific material from areas you know something about. Because I more or less dropped out of what's called "the world" in more or less early middle age, what I daydream about best is getting back into it in some big-deal way. And because what I used to be "in" was publishing, a lot of my daydreams have to do with that—but not all of them, not by any means. The basic technique I use is that *"they" come to me.* They come to get me out of retirement because they realize that I'm the only man who can do whatever it is they want done right. This utilizes a lot of my best stuff.

I Wow Them with My Idea for a TV Show

For instance, a daydream I find pleasant and useful is that they come to me in the form of two network producers who have heard my idea for doing a once-a-week, hour-long television series drama about a pro-football team, to be called either "The Team" or "The Coach."

"It's a real great idea, Rust," they say to me. "Out of *sight*." They are as convinced as I am that not only all those millions and millions of pro-football fans will watch the show, but so will all their wives and kiddies, because of the dramatic interest. *Everybody* will watch it, they feel; the other channels might as well suspend broadcasting in our time-slot. And with the kind of ratings we'll get, the network will have to let us do Real Good Serious Stuff. The coach is to be an angry, attractive man, like the old snarling Ben Casey; many of the shows are to be written so the plot can be resolved in action on the field. It'll be a real breakthrough, because there's never been a successful sports drama on TV before. I'm to act as producer and story editor, with a big budget and enough freedom to get important writers to do script ideas.

"Ted here and me," says one of the producers, "we'll handle all the business and technical stuff, make sure things go easy for you. The network says they will give you a huge share of the action, and when the reruns start, believe me you'll clean up."

I Cut Proust

Or they come to me as two old acquaintances who work at Random House.

"As you know, Rust," they say to me, "Proust's *Remembrance of Things Past* is mostly available in America only in that big, boxed edition that Random has been selling like mad for years and years. There's more to publishing than just making money, though. We're worried that not everyone who buys the book, reads it. You have any ideas?"

"Well, fellows," I say confidently, "as *you* know, Edmund Wilson makes the distinction between Proust the philosopher and Proust the social novelist. Proust is much admired as a philosopher in France, but in England and America what we relish is his incomparable ability as a novelist. For many readers, unfortunately, Proust's story telling proceeds so slowly, clogged by his philosophizing, that they stop reading. I suggest an abridged Proust—wait, don't look so shocked, fellows, let me explain—a shortened version of the whole book that would emphasize Proust-the-novelist. It would be a big book anyway, perhaps six or eight hundred pages. With a few transitional, explanatory paragraphs that we could insert in italics, the story would emerge luminously. Reading just *Swann's Way*, or only part of it, is actually a far more violent abridgement of the whole than is the condensed version I'd prepare. How alert of you to think of me to do this!"

"Listen, Rust," the editors say excitedly. "Your idea is exactly what we think we had in mind. Could you do it in a year? We'll give you a good royalty and a fat advance and help you get a grant from Rockefeller or Ford. We assume you'll want some travel money to go around and discuss the project with the leading Proust scholars. They'll be envious of you, of course, but they'll realize that a trained fiction editor is what's needed here and that as a long-winded writer yourself, you'll just naturally know how to cut the daylights out of Proust. If you want, why don't you go live in Paris for the year you're working on it?"

I Benefit My Country in Two Ways

Or, they come to me from the Treasury Department, having heard of my great idea how to supplement the federal government's revenue and benefit America at the same time. It's to put a one-percent tax on advertisements placed in all media: if advertising is, say, a three-hundred-billion-dollar industry, then the one-percent tax would produce three billion dollars each year, which would be turned over to education, just as the tax on gasoline is turned over to road building. My tax would benefit America by discouraging advertising, which is bad, and by encouraging education, which is good.

One of the Treasury Department men looks very much like a man I had to spend three awful hours with discussing my income tax. "Everyone in Washington is very impressed," he says, in his distant, meticulous way, "that a man who self-admittedly hasn't much of a head for figures could come up with such a viable idea." It turns out that they want me to come down there and "head things up" for them until the plan gets started. "It would be a service to your country," they say, "and you might enjoy spending a year in Our Nation's Capital." Every time a letter arrives from the Internal Revenue Service, I think it will be about this, but it isn't.

The Yaddo Caribbe

Sometimes in the early winter, when the sun's about to go down at three-thirty in the afternoon and the house is drafty from the north wind and there's no one around and everyone there is is boring, they come to me about what to do with this Caribbean island. A distinguished committee comes to me from Columbia University, comprised of faculty members and two or three trustees in banker's gray with very faint pinstripes. It seems that a millionaire has left Columbia a small Caribbean island with just the millionaire's mansion and a dozen or so guest bungalows on it. The university had considered selling it to add to the general endowment fund, but it seemed too ideal a place not to use in some way. . . .

"Writers!" I say to them. "A place for writers!"

"You mean a writing school?" says the chairman, pursing his lips and looking at the others as if to say: Not a bad idea.

"Well, yes, that's part of it," I say, thinking fast. "A graduate school of writing, offering a Master of Fine Arts degree, run something like the famous Iowa Writers' Workshop, except it wouldn't be way out in cold Muddy River City, Iowa, but on this neat hot island."

"But listen," I say to the committee, "if this island is all you say it is . . ." They nod to reassure me of the beauty of its beaches, its superb climate, the elegant accommodations. ". . . then it can benefit American literature in a far more significant way. What I have in mind, gentlemen, is a sort of writers' retreat, like The MacDowell Colony or Yaddo. It would be a sanctuary for our writers to create in, away from all the turmoil and boredom of their households."

I hear approving murmurs from the committee and notice them turning to smile congratulations to one another for having come to the right man with their island problem.

"All the major American writers would want to have a resident term there," I continue. "They wouldn't have to *teach* the students exactly, just expose themselves to the ones they were interested in. . . ."

"Mr. Hills!" warns the chairman, glancing at the trustees.

"You know what I mean," I say. "The thirty young, inexperienced, golden-tanned writing students would learn technique from the established older authors just by being in close proximity night and day."

"A Caribbean Yaddo . . ." I muse to myself, beginning to daydream in the middle of my daydream. It seems to be the morning after a great debauch, and we're all lying on the beach recuperating. I overhear two golden students on a nearby beach mat:

"That was a *marvelous* discussion last night, wasn't it?" says one girl.

"*I'll* say," answers the other. "But it's always real great when Saul and Norman and Vladimir get to arguing about techniques of point-of-view method with Rust. He's really smart, that guy."

"But *kindly*, too," says the first.

I Save Life

Sometimes they come to me in the form of just one person, whoever it is runs the Time-Life organization, Henry Luce, say, back from the grave; and on his way home from Rome or China or somewhere, he wants to stop and see me here in Connecticut in the country, where we can talk quietly, away from the distractions of his hectic life. He offers to take me out to lunch, but I decide we'd really have a better meal at home. At the table I made, looking out at the cove through the bow window I put in, we have a delicious cheese soufflé or chicken salad or something, and over a good bottle of light wine we get to talking about what he's come for.

"Well," he says, "Rust, I don't know if you've got wind of it up here, but we're in trouble with *Life:* advertising's soft and circulation's expensive. Television news has sapped the vitality of the photojournalism we used to do so well, and there's a feeling the magazine has lost its rationale. Casting about for a new concept, I've come up with what I think is one hell of a good idea: if I can find the right editor for it, I'm ready to switch *Life* over to run nothing but fiction. I believe serious literary fiction has a very great deal to tell us about how we live now in this country, and I know that you do too. You could pay absolutely top rates, have three or four major novels running in serial simultaneously, eight or ten stories by

Famous-Name Writers and Promising Young Writers, plus a couple of novellas, *each week*. You can imagine how a market like this would revitalize the American novel and short story! We'd handle all the business stuff; you'd have a completely free hand editorially; make your own hours and choose your own staff, of course. You'd start at a real good salary, and there are a lot of fringe benefits at Time-Life. If the magazine makes the kind of turn-around I think it will in your hands, you'd be a very wealthy man in just a matter of years."

There is a pleasant pause while I consider my answer. Henry Luce, or whoever it is, sighs. He raises his wineglass and considers it in the afternoon sunlight coming through the coveside window, then sips it appreciatively: "Well . . . ," he begins, but then interrupts himself: "Those ducks are buffleheads, aren't they? Isn't it amusing how they dive down and bob up that way?"

I smile in agreement. In the winter, when the cove isn't frozen, I spend far more time watching the buffleheads than I care to admit to this busy man.

"Well, Rust," he says. "You don't want to see *Life* go the way of *Collier's*, the *Post* and *Look*, do you? I've looked the whole field over, Rust; I'll level with you about that. But you're the one I'm coming to first. I've come to you because you are the only magazine fiction editor who can do this thing *right*. You interested at all?"

"No," I say, gently restraining the mounting enthusiasm he feels for his plan. "No, you must give this power to one of your *young* editors, not to a soured old veteran like me." I smile at him. "Your offer is of course very flattering, but I don't think I'd care to go back into publishing again. I'm sure you remember what Thoreau said in explanation of his leaving Walden Pond: 'Perhaps it seemed to me that I had several more lives to live, and could not spare any more time for that one.' No, I don't feel I could make as substantial a contribution in publishing now as I could in some other area."

"Well," he says sadly, "publishing's loss will mean a tremendous gain to some other field. You are one of the few people in America today who knows his own mind. Here's to your future—I know it will be brilliant." He drains his glass. "This wine is really superb. Would you be terribly affronted if I took the label and had Sherry-Lehmann send you up a half-dozen cases as a slight token of my appreciation for the time you've given me?"

Then he leaves, and I'm left just sitting here, still with nothing whatever to do—except look at the damn ducks. Also, I worry that he'll have some way of knowing how often I use that Thoreau quote. But then when I mull over things that he said—like being able to publish eight or ten stories a week, and becoming a very wealthy man in just a matter of years—then I know I've had a good daydream, and I'm almost sorry I turned the offer down.

I Am Approached for the Biggest Job of All

A day or two later, a half dozen of the most powerful politicians in Washington all arrived in a limousine. They'd come to plead with me. They were all stepping aside, forgoing their own ambitions—"for the sake of the nation," as they put it. They all wanted to help organize my campaign as Democratic candidate for the Presidency of the United States. That's because they'd finally heard my great plan for How to Solve America.

❦

How to Solve America

MY SOLUTION to the problem of America came to me shortly after— and more or less as a result of—reading the newspaper on January 19, 1968, an historic date. It's not historic, even to me, because that's when I thought of my solution for America: I've told God's own amount of people about my plan, and while everyone agrees that it's a great plan, no one's implemented it yet; and obviously it's no good just having a plan, you've got to implement it; otherwise you might just as well not have a plan at all. No, January 19, 1968, seems to me historic because surely the American low point was somewhere about that time: Lyndon Johnson was our President (which for me was a lot of low point just on its own); we were still escalating in Vietnam (toward our low point there, the Siege of Khesanh and the Tet Offensive, not much later); we'd had eighty-three straight months of economic growth (you'll see why that's bad in a minute); and there were all kinds of other things wrong. I keep thinking things have gotten somewhat better since, but I'd be hard put to explain exactly how. Maybe that's just because after I got the solution I became less interested in the problem.

At any rate, the newspaper I read that morning was the *New York Times*, and reading it started off like reading it every morning: so many ironies, so much to deplore. I remember how my grandfather used to rattle the paper in rage at FDR, but I am convinced that that was different: Roosevelt's policies threatened my grandfather's personal financial interests. The rage, the outrage I feel, stems from a similar sense of frustration—a sense that everything's being done wrong, and that I'm powerless to stop it—but it is different in that usually there's nothing in the newspapers that threatens my own personal financial interests. But maybe that's just because I don't actually have all that many personal financial interests.

Every once in a while, though, there is something that strikes, as the cliché goes, *close to home*. Reading the paper that morning, I was struck rather closer to home than usual by the opening passage of Eliot Fremont-Smith's review of an edition of the poems of the late Frank O'Hara:

> "Hell," cries the painter in Frank O'Hara's dramatic mono-
> logue, *Franz Kline Talking*—"Half the world wants to be like
> Thoreau at Walden worrying about the noise of traffic on the
> way to Boston; the other half use up their lives being part of that
> noise. I like the second half. Right?"

This indeed and quite literally struck me close to home. The place I care most for *is* my home—my house and outbuildings and twenty acres of land on a cove in Stonington, Connecticut, between New York and Boston. It is also between New London and Providence, between Mystic and Westerly, Rhode Island, and between Route 1 and Interstate 95. I-95 is just barely too far away for us to hear, although one winter night when the cove was frozen over I walked out on the ice in the starry night and clearly heard the faint high whine of truck tires in the distance. Route 1 crosses a bridge perhaps a quarter-mile from the house, down-cove toward the mouth; and when the wind is fresh and from the north, we never hear the traffic on it either. But when the wind is from the southwest (and that is the prevailing summer wind), the sound of traffic can be clearly heard—if one listens. If one doesn't listen, one doesn't hear it, for the noise is not loud and there is much else to hear: birds, dogs, barking, children calling, outboard engines, someone shouting as a horseshoe clangs on the stake—all the noises of a country place.

Yet sometimes, I find myself alone there in the late fall or early spring. It is an important time for me. There are days that are cold and wet and foggy, when the sky seems low above, when the wind has dropped, and the birds and dogs and outboards are all still. I am perhaps working about the place, or maybe just walking around, looking at my land, my trees, my dock. Suddenly I look up, perceiving the extraordinary noise. Out of the mist, across the water, the water itself acting as a great sounding board, megaphoned up the cove from the road, comes the growl and whine and roar of traffic. It lets up, shifts, grinds, socks in again with a sort of a whoosh and thump as two trucks pass, lets up again, and I hear the sound gradually fade away, and then the growing wail of another car approaching in the distance. I put my hands over my ears. I love this place. It is what I have always wanted. Why do I let this noise bother me? It is not so bad, or it is only some days that it is bad. Yet each day it grows worse, as strip-development continues between Mystic and Westerly; and someday, I know, Route 1 must be widened to four lanes.

One half of the people in America, Frank O'Hara has Franz Kline say, are "worrying about the noise of traffic on the way to Boston." It is for me so literally the case that I have to make an effort to see how it can function as a symbol in his poem. Yet I know that it does, and it is a good one. It is a symbol of that one half of us who are the old, the fussy, the retired, the out-of-it, the complainers, withdrawn and frustrated and powerless, the constant deplorers. And there's "the other half who use up their lives being part of that noise," those who are busy and active and energetic, effective, and perhaps powerful, doing things, getting things done, going places, getting somewhere, making it. O'Hara/Kline say that they like the second half: they want their art to be with-it, to be part of ongoing life.

For some reason I clipped the O'Hara review from the paper that morning and happened to turn it over. There on the back was James Reston's column, headed "Washington: 'Why, Then, This Restlessness?'" Reston was referring to something President Johnson had said in his State of the Union message to Congress two days earlier. Here is the passage of the speech in which it occurs:

Now let me speak of some matters here at home. Tonight our nation is accomplishing more for its people than has ever been accomplished before. Americans are prosperous as men have never been in recorded history.

Yet, there is in the land a certain restlessness, a questioning.

The total of our nation's annual production is now above $800 billion. For 83 months this nation has been on a steady, upward trend of growth. All about them, most American families can see the evidence of growing abundance.

Higher paychecks; humming factories; new cars moving down new highways; more and more families own their own homes equipped with more than 70 million television sets; a new college is founded every week. . . .

Why, why, then, this restlessness?

Because when a great ship cuts through the sea, the waters are always stirred and troubled.

And our ship is moving—and it's moving through troubled and new waters, and it's moving toward new and better shores. . . .

I remember seeing President Johnson give this speech on television. There was always something about the manner of that man when he was in the White House that drove me up the wall—my dislike of him was certainly as great and perhaps as irrational as my grandfather's dislike of Franklin Roosevelt. I grew cold with rage when I heard him talk about "new cars moving down new highways" and "more than 70 million television sets"—as if it were *good,* all this. "Who needs it?" I kept saying. "Who *needs* it?"

Can it be true that this nation is in fact divided between those who want more new cars moving down more new highways and those who think what we need is *fewer* cars moving down *fewer* new highways? Divided between those who love to be always zipping up to Boston to do whatever it is they do there, and those who sit by the side of the road hating the noise they make.

James Reston, in his analysis of the President's speech, makes the point that seems so obvious:

This is a divided nation today not alone over economic but over fundamental moral questions. . . .

We have come to see that prosperity is not, after all, the goal

61 ≈

in the "pursuit of happiness," and that after all the boasts of 83 months of economic boom something is still wrong.

Even in prosperity we feel that something is wrong in America. That is, it seems to *some of us* that something is wrong. To those who are getting their first new car, their first television set—those who don't *have* twenty acres on a cove—it must seem a different matter. Can it be that this "fundamental moral" division in America is nothing more than the tedious, traditional, bitter old one between the haves and the have-nots? Who needs it indeed? Who needs it is who hasn't got it.

We are coming now to what I believe is called the crux of the matter. Here it is, *the crux:* We've already got too many cars, say—let's take just cars, because they strike so close to home. Yet there are still a lot of people who don't have cars, and they want them. You can't keep them from having cars if they want them. How would you like not having a car? But if we get many more new cars going down many more new highways, our countryside will soon be all turnpike-and-parking-lot. This is simpleminded, I know, but it is the crux of the matter: continued economic growth, more "progress," and more "abundance" are going to make this country not worth living in.

My solution for the problem of America resolves this paradox, takes into account all the psychological-sociological aspirations of the citizenry, and at the same time cures all our economic ills. In fact, my idea for how to solve America could solve the rest of the world as well.

That's because the rest of the world still sees our problem as its solution. In that same newspaper there was a series of stories on Japan's fantastic rate of economic development. This is the sort of thing no normal man would ever dream of reading, but being struck close to home isn't very pleasant, especially in the morning when one is having his coffee and reading his paper, and it tends to make one read the rest of the news more sensitively:

> TOKYO.—According to economic analysts, every Japanese aspires to own the "Three C's"—color television, car, and cooler (air conditioner).
>
> In too many cases, economic prosperity has been gained at the cost of certain individual sacrifices, and developments in one

field have caused disruption in another. Critics note a deterioration in family and neighborhood relations as the pursuit of material comforts assumes greater importance.

This Tokyo story came from a special supplement in the paper, "The *New York Times* Economic Survey of Asia and the Pacific." Every country mentioned in it appeared to have made the same commitment: to some insane conception of "progress" as an end, to achieve economic "growth," as if growth were something that could ever be achieved. Every underdeveloped country wants to become a modern industrial power like the United States or Japan. Isn't there one country somewhere that can see that what's paid for the color television, the cars, the "coolers," is never worth it? Not only not worth it, but that the cars and televisions aren't advantages anyway, but disadvantages? And that air conditioners aren't necessary if you don't pollute the air with factories making them? Hasn't this all happened enough times and enough places already for anyone anywhere to have learned anything? Is it all going to go on and on until the whole world looks like Queens Boulevard?

> HONG KONG.—One of the most picturesque aspects of Hong Kong is coming to an end. The boat people are gradually coming ashore. . . .
>
> For more than a century of Hong Kong's existence as a British colony the boat people have been one of its colorful human spectacles.
>
> Until they began to move ashore some years ago there were 100,000 to 150,000 who passed all their lives aboard craft clustered in vast, bobbing fleets of wooden hulls, soaring masts and reefed sails at a half dozen main sheltering sites.
>
> Cheerful illiterates, the boat people sing and laugh, dress in tattered garments, wear jade bracelets for luck and set off firecrackers to scare away evil spirits. . . . Children start helping with boat chores as soon as they can walk. . . .
>
> Years ago the Hong Kong government began to encourage the boat people to move ashore. . . . Huge blocks of small apartments have been built for them and about 45,000 have been lured to life on land.
>
> "It's like dragging cave-men out of the forest," said a

resettlement officer. "They are bewildered by a kitchen and haven't the slightest idea what a toilet is. It takes them years to accommodate to apartment living."

Why should they want "to accommodate to apartment living"? I lived in an apartment a good deal of my life and I sure as hell don't see anything so great about it. Living on a boat is much better: wealthy industrialists spend millions on yachts and never have the time to use them. I suppose it's humiliating to be part of "a colorful human spectacle," rafted up as a tourist attraction; yet look at the quai-side in Cannes and you'll see rich people doing it for pleasure. "Children start helping with boat chores as soon as they can walk." Why is it better to get them ashore in an apartment to watch color television?

Why? Why? Why? That's the whine of the man who deplores the noise of the traffic on the way to Boston, and it's no more pleasant than the whine of the traffic itself. Why the Vietnam quagmire? Why the space race? Why a new lousy college every week? Why drag "cavemen out of the forest"? Why drag these happy underdeveloped countries into the wretched modern world? Why ruin their country-side, their waterways, the very air they breathe?

Clearly America leads the way in all this, like a Judas goat; clearly all the other countries follow, like little lemmings determined to get their share of the future. Yet Americans are manifestly more nervous and insecure and restless—less happy—than the "simple" people of these "underdeveloped" nations. Even President Johnson noticed this. He said it was because when our great ship of state is on the way to better shores, the boat's bound to make waves. But some of us, up to our necks in this crap, mumble the punch line of the famous joke: "Don't make waves." And anyway, we're *not* on our way to better shores; we're on our way to *worse* shores. That's what makes some of us who sit by the side of the road want to get off the boat. We are all dismayed by the quality of our life. There's nothing wrong with the quantity, I guess; unless, as I say, there's too much of it. The country as a whole—the countryside and the cities, the look of America—is getting uglier and uglier. Mrs. Johnson's beautification campaign did just what we expected it would: nothing. Each reader can fill in the specific things he specially deplores about modern America; but the point, again, is that everything is getting worse instead of better. Everyone knows this, but let me give some examples so that you deplorers can nod in agreement and cluck your tongues.

When a building is torn down in New York City or anywhere in America, the building that is put up instead is, with some very few exceptions, uglier and worse built. Even the brownstone tenements are better buildings, solider and better-looking than the slum-clearance architecture that replaces them. The old rambling farm buildings are better than the flimsy development houses. Factory architecture in this country has gone from solid old stone buildings, beautifully windowed, through red brick, to tinny aluminum sheds with fluorescent lights. It is now too expensive, or something, to put up good buildings. Older buildings are almost always better—houses, apartments, factories, whatever. Everyone knows this.

What is true of buildings is pretty much true of everything. *Boats:* The old wooden sailing yachts with their lovely lines were infinitely better than the awful molded-plastic, humpbacked modern ones. *Roads:* The beautiful old winding country lanes were incredibly much better than the snarling new superhighways; they were lovelier and made less noise, and that's better. And what is true of buildings, boats, and roads, is true of virtually *anything you can name:* always the old was substantially, demonstrably better than the new.

Everything was better before. Everyone knows this, and aside from a few real estate developers, who just want to keep on going the same dumb wrong way, everyone admits and deplores it. No one can ever actually be made happy by the way things are going, with all this growth and progress, everything growing worse and progressing in what's clearly the wrong direction.

The problem of America, then, is one hell of a problem.

But, fortunately, my solution is also one hell of a solution.

So what am I going to do about it? How are we going to solve America? You can't slow down or stop all this growth and progress without causing disaster to the economy; we know that. My solution for America takes this into account. It takes *everything* into account.

How to solve America is profoundly and beautifully simple: *just turn everything around and start going the other way.* This would keep America moving, but now we'd be moving in the right direction, backward—from the complex back toward the simple, from the new back to the old, from the ugly and shoddy back to the lovely and the sturdy.

The idea, basically, is to decide today to undo tomorrow what was done yesterday. Then day-after-tomorrow undo what was done day-before-yesterday, so that two weeks from now we'd be undoing what was done two weeks ago. And so on, with some important variations and refinements—backward in time, until we get just the kind of America we used to have and liked so much.

This would cause no unemployment, because there'd be just as much work undoing all the things we've done recently as there was doing them; actually it will be *more* work, the way we're going to do it. The real cause of unemployment is mechanization, right? Well, not only are we going to demechanize America, we are going to demechanize her, insofar as possible, quietly and slowly, without using any noisy machines, and that's going to be a lot of work. No de-assembly lines: men will take computers apart using just screwdrivers and pliers. So actually this job of painstakingly dismantling modern America would require fantastic amounts of manpower—and rebuilding the old America would take even more, for we'd have to relearn the skills and attitudes of good workmanship. For instance, the tunnels under the rivers around Manhattan would have to be undug, and the bridges unbuilt—both dangerous and time-consuming jobs. Then the ferryboats that the tunnels once replaced would now have to be rebuilt to replace them—and because wood is going to be at a premium in this new, older society, until we can get some trees to grow again—the ferries would have to be built of available scrapwood by skilled shipwrights. Taking down skyscrapers will be done carefully, too—with no noise or dust. Hardhats will stand proudly and respectfully and quietly as the mayor says a few grateful words to them at the joyous ceremonies celebrating the unlaying of a cornerstone. Taking up the asphalt and concrete would be done by friendly groups of overweight businessmen working easily together with sledgehammers and crowbars, for the sound of the air compressor and the jackhammer would pass from the land. And as the good earth is revealed again under all the crud we've put over it, how lovely it will be! Perhaps a tenth of our men and a quarter of our women will have to work as landscapists and gardeners for a while—not just as a hobby, as they do now, but as their work. Imagine finding pleasure in work!

There would be a great need for people to raise and train horses. What a job it would be to dismantle all the automobiles, melting down all the steel and ultimately replacing it in the ground in a form as close to iron ore as possible. Everything—steel, concrete, plastics—all would go back into the earth where it came from. What planning it would require to get it all put back neatly into place! Archivists would search the records to determine what existed previously in each area; long-range planners would speculate about what existed even earlier; and implementers would plan older, slower ways to achieve it.

The intention wouldn't be to take the nation as a whole back to an aboriginal state, living in caves and tepees and hunting from ponies, or anything like that—although that style of life would be available for those who wanted it. What's to be achieved is a return to some sort of approximation of the American ideal, having the best of each era, without anybody being exploited.

Thus, most Americans would live in small towns, but there would be isolated rural areas and there would be moderate-sized, tenable, livable cities for those that wanted them. The economy would be basically agricultural—small farms, unmechanized, family-owned, and family-worked—but there would also be small, local industries manufacturing things *well.* There would be traveling companies of repertory players, putting on plays in renovated movie houses of each village. Books would be published in each city, sold in the bookstore in each town. Everything would be much cheaper, the way it was before we got mass-production. Saturday afternoons there would be baseball games, and one would play—or watch men one knew play—against the teams of other towns. People would once again know where they belonged, who they were.

We would take something of the best from each era, but very little of the very modern would endure. There could, for instance, be a few quiet old-fashioned airplanes, kept as museum pieces for those that wanted them; but no jetports, nothing remotely resembling a jetport. There would be old, grand, luxurious trans-Atlantic liners and romantic tramp steamers, as well as lots of sailboats, not just yachts, but fast clipper ships and working schooners. An adequate train service might remain, or be recreated—with elegant dining cars, as in days gone by. All the elevated highways and the throughways and the parking lots would be replaced with trees and grass, of course; but there might be a few hundred cars left, for the nuts. Telephones would go through local switchboards, calls placed by friendly operators.

All the noisy inconvenient "conveniences" of modern life will disappear more or less in reverse order of their appearance—the jet ski and the snowmobile taking precedence over all others, however, no matter what newer horrors they've thought of by the time we start this.

The family will assume a vital role again, as demechanization creates chores inside and outside the house for older people and for children. In coastal areas children may be able to help with boat chores as soon as they can walk. "Community" will come to mean something good again, too, as the process of urbanization is reversed.

There'll be a need to subvert and eventually obvert our national mania that "growth" is a good, that it is "vital." A nation that is really vital, we can say, is one that endures in its best phases, that refuses to grow toward its own extinction. We must make our Gross National Product *less* gross, more refined. Those in charge of our bureaus of government must show a substantial decrease in all aspects of their organizations at year's end, or be replaced by can-undo men who will.

How would it be paid for? How, I ask you, was all this mess built in the first place? People were somehow sold on the idea that they wanted all these junky new things. Already we find many Americans seeking just the opposite: *paying* to go on a boat ride around Manhattan, even if the boat doesn't take them anywhere, the way the old ferries did; *paying* to have a cottage way out in the country somewhere; *paying* to go on camping trips—and the more primitive the conditions, the more they pay. Do you know what it *costs* to ride in one of those horse-drawn carriages through Central Park, or to ride and keep a horse anywhere? It would be twice as easy to persuade Americans to get rid of all this junk as it was to persuade them that they wanted it in the first place. In fact, once a kind of conspicuous *de*consumption pattern started, it would be hard to control. No one would want to be last on his block to get rid of his color television set, especially after all television programming had ceased forever.

Of course the plan has to be implemented collectively, and the best way to persuade people to do something collectively is to pass a law saying they have to. I suggest that on the federal, state, and local levels, all legislatures pass a law with the same wording, to show we're all behind it, and the executive departments of government agree, and the courts declare it legal in advance, and all the media support it and promote it and explain it and analyze it, the way they do, so that everybody's clear about it: that we're going to turn America around and start going the other way.

Doesn't it all sound nice? An ease and a peace will come over the restless, troubled people of this land, as gradually out of the noise and grime and busyness of our "civilization" appear once again the rolling plains and the farms and the wooded hillsides.

Isn't this a good plan for how to solve America? I know you're anxious to get started, but I don't really recommend our doing it on an individual basis. I mean, if you and I, say, and our families, started undoing tomorrow whatever it was we did yesterday, and so on back the way the plan has it, but just all by ourselves, we're not going to have any effect on the traffic on Route 1 or on anything else for that matter; we'll just end up further behind than usual.

POSTSCRIPT

Delight in Order

It is beautiful to see the footgear ranged in a row according
to its kind; beautiful to see garments sorted according to their
use, and coverlets; beautiful to see glass vases and tableware
so sorted; and beautiful, too, despite the jeers of the witless
and flippant, to see cooking-pots arranged with sense and
symmetry. Yes, all things without exception,
because of symmetry, will appear more
beautiful when placed in order.
—XENOPHON, *Economics*

THERE IS a sign, installed over our kitchen sink, the most appropriate place, inscribing more or less permanently one of my most oft-iterated and deeply held convictions:

> **CLEANING UP AS YOU GO ALONG
> IS HALF THE FUN**

Then, over the kitchen cabinets is another sign:

> **ONE OF LIFE'S GREATEST PLEASURES
> IS PUTTING SOMETHING BACK
> WHERE IT BELONGS**

Our kitchen's beginning to look like Montaigne's famous tower room, where he had quotations from his favorite classic authors painted all around the walls—except all ours has are my own admonishments.

≈ 70

What I think would be nice to have next is a lovingly designed, carefully embroidered sampler to hang over the eating table, again the most appropriate place. It would say:

CAREFULNESS IS LOVE

LOVE IS CAREFULNESS

Then a parent could simply point up at it reproachfully if anyone spilled. Children who love their parents, one always heard, took care never to spill or slop or speak with their mouths full. Tidy rooms and a clean kitchen show a loving, careful spirit.

There's a whole psychology that claims the opposite is true: that the careful, tidy person is anal, authoritarian, rigid, irascible, and unloving. Careful people know how false this is; we know how much love is locked in our hearts, waiting for others to be tidy enough to deserve it. We in fact watch the others constantly, looking for the sort of carefulness we could give our love to. And all they (the others) say is that our watching them that way makes them nervous and that's half the reason they spill. The world's psychologies and philosophies are full of justifications for the sloppy, the careless, the accident-prone—while we fussy are left without defense. Never mind—perhaps we can have another sign made, appropriate, I'd say (or admit), this time for the bathroom, that would provide us some solace:

**FUSSINESS
IS ITS OWN
REWARD**

For the ultimate sign, after I've flipped completely, I'm going to the zoning board and ask for a variance so that I can install a giant neon sign on the roof, one that flashes on and off, with a twin message to the world. First it would say:

DISORDER IS THE ULTIMATE EVIL

Then that would blink off and this would flash on:

ORDER IS THE INITIAL GOOD

And they'd alternate that way, all through the night, lightening the dark, spreading truth through the land.

Notice that we're speaking of disorder as the *ultimate* evil, while all we claim for order is that it is the *initial* good. No one would claim order as any kind of ultimate virtue; it's probably the most boring of the virtues, and they're all pretty boring. But just as disorder is the end result of all the vices, so order is the beginning of all the virtues. Take a vice like sloth: it leads to disorder. So does adultery—they all do. The beds never get made; where Vice reigns, Mess stands close beside the throne. On the other hand, the virtues all flourish in an orderly environment.

The thing about both order and disorder is that they spread. Disorder, as is well known (i.e., a cliché), spreads like wildfire—that is, I suppose, much too fast and out of control. But order spreads too—not far, not fast, not like wildfire certainly, but it still spreads. How order spreads is in an orderly way: slowly, calmingly, carefully, even neatly. But the key thing about how order spreads is that it spreads from the inside out.

Imposed order is worse than no order. You can't run a household by posting a lot of rules. If a nation is controlled by a repressive regime, it is an indication the society is disorderly, not orderly. Order need not, indeed ought not, be hierarchical—we've had all that in the social structures of the past, and the people on the bottom didn't like it as much as the people on the top and because there were more of them, this misorder created disorder.

Rules, regulations, forms, controls—all such aspects of a managed and manipulated society—aren't at all the kind of order I'm trying to praise. Any "New Order," national or otherwise, that sets out to straighten the world by ruling it, is hateful, disruptive, intolerable totalitarianism. And any kind of order that seeks to regulate even without ruling is appalling, intolerable creeping bureaucracy. None of these is the kind of order one can delight in. One wants to regulate his own life, not have it done for him.

If you get yourself straightened out and settled down, it's going to help your spouse to get in order too; it's bound to. And this in turn will have a good effect on the kids. Maybe even the dog will get less yappy and nervous, and that will please the neighbors. Order spreads slowly, but it spreads. Real order, the order which is worth seeking, begins with the composed, balanced, secure individual (you); spreads (one hopes) through the composed, balanced, secure family; extends (perhaps) to the composed, balanced, secure community; and thence (with the participation of millions) to the nation; and from there (triumphantly) to an ordered, composed, balanced (and grateful) world. But you have to start with yourself—you first, then your spouse and kids, and only after the dog do you tackle Town Hall.

On the refrigerator, a great big good old solid GE monitor-top made God knows when, the kind my father used to sell when he worked for Rex Cole, who used to be sole distributor for General Electric appliances in the New York City area and you can imagine how long ago that was—on this refrigerator, which is the one thing we have that never seems to break down (touch wood), and the reason it never breaks down, I swear, is because it was made so long ago it doesn't realize it's entitled to—anyway, *on* this refrigerator, it says:

ONLY THE BORED WELCOME THE UNEXPECTED

another of my admonishments, one that now seems to me to cut two ways.

Originally I composed it to persuade householders to mark on the calendar, which is stuck to the side of the refrigerator with magnets, in advance any invitations extended or accepted, so that fewer comings and goings would occur unexpectedly. But it doesn't seem as apt to me as it once did. One is sometimes bored enough to welcome *anyone* who drives in—unexpected or not—that's true. But when you're *really* bored you enjoy anticipating a major event like going out to dinner, want to know about it as far in advance as possible, and rather lament the waste involved when someone asks you at the last minute.

This suggests my admonition's other edge. It seems to me now that it takes basic order (boredom in this case, but there's more to it) to delight in disorder (the unexpected, but more there too). The sign over our boathouse workbench:

DELIGHT IN ORDER

of course plays off Robert Herrick's famous poem:

Delight in Disorder

A sweet disorder in the dress
Kindles in clothes a wantonness:
A lawn about the shoulders thrown
Into a fine distraction:
An erring lace, which here and there
Enthralls the crimson stomacher;
A cuff neglectful, and thereby
Ribbands to flow confusedly;
A winning wave (deserving note)
In the tempestuous petticoat;
A careless shoe-string, in whose tie
I see a wild civility:
Do more bewitch me than when art
Is too precise in every part.

Now I know that as a somewhat sloppy person you've always been very fond of this poem, and I'll have to admit it's real good: all the slippery, sloppy, slithery S-sounds, as if sexy, silken slip-straps were ceaselessly sliding off seductive shoulders all over the place; and the functionally irregular and disordered stresses leading up to the precisely iambed couplet—

Do more bewitch me than when art
Is too precise in every part.

—parodying by epitomizing the very perfection it mocks; all these
sounds, and more, enhance the sense superbly. But now just what
in fact is it you're saying the sense of the poem is? What is its meaning in this order-disorder argument? Does the poem set forth a theory of art—extolling some loose "natural" romantic or gothic notion
of art over the refinements and internal unities and harmonies of the
classical and neoclassical art that are too precise in every part? Or is
it a statement on laws and ethics? Or maybe it's just a kind of lecherous lyric? The idea is there, surely, that a woman who is a little
careless in her dress may be a little careless with her virtue—which
is what I think of as the messy-is-sexy fallacy.

But notice how qualified what Herrick says is. He speaks of "a
sweet disorder," "a *fine* distraction," "*an* erring lace" (i.e., *one*, not
the whole bunch), and a "civility" that may be "wild," but is still
civility. I think all you've got here is the poet saying that so long as
there's a good basic order it's kind of nice and exciting sometimes
in a strange way to have a *little* disorder. No one's going to deny that.

In fact, I wish it said over the inside of our front door, so we'd all
see it on our way out:

ORDER IS THE MOTHER OF FREEDOM

You can't believe how liberating order can be, or could be, if it
ever were achieved. I once spent four hours making a list of 183
things to have for dinner, so my wife wouldn't have to plan menus
more than twice each year. She claimed she lost the list, and you
can't help that, but that's the kind of potential labor-saving, decision-
eliminating ordering and planning that *could* produce freedom of
mind and time. Oh, an ordered household is much less work and
worry! You don't have to fret so much about when to do something
or the best way; you just do it how and when you always do it. You
don't even have that awful worry about what you ought to do next;
just do whatever it is you usually do then, that time of day, that day
of the week, that time of the year. Having fewer options to reject may

not sound like freedom on the face of it, but in our option-ridden, option-*burdened* society, it is, it is.

And if boredom with routine ever sets in—and while I'm not enough of an optimist to believe that a regular household routine could ever really be established these days, I'm still enough of a pessimist to realize that restlessness would move right in behind it—then you can (or could) do something else, perfectly certain that you do in fact *want* to do it, and secure that your household, your family, and your own real life will still run along in its well-run way. Q.E.D.: Order is the mother of Freedom.

I don't know the way everybody lives now, but how the people I used to know lived was in the city, with a house in the country, two or more kids, two cats and/or one dog, a live-in Dutch girl or West Indian babysitter, a two-day-a-week cleaning lady, a once-a-week laundry lady, and arrangements for extra babysitters for Sundays and for Wednesdays when the Dutch girl goes to her English class and for the other nights when she goes out with her boyfriend, which is happening more and more often and is not just a nuisance but a worry because the boyfriend is a slick guy with no job and gives her a hard time. The wife works part-time; the husband works *all* the time. There just can't possibly *be* any more complicated way to live than this—I've lived more or less that way myself, and I know. The house in the country requires having at least two of everything (everything!) or else jackassing everything back and forth every Friday and Sunday night in the Volvo station wagon. Someone someday will write a great epic poem about these heroic people—cataloging their possessions, celebrating the complexity of their arrangements, chronicling their comings and goings—some Homer of Manhattan's East Nineties. Or perhaps a Sophocles is needed, or an Allen Ginsberg, to show the finest minds of our generation in despair, deranged by the Home Management Muddle.

Most of the people I know seem to be getting divorces. And of course it's no wonder. One or the other in each couple is insisting on what he or she calls "a chance for a new life before it's too late." Who can blame them? Not even the person they're married to blames them much: "Yeah, well," the other one says, "I wouldn't mind a new life myself." And they add to this, when you have lunch with them separately: "I want to begin over, *more simply.*"

I've nothing against divorce, God knows. It's the unhappiness that causes the divorce that I find hateful. And what causes this unhappiness is the inability to cope, the impossibility of keeping "on top" of all the things that keep popping up, the sad inadequacy of our efforts to keep together in our lives and to keep our lives together. And what causes this inability to cope, this disorder, is the complexity of the way we attempt to live.

What we middle-class people want or need or yearn for and try to establish is something to resemble the Old Order, the kind of order our parents, or if not them then our grandparents, used to be able to maintain in their homes, whether they had less or more money than we do now. We want something of the old, less chaotic, more structured world of value-oriented, careful, mannerly behavior, where things made sense, and there was time to read. This kind of Old Order is simply not available to us—the chaos and complexity and tempo of modern life flatly disallow it. The rich can, or could if they wished, perhaps achieve something like the old middle-class order now, could isolate themselves from the chaos and complexity if they chose, could slow life down to something like the old pace. But we want all the accoutrements of the rich—the house in the country, the apartment in town, or the big suburban house and grounds, the private schools, or the five-acre zoned-residential area in a good school district, the clothes from Brooks or Bergdorf's, the two cars, one a sports car, the vacations in foreign lands—without having anything like the kind of backup money not just to pay for them but to maintain them. These poor, very-well-paid (but heavily taxed) professional or business people *have* all these things, but they haven't either the extra money to hire, or the experience to train, competent people to manage and carry for them, for most of these professional people are too liberal, or too kind, to exploit servants: they don't "handle" them "right." And there's no real room for servants either, in the apartment, the summer house, and the Volvo.

And there's no real reason either, now I think of it, that somebody else should break his ass just so *you* can try to live the elegant life like your grandfather.

It should be clear, then, that it's necessary to simplify our lives before we'll be *able* to order them.

On the inside of one cupboard door, it says:

SIMPLIFY. SIMPLIFY. SIMPLIFY.

but inside the cupboard itself is an extraordinary disarrangement of mixing bowls and baking dishes. There seems to be no way to keep these in neat piles, a smaller one nestled cozily inside a larger, the whole pile taking no more room than the largest bowl itself. Some of the baking dishes are square, some rectangular, some are round pie plates, some Mexican, some Pyrex. The bowls are not a set, but an assortment: nice old pale-brown bowls that we like. They don't fit with one another and there are too many of them anyway, far more than are ever needed or used. None of our coffee cups and saucers match either, but they too are sort of old, and we like them.

What I'm getting at at the moment is not another of my admonishments, but one of my L C Ts. Surely it is one of Life's Cruel Truths that "things are nicest just before they wear out." This is true of all clothes – of soft khaki trousers and faded blue jeans, old frayed neckties and favorite jackets with leather patches and torn linings. It's true of wooden boats and frame houses and beloved old green convertibles. It is true of nearly everything – except maybe marriage.

The ramshackle is a falsely simple stage: difficult to achieve and even harder to maintain. It's said of the things I build – floats and porches and bookcases and kindling boxes and so on – that they look old as soon as they are finished. That's because I thriftily use wood that was once something else, so it's battered and somewhat warped just to begin with. The driveway as I like it has grass growing through the gravel – it's just at the point where you really ought to do something about it or you're in for a lot of work later. A rickety pier is what we all love to look at and to feel its silvery weathered wood – but we know next winter's ice will take it out. The ramshackle is lovely to some of us – not because it's fragile, but despite the fact it is. Despite *ourselves* is how some of us like the ramshackle, *despite* our rage for order.

> A lawn about the driveway grown
> Into a fine distraction . . .

These are aesthetic indulgences that the ordered life permits, or ought to. Order is an aspect not of compulsion but of tranquillity, or should be.

When the refrigerator has to be cleaned out from time to time, I never fail to say: an icebox should never *need* to be cleaned. Just don't ever put anything dirty *into* it, just keep track of what's in there, *use* it regularly and systematically, and you'll never have to clean it out or ever throw anything away. If I lived alone, I'd never have to clean out the icebox, I know. I'd never put anything in unless I had the *definite intention* of taking it out and eating it soon, or fairly soon. Defrost now and then I might have to, yes; but clean it out, never.

But is there anything sadder in the world to contemplate than a big old GE monitor-top used solely by one fussy man? Instead of bursting with stuff—God knows what it all is!—there'd just be a few jars, tidy and righteous and lonely, in one corner. No good. A fussy man needs something to be fussy *about*. We wouldn't like it living alone, my admonishments and me.

There are, thus, also emotional considerations that the ordered life takes into account, or ought to. Again: Order is an aspect not of compulsion but of tranquillity, or should be. It's an approach to life, not the absence of life.

What I mean by order, when I'm being serious, is not neatness and tidiness and cleanliness—but it is establishing so far as possible a sense of a regular, regulated, on-going household, so the family can come and go in freedom, knowing there's definitely a place to come back to and what it'll be like when they get there, get home.

What I do mean by order is not taking on more than you can manage without still being able to do what you "really" want. What order is, is not purchasing a lot more stuff than you can fairly easily pay for—not because debts are "bad" as such, but because they end up worrying you and because you don't really need the stuff anyway and you have to maintain it and lug it around with you and get it fixed when it breaks. Order is the opposite of complicating; it's simplifying. Order is not getting deeply entangled with another woman, so you don't get her problems on top of your own. Order is like not wasting a lot of time trying to find things. Order's avoiding a lot of recriminations because you didn't do something you said you would; and maybe it's not saying you'll do a lot of things to begin with. Order is scrupulousness and meticulousness in arrangements with others, so neither of you gets screwed. It's doing things right, or fairly right, as right as they'll let you do them (the things).

The trouble is, the disorder in our lives accumulates so gradually that by the time it bugs us it seems too late to do anything about it and we're not sure we want to anyway. This is especially so in our married lives, but is true of other aspects too, our business and general busyness. The growing complexity seems a natural part of growing older and assuming responsibility. Children, promotions, possessions, are in fact all very much wanted when they arrive. A lot of the "things" we own—the extra car, the summer house, the children's television—are acquired in the delusion that they will make things "better" and (especially ironic) "easier." They ultimately do not, of course, because most of them do not simplify but only further complicate. All these wretched noisy "conveniences" that could do so much to help us establish a little order in our lives—all the dishwashers, washing machines, disposals, electric coffee pots, irons, dryers, knife sharpeners, grinders and blenders and mixers, vacuum cleaners, faxes and freezers, electric alarm clocks, and so on—that are supposed to have replaced the servants of the Old Order and brought a new leisure to the home, that are supposed to do the work, *don't.* They help, maybe; but they don't *do* the work. And there are so *many* of them now that there's always at least one of them that isn't working that we have to "service." *We* service *them* almost as much as they service us.

Part of the trouble is that no one knows how to fix things any more. Not only don't we know how to fix these things ourselves, but neither do the people who sell them to us. All they know how to do is sell us new ones. One reason, of course, is that mass-production methods require a mass-distribution system that licenses dealers as authorized maintenance and repair agents. So of course when you phone a dealer to repair something, he's going to sell you a new one instead. He knows a conflict of interest when he sees one.

One accommodates to this, of course, or tries to outwit it as best one can. One buys a television cheap enough to begin with, so that when it stops working one can afford to throw it away and get a new one. I haven't in my whole life ever owned a decent watch—a watch like my father's or grandfather's that was a pleasure for them to consult, to wind regularly, to handle, to fondle even. All I've ever owned is a succession of rather nasty Timexes, purchased for a very few dollars—they are disposable watches. Accommodating to modern life means accepting the shoddy and expendable instead of enjoying the valuable and permanent.

There are analogies here, you know. I'm not just running off about the machines, although they really do bug me and they really are a part of the problem as well as analogous to it. It appears that nowadays we can "buy" a new life for ourselves, just as we can buy a new anything else if we're getting tired of it or it doesn't seem to be working too well. Then it seems that modern marriages are as expendable as mass-produced machines; they seem in fact to have a built-in obsolescence factor like our autos: they last about six to eight years—more if it's a cream puff, less if you get a lemon. Also, like the modern machines, which are far and away too complicated for any normal ordinary man to fix, our modern lives get so complicated that even the specialists (the lawyers, the marriage counselors, the shrinks, and so on) may tell us (as do the manufacturer, the dealer, and the repairman) that it's "simpler" to start all over with a new one.

This is modern all the way; you can't deny it, and even to deplore it is out-of-date. The best we can hope to do with our lives and marriages is try not to let them get too run down in the first place. As with the modern complex machines you can't repair once they break, the thing to do is maintain them in good order, and hence avoid having to put up on our own lives the sign that says—

OUT OF ORDER

—which is perhaps *the* sign of our times.

Book Two

How to Retire at Forty-One

OR,

Life Among the Routines
and Pursuits and Other Problems

PROLOGUE

How I Happened to Quit Work

And because I found I had nothing else to write
about, I presented myself as a subject.
—MONTAIGNE

IN MARCH of 1965 I bought a place in the country and six months
later quit work. I could have done it the other way around, of course—
a lot of people do. Quitting work and buying houses in the country
seem to go together somewhat like Sloth and Melancholy: you can't
tell which one causes the other.

We started calling the place "Coveside," at first as a joke, but the
name stuck. It is on the Connecticut coast, very near Rhode Island,
halfway between two interesting towns, Stonington and Mystic. It is
on the east side of an inlet called Quiambaug Cove, and at twilight
with the sun setting behind the hills on the far shore, there is a quality
of light that I know I have never seen anywhere else. It once belonged
to an oysterman, one Captain Wilbur, and my deed specifies riparian
rights in four acres of oyster beds right out in front of the house. They
are now in eel grass, but I have a blueprint map (dated 1888) that
shows how they were once laid out. There is a sort of not-very-
elegant but awfully cozy house with seven small bedrooms and three
bathrooms and a low-ceilinged living-room/dining-room/kitchen
complex I devised, with a bow window I put in looking right onto the
cove, with a screen porch on the west, and on the east a ramshackle
kitchen porch I added myself, built with wood from a long unnecessary fence I tore down. By the waterside, there are also a garden-
tool shed, a tractor shed, and a big garage, all sort of vine-overgrown.
There's a separate studio (the previous owner had been an amateur
painter), which I insulated, lined with all my books from the city,
and where I installed a Franklin stove and a big refinished table from
the Connecticut College Library. There's also a boathouse (ah, the
boathouse!), a flagpole, a lot of lawn, trees, a dock, and a big wooden

float. And uphill there are woods, and farmfields going back to woods. It's twenty acres in all.

I have to admit it sounds pretty ideal, this place, as I describe it this way. But that's just because I describe it this way. You ought to hear me when I describe it the other way! It may seem overdramatic to say so, but the place came close to ruining my life—or I think so sometimes. Coveside seemed somehow to have implicit in it all the potential for the success of my retirement—as well, of course, as the potential for failure.

But I can see even now why I was unable to resist buying it. It was the boathouse that really got me. My grandfather had owned a small island, "Potato Island," one of the Thimbles, off Pine Orchard and Stony Creek, in Long Island Sound, and I'd spent summers there as a boy until the hurricane of 1938 pretty much wiped it out. There'd been a boathouse there (washed entirely away in the hurricane), and the boathouse at Coveside was eerily like it: the same size and construction, and I'd swear it had the exact same workbench with the exact same big iron vise where I'd sawed out toy boats from scraps of wood thirty years before. I fancied that the '38 hurricane had swept the workbench fifty miles upcoast into Quiambaug Cove and old Captain Wilbur had thriftily reinstalled it here, vise and all. So when I built that landing float, again with wood from that torn-down fence, I designed it from memory to be like the one on Potato Island, heavy and huge, two-by-eights on nine fifty-gallon steel drums; and often it made the same thunking noise, as temperature changes inside the drums caused them to expand or contract.

The urge to resume or revive our grandparents' lives—to reestablish "the grandfather place"—is deeply there in some of us middle-aged, middle-class WASP losers. We remember those places, with their launches and lawns, the various canoes, the rum cocktails before Sunday lunch (when all the grownups were especially cheerful), the big regular on-time meals, the jolly guests who would come on weekends; then, after the men went back to the city to their work, the long days of the week in-between, with their different, less formal schedules, days to be filled by nothing but play. The trouble is that of course we aren't rich enough to have it all set up and kept running the way it was then, or even some less elaborate way we might want it now; nor are we really established and old-and-retired enough to be able to just sit and enjoy it anyway, having other things we want to do, or think we want to do; nor are we children, so ignorant of what work is required that we just play.

My specific trouble (put schematically) was that when I wasn't working I never had the dough to do right by Coveside (painful), but if I *was* working, then I wasn't there to enjoy the place (equally painful). Obviously this is more or less a self-created problem, but it is an LCT (one of Life's Cruel Truths) that self-created problems are the hardest problems to solve. Only a simpleton would think he'd created a self-created problem if he knew what the solution to it was.

In the autumn of 1965, when I was forty-one, I had been "in" publishing, as they say, in New York City, for nine years, and I was pretty fed up with it. For the past two years I'd been working as the fiction editor of *The Saturday Evening Post.* They'd been troubled but interesting years (to say the least), and things had finally gotten a lot calmer (dull). Before that, I'd worked for seven years as the fiction editor of *Esquire.*

Before that—let's get my life story over with in a paragraph—before that, I'd been in Europe for four years or so, teaching freshman English, off and on, at various U.S. Air Force bases in England for the University of Maryland Overseas Program. And before that I'd worked a year in the college textbook department at Henry Holt & Company. And before that I'd taught a year at Carleton College in Northfield, Minnesota (cold!). And before that I'd been at Wesleyan University in Middletown, Connecticut—M.A., 1949; B.A., 1948—running backward like this, it's beginning to sound more like a resume than a life story. Well, before that I'd been through the U.S. Merchant Marine Academy at Kings Point on Long Island and a third mate on Liberty ships toward the end of World War II. And before that I'd been one year at Kenyon College in Gambier, Ohio. Before that, a miserable adolescent in East Williston, Long Island; and before that, a whiny child in my parents' apartment in Flatbush, corner of Caton and Ocean; and before that I don't really remember.

The point I'm trying to make is that I've quit work a lot of times in my life. It hasn't been because I was an out-and-out failure at these things I've done either, or at least I don't think so. I know, for instance, that I goofed up a lot in the Merchant Marine, but the last of the four Liberty ships I was on had a good captain and a good chief mate and was under charter to the United Fruit Company, and the two of them wanted me to stay on with them in the company, now the war was over, as a kind of team, moving to larger ships and eventually (they said) cruise ships. I haven't thought of this in years. What would I be like if I'd stayed on? But anyway, I was fed up with merchant ships (lonely!), and just had to get *off*. I'd saved some money and wanted to go back to college. It was the same with teaching at Carleton: I'd saved some money and wanted to drive around the country. The same with copy editing and college traveling at Holt: I'd saved some money and wanted to go to Europe. With the University of Maryland, I'd work one or two eight-week terms at a couple of air bases in, say, East Anglia, then take off for Spain or Italy, then come back for a couple more terms, save some more money (PX cigarettes, Class VI booze, low rent in some English cottage; with a good American salary), and quit again. I am *very experienced* as a quitter. But when I quit the magazine business in 1965, at forty-one, it was somehow as if I had to begin a whole new life.

As fiction editor of *Esquire* I had sort of "found myself," as they say. There were a lot of reasons for this. I'd lurched back from four years in Europe determined to stop screwing around and *do* something for a change. Also, at about the same time (1956) *Esquire* was trying to revitalize itself–to differentiate itself from the new magazine *Playboy*, and to establish itself as a "quality book" so as to get some of the advertising being taken by two other postwar magazines, *Holiday* and *Sports Illustrated*, the real competition at the time. Arnold Gingrich, the founding editor, had returned, and there were four new editors: Clay Felker, who went on to fame as editor of *New York* magazine; Ralph Ginzburg, who went on to fame as publisher of *Eros, Avant-Garde, Fact,* and *Moneysworth*, and went on briefly to jail too (as Gay Talese once said: "Ralph Ginzburg was ten months ahead of his time"); also Harold Hayes, who went on to be *the* editor of *Esquire* in its glory years; and L. Rust Hills, since gone on to you'll soon see what.

Those were exciting days at *Esquire*. I was able to stand a bit apart from the competition of the others for the managing editor's job, because I took responsibility for what I was interested in: fiction. I wanted to publish what I called "literary" fiction in a national commercial magazine, and because Arnold Gingrich had done this himself successfully in *Esquire* in the prewar years (publishing Hemingway, Fitzgerald, Wolfe–most everyone, really), because *Esquire* was so receptive to change just then ("expect the unexpected" we used to advertise, trying to make a virtue out of a vice), and for one other reason, I was able to do what I wanted. The other reason was that, except perhaps for *The New Yorker*, there was then little competition from any other big magazines for the work of the major literary writers, and there were at the same time just then and coming along a bit later, an extraordinary number of marvelous fiction writers—Bellow, Malamud, Roth, Barth, dozens of them—who had rarely if ever published short fiction outside the so-called "little" magazines. At first they were skeptical about *Esquire*'s interest, but then they'd send something and we'd run it.

I was really busy, happily busy, in those years: searching out new writers, editing stories, excerpting novels, arguing with the other editors for more space for fiction, making "scouting" trips, giving talks at colleges. I had expense-account lunches with writers, literary agents, and book publishers lined up for a month and a half in advance. "You've got to be kidding," an agent would say to me sometime before Christmas. "You mean you can't have lunch with me until next *February?*" Also I was busy promoting the fiction: we got out anthologies of *Esquire* stories, ran contests with Houghton Mifflin and other publishers, and I organized the sequence of *Esquire* Symposiums on "The Role of the Writer in America," where each year we'd take four well-known writers to different campuses under *Esquire*'s auspices. Somewhere toward the end of my time at the magazine—1963 it was—I prepared my monstrous chart of "The Structure of the American Literary Establishment" for a special "literary issue" of *Esquire*, and gathered for that an account of what "everyone" was writing, along with samples of Work-in-Progress. Even the things I did on the side—like teaching short-story writing at Columbia and The New School, or running a summer writers' conference on Staten Island—seemed somehow related to the job of being fiction editor of *Esquire*. It all worked well, for the magazine and for me. I really *had* somehow "found myself" in that role: I had a complete sense of what I was supposed to be doing and (hence, I guess) a sense of "who I was."

But after seven years I began to get bored, and perhaps a bit discouraged. There didn't seem to be so many good new writers to get, everything had somehow been done. Harold Hayes printed so much of the good "New Journalism" that all but demonstrably brilliant stories got crowded out of the magazine. When the chance came (at double my *Esquire* salary) to do the same thing at *The Saturday Evening Post* (which could publish as much fiction in a week as *Esquire* did in a month), I tried it. But it didn't work there. Let's just say that "events," and perhaps "circumstances," too, conspired against it. Besides, it was more or less the same work. I was getting fat from the expense-account lunches and drinking way too much, occupational hazards. And I was really sick of seeing the same 180 publishing people at lunch, cocktail parties, dinners, and weekends. I'd spend long hours staring at a huge, marvelously small-town Norman Rockwell in my New York office at the *Post*; then I'd swivel around and spend long hours staring out the windows, thinking of all that needed to be done—all that I so much *wanted* to do—at the place I'd bought in the country, Coveside.

Finally I had the feeling I just couldn't go on the way I was. There was no other job in publishing that interested me, so I thought, Hell, I'll take at least a year off, maybe two, "to think things over." I can always get another job or some kind of part-time work, and meanwhile I'll get Coveside all fixed up (what a laugh!), and see what happens.

It seemed a cliché to retire at forty, so I waited until November, when I became forty-one, even though that meant beginning my new life in the country just at the beginning of winter.

CHAPTER ONE

Life Among the Routines

To know how to free oneself is nothing; the arduous
thing is to know what to do with one's freedom.
—André Gide, *The Immoralist*

Prerequisites to Retirement

IF YOU want to retire at forty-one, it seems to me that there are *at least* three absolute prerequisites. (It always turns out somehow that there may be more, is why I say "at least.") First and foremost is that you *be* forty-one and have a job to retire *from*. Second, you should be somewhat fed up with your work; otherwise, there wouldn't be much point (in fact, no point whatsoever) in quitting, not if you were enjoying it. Third, you should have done fairly well when you were working, so you won't feel your retreat is some kind of defeat. Fourth—and this may not seem as important as the others, but is pretty much what all that follows is about—you should have some idea of how you are going to use up all the time that will suddenly become available.

"And fifth," you say, "is that I have to have some money to live on."

That's nonsense. I discount the money problem more or less entirely. If you *really* want to quit work, you could do it tomorrow—you know you could. Certainly you could do it within six months, after simplifying your life and making certain arrangements you've got in the back of your mind. *Anybody* can quit work—even if it means drawing unemployment insurance, camping out, and living on welfare.

The thing is, it's far more expensive to work than we ever realize. The place you live, the way you move around, the kind of entertaining you do, the taxis you take and the taxes you pay, all the things you pay others to do because you don't have time to do them yourself, the very clothes on your back—all these, and in fact virtually all aspects of your life, financial and otherwise, but financial is what I'm talking about now—all are determined by your work. And all of them are more expensive because you are working than they would be if you were not.

No matter what money you are making, most of it gets slurped right back by how you have to live to do your job. Working in publishing, for instance, you have to have a big apartment or a small brownstone in New York City, a summer- and winter-weekends place in some reasonably fashionable exurb, cars (one garaged in the city at a huge rental every month), kids in private schools, some kind of live-in or nearly full-time help, lots of taxes to pay, the pleasant "necessity" or "justification" for taking taxis hurriedly everywhere, people in to dinner all the time, expensive nights out on the town, and so on. It's all more or less "required," isn't it?

But none of it would really be *required* if you retire, would it? So your decision to quit work will also have to be a decision to give up a lot of those pleasures of your working life-style—assuming you still think of all those complexities as pleasures. Those luxurious "necessities" are immediately seen to be unnecessary luxuries. That's all expense-account living, and when you quit work you give up the expense account as well as the salary. But you can make some money anyway, if you want to, doing odd bits of work in your spare time, now that you'll have time to spare. And you get to deduct a whole lot of your living expenses if you work out of your home rather than in an office on straight salary. But even if you do have to alter your living arrangements drastically, I feel that's good for you: it emphasizes that you're beginning a whole new life that you'll have to adjust to. One can get by on remarkably little. Money's not the real problem in retiring at forty-one, not at all.

We'll consider the real problems peculiar to the retired life as we consider the peculiar solutions. Let me just say now that the change from work to leisure is very tough, gets to be very *painful,* as any major change in life is always painful. And it is somehow possible to *fail.*

How can you "fail" in retirement? It's not exactly like failing in business, but it's not exactly unlike it either. Your investment in your retirement is personal rather than financial, but it is nonetheless substantial. You go into it with such hope about yourself, with such an expectation of achieving a higher, better life of true leisure—and there is such a risk of it ending in a kind of emotional and spiritual bankruptcy.

You have to know what you are doing. It is perhaps the least thing to say about the great French writer Michel de Montaigne, but he was a very successful retiree. He did it at thirty-eight, but he knew exactly what he was up to:

> Being long out of patience with public duties and the servitude of the court, I retired to my own house in the year 1571, when I was thirty-eight and still in good health. I planned to pass in peace and security the days that remained before me in this sweet paternal abode, and consecrate it to my independence, quiet, and leisure.
>
> I did not flee from men, but from affairs. We have lived long enough for others: let us live the rest for ourselves; let us disentangle ourselves from the clutch of things which hold us elsewhere and keep us from ourselves. The greatest thing in the world is to know how to belong to yourself.*

Montaigne did find out how to belong to himself, and you who are about to retire will be inspired by his saying that it is "the greatest thing in the world." But Montaigne goes on very sensibly to warn:

> If you plan to withdraw into yourself, first prepare yourself a welcome. It is folly to trust yourself in your own hands if they cannot hold you. And man can fail in solitude as in society.

Everyone knows retired men who have failed. They are a mess: frittering their days away in elaborate time-consuming routines; frittering from superficial involvement in one pursuit to another, cabinet making one week, ecology the next. Absolutely out of touch with the

---

*Montaigne will rejoin us later from time to time. I think you'll find he is the best company there is. Many of my quotations from his work (the one above is slightly shortened, by the way) are from Marvin Lowenthal's rearrangement of the essays as *The Autobiography of Michel de Montaigne*. This splendid book would be a complete delight if only one didn't feel so guilty about reading it instead of the essays as they were originally written. For the solution to this problem, see the footnote on page 138.

way things really are, irascible and fuss-budgety, either lushes or
AAS, opinionated yet indecisive, they live empty, purposeless, wasted
lives. When a man retires, he feels sure he can avoid becoming like
that; perhaps those already retired feel they *have* avoided it. The
trouble is—*one* trouble is—that there's no outside judgment on you:
you don't get promoted, nor do you get passed over for promotion.
It is much harder in solitude to *know* if you've failed than it is in
society.

My own attempt to retire at forty-one, while not perhaps an out-
and-out *failure*, has to be considered as something less than a roaring
success. I mean, I *did* retire when I was forty-one—oh, God, yes—
but the retirement itself left a good deal to be desired. *Quite* a good
deal. Does this disqualify me from telling *you* how to do it? Not at
all. Was The Ancient Mariner disqualified from telling you about
the albatross simply because his ship sank? I can always preach
much better than I can practice anyway. Do as I say, I always say,
not as I do.

The "Problem" of Retirement

THE MAIN problem in retirement is that one's life is utterly unstruc-
tured, with no schedule, no "hours," no order to the day's or week's
events, except what you establish yourself. Other aspects of the problem will come up as we consider various solutions, for I'm becoming
more and more convinced that a great deal of the problem lies in the
solutions. I don't mean to be enigmatic or (God knows) epigram-
matic; what I mean by "the problem lies in the solutions" (It does
sound a little mystical, doesn't it?) is really very simpleminded. The
central problem of how to retire at forty-one is how to know what to
do with all that available time.

You say, "Nothing. I'm just going to relax and do nothing." I say,
Nobody can do purely *nothing* for more than about two days. Just
take my word for that. You'll see when you try it.

All right, then: *something* must be done. Whatever is done, whatever one attempts to *do*, is a potential "solution." It is in the failure
of a sequence of these *solutions* (and the resultant debilitating effect

on the individual who makes these attempts) that the *problem* of an early retirement occurs.

For, you see, what you have to do in order not to fall apart is really quite difficult: you have to plan and organize everything so that you won't suddenly be just left there dangling with nothing whatsoever to do.

It's frighteningly as though all the laws of regular life were suspended, or perhaps reversed. It's not true anymore, for instance, that "work expands to fill the time available," because there is no work *to* expand, and there is an *infinity* of time available. Other "rules" of life are similarly revoked. The old cliché "Time is Money," for instance, no longer holds true, since there's no way to make money (through earning a salary or making a deal, or whatever) in any time saved. In fact, time saved is really money *lost*, because you may have to pay something (for a magazine or a movie or a trip to Europe) to fill it up. Everything is backwards: it's a new world, a looking-glass world.

Out of the rat race, then, and down the rabbit hole. Let's consider these solutions that define our problem. The traditional solutions to the available-time problem of not working have always been of two kinds: routines and/or pursuits. By "pursuits" I mean all the various so-called leisure pursuits—such as outdoor pursuits, travel pursuits, intellectual pursuits, and pursuits of "interests" of all sorts and kinds. But we'll discuss pursuits later, routines now.

❦

The Rationale of Routine

LEISURED PEOPLE of the upper class traditionally have tried to establish the most elaborate time-consuming routine for their lives as possible: long meals, changing clothes as often as possible during each day, calling on people or being called on in a ritualistic way—all that rich sort of thing. That kind of life is pretty much gone, of course—but not because it didn't do the job of filling up the time. It just took too much money, too many servants, a degree of exclusivity which is now hardly possible, and also a lot of skill and practice and training. It all constituted "a traditional way of life" which has little relation to the more informal contemporary life-styles. But we middle-class Pioneers of the New Leisure have a lot to learn from the theories *and practices* of the Old Leisure Class, and in our preoccupation with pursuits we must certainly never underestimate the time-consuming virtues and the numbing powers of good old-fashioned routine.

In the modern world, routines are not likely to be formal and ritualistic, but informal and (to some extent at least) functional. They often bear a close resemblance to Chores & Maintenance. Chores & Maintenance, for some retired people, often become pursuits (cooking meals as a hobby; the do-it-yourself "fun" of home repairs, etc.), but for most people they are more usefully incorporated into routines.

Thus it is that things you'd just do routinely in the regular working world on the way to or from work—taking clothes to the cleaner's, getting a haircut, having something repaired, reading a newspaper, buying a new pair of shoes, getting gas for the car, and so on—things that just get done somehow, anyhow, when you're working, become ends, objects, tasks. They are made into something very like *work itself* when you're retired.

A Sample Comprehensive Day Plan

EACH EVENING before going to bed, you should make a list of what you intend to do the next day. This is useful in counteracting the dreadful moments of emptiness and purposelessness and uncertainty that assault one upon awakening each morning.

So it is that first light will find you already up. Busy day *ahead!* A quick breakfast, gulping coffee while checking over the list of "Things To Do Wednesday" prepared the night before. Some of us like to put it in the form of a schedule, in which case it serves as a Comprehensive Day Plan, or as we know it around our house—"The C.D.P."

THINGS TO DO WEDNESDAY

Prelude

6:45	arise
7:00–7:30	shave, wash, etc.
7:30–7:45	have breakfast
7:45–8:15	check over this list
8:15–8:40	prepare things for errands:

        outboard engine from rowboat to truck
        laundry to truck
        measure cracked pane pantry entrance door
        check name good kind honey
        remember take check and $s
        other?

Major Activity I: *Errands in Mystic Area*
(8:40–11:00; 1 hour and 20 minutes)

8:40–8:50	drive to Mystic (5 minutes)
8:50–8:55	stationery store (5 minutes)

    NY Times
    new *Newsweek* in?
    black Bic ballpoint (not fine, *medium*)
    Swingline "Tot" staples

8:55–9:15   Old Mystic Marina (20 minutes, including travel to this, the farthest point)
    leave outboard
    ask when ready
    got a tide table?

9:15–9:30   The Honey House (15 minutes)
    get good kind honey

9:30–9:40   Ella's Bakery (10 minutes)
    6 sugar buns
    ask: any cinnamon twists today?
    if not: which day?

9:40–10:00   Cottrell's Lumber Co. (20 minutes)
    ask: dishwasher silver basket ordered in yet?
    new pane of glass for pantry entrance door
    extra Elmer's glue

                          Cabot's tree paint
                          small nails
10:00–10:20   A & P (20 minutes)
                          paper towels
                          beef kidneys for dog
                             (or chicken giblets if no kidneys)
                          Eversharp hotdogs
                          Mott's applesauce
                          B&M beans, pea, New Eng style (molasses)
                          Boston brown bread
                          5 pounds onions
                          lemons!!!
10:20–10:30   Puritan Laundry (10 minutes)
                          leave off laundry
                          pick up laundry if ready
                          if not ready, when ready?
                          when *this* laundry ready?
10:30–10:45   Jim Esso's (15 minutes)
                          fill up with gas
                          get them to check: oil
                                         water (radiator)
                                         water (battery)
                          ask: has new windshield wiper blade come in yet?
                          ask: why haven't they sent bill?
10:45–10:55   Cove Fish Market (10 minutes)
                          flat fish for lunch
                          if no flat fish, see what else they have
10:55–11:00   drive home (5 minutes)
11:00–11:30   catch breath
                          have coffee
                          read *NY Times*

                          Major Activity II: *Replace broken glass pantry
                          entrance door*
                          (11:30–12:20; 50 minutes)
                          things needed:
                             trash can from garage
                             putty and putty knife from boathouse
                             the little goomies that hold the glass

hammer
new pane of glass from truck
steps to take:
  break out old glass remaining
  scrape away the old dried putty
  put in new glass, goomies, then putty
  return all above things where they belong

Intermezzo

12:20–12:40	prepare lunch
	hot dogs, baked beans, brown bread? flat fish?
12:40–1:00	eat lunch
1:00–1:10	clean up lunch dishes, etc.
1:10–1:30	get mail from mailbox
	read mail (if any)
	read *Compass* and other circulars
1:30–1:45	pay bills – Jim Esso?
1:45–2:15	write letters
	write Sears Roebuck re power saw parts
	write Shelley re his new job

Major Activity III: *Errands in Stonington*
(2:15–3:50; 1 hour, 35 mins)

2:15–2:25	drive to Stonington (10 minutes)
2:25–2:45	Roland's Market (20 minutes)
	dog kidney (if none at A&P)
	1 pound hamburger
	1 pound slab bacon
	2 pkgs frozen petite peas
	2 pork chops
2:45–2:55	Paul Schepis' Liquor Store (10 minutes)
	1 B&L scotch
	1 Wilson's blend
2:55–3:00	Frankie Keane's stationery store (5 minutes)
	New London *Day*
	new *Newsweek* in? (if not got in AM)
	Bic pen as above (if not in AM)

3:00–3:30	Bailey's (20-minute visit)
	return Annie Bailey's sweater
	*remember take sweater
3:30–3:40	Stonington Bank (10 minutes)
	cash check
	*remember take check
3:40–3:50	Post Office (10 minutes)
	mail letters
	get book of regular stamps
	*remember take letters
3:50–4:00	drive home from Stonington (10 minutes)
4:00–4:10	sit in truck
	catch breath
	carry stuff in from truck

Major Activity IV: *Cut broken limb off maple tree*
(4:10–5:35; 1 hour and 25 minutes)
things needed:
    Cabot's tree paint from truck
    stepladder from garage
    pruning saw from tool shed
    lawn mower-tractor from garage
    paint brush from boathouse
    ax from tool shed
steps to take:
    saw off limb, remembering to make undercut first
    paint with tree paint (the tree)
    lop off leaves, etc.
    cart them to mulch pile
    drag limb to wood pile place with tractor
    return all above things where they belong

Coda

5:35–5:45	get Cabot's tree paint off hands w Lava Soap
5:45–6:00	burn trash
6:00–6:30	read New London *Day*
6:30–6:40	bring in fireplace wood
	set fire

---

*I always put an asterisk (*) when I have to remember to take something.

6:40–6:50	put on pork chops
	applesauce into bowl
	make coffee
	set table for dinner, etc.
6:50–7:00	make whiskey sour
7:00	light fire
7:00–7:30	enjoy fire
	enjoy whiskey sour
7:30–8:15	eat dinner
8:15–8:30	put dishes in dishwasher
	turn on same
	clean all up, etc.
8:30–10:00	make list: "Things To Do Thursday"
10:00–10:15	listen to ten o'clock news
10:15–10:30	walk with dog
	enjoy night air
	turn out lights
	shut house, etc.
10:30–10:45	get ready for bed
10:45–11:00	read?
11:00 sharp	lights out! Big day tomorrow!

Oh, a list schedule of the sort presented is really invaluable. One should make it out faithfully each night and keep it somewhere about him all during the day. The schedule part is a great help in *knowing what to do next,* because retired people are in very great danger of becoming totally immobilized. And the list part is useful for when people say to you: "Well, what do you have to do today?" Then you can wave the sheaves of paper at them and answer: "Oh, Good Lord, what *don't* I have to do today! Just look at this *list* a mile long!"

❦

Mapping Out the Errand Routes

SOME DAYS, of course, will have different routines (too bad, but *true*). Of course you won't stop at the gas station every day. (If you ask them to "Fill it up" when the tank is more than three-quarters full, it shuts off almost right away and they look at you funny.) But there is usually *some* laundry or cleaning to pick up or leave off, or something to leave off for repair or pick up afterward or even just see if it is ready yet. You can spend a whole morning driving around seeing if various things are ready yet, but if you do it more than once a month, people begin to realize that you don't have anything better to do.

Some days the routines you use to kill time may be very different, but because it is all written down and scheduled, it still seems like routine, even though it varies.

Everything is scattered all over in a way that requires fantastic planning and scheduling and a strong geographical-historical grasp or *vision* of the shape and sequence of the errand expedition as a whole. Ideally, one would go into a sort of out-of-body trance to achieve a bird's-eye view of where everything was and look down on it to determine the best routes and order for the errands – a *futuristic* out-of-body experience so that you could see it all in advance to permit better planning.

It seems one is always having to go from town to town to get this best product or that best service, yet of course things being what they are in this country today, most of the buying isn't done in any of the villages at all, but in the shopping centers located between them. Everybody must have these problems.

But I don't know. Maybe everyone *doesn't* have these problems. I just finally had to buy some trousers, and I was in Bendett's in Mystic the other day for about an hour, resolved that I *would not leave* until I'd bought something.

Me: "What I want is just some regular old khaki trousers like they issued me at the Merchant Marine Academy in World War Two."

Patient Clerk-Owner: "Well, we've got some khaki-type trousers over here."

Me: "Do they have the permanent press?"

Patient Clerk-Owner (proudly): "Oh, yes, sir. All our washable trousers have permanent press."

Me: "Don't you have any *without* the permanent press?"

Patient Clerk-Owner: "Don't you *want* permanent press?"

Me: "No, I really don't. I hate to seem to be against progress, but I don't."

Patient Clerk-Owner: "Why not? They save ironing. You just put them in the washing machine and they come out looking good."

Me: "But I don't put them in the washing machine. I send them to the Puritan Laundry. You know? Over on Route 1, behind the Carvel ice-cream stand?"

Clerk-Owner: "Yes."

Me: "Well, they have two ways of doing the laundry: 'rough-dried' is one, 'finished' is the other. I have the shirts finished – that is, ironed, with no starch. Everything else is rough-dried, just folded, which isn't very nice, but it's a lot cheaper. If I have the trousers rough-dried, they come out all wrinkled and crinkly. If I have the trousers *pressed,* they come out with two creases: one the permanent-press crease, the other the Puritan Laundry crease. See? Here." (I show him.)

Clerk-Owner: "I see."

Me: "Doesn't anyone else have this problem?"

Clerk-Owner: "I don't know, sir. Certainly no one else has ever carried on so about it."

Or I go into a big sort of self-service drugstore so as to save a bit of money; among the things I want to get is a tube of Unguentine. To save a bit of time, I ask the lady at the cash register where the Unguentine is.

"Third aisle, sir, almost all the way down, on the right."

"Thank you," I say, then proceed as directed, and start looking.

Meanwhile the pharmacist, who had been at the cash register, is walking down the next aisle on his way back to the glass-enclosed area where he fills prescriptions. "Finding it all right, sir?" he asks me.

"Well," I say, "as a matter of fact I'm not. I feel very stupid. I know it's yellow, and it must be right here in front of me somewhere, but I just don't see it."

He comes around the rear of the store into my aisle, reaches down right in front of my nose, where if it had been a bear it would have bit me, and picks up a tube. It's sealed onto a piece of cardboard in a plastic casing. "New Improved Unguentine," it says on the cardboard, among other things.

"But it's not *yellow,*" I say to the friendly pharmacist. "It's red, white, and blue."

"Well, they've changed it recently," he says, smiling. "They've improved it."

"I hope they haven't changed the smell," I say. "I used to love the smell of Unguentine."

"I don't know about that," he says. "Just what did you want to use it for, sir?"

"Oh," I say, "for sunburn and mosquito bites and like that. It used to have a pungent, sort of *soothing* smell, very evocative of summer."

The pharmacist is moving back toward his glass-enclosed booth, so I call after him: "I don't suppose there's any way of opening it up to see if the smell's changed, is there? It's all sealed up in this plastic-cardboard case."

"I'm afraid not, sir," he says. "You'll just have to take your chances."

I stand there and consider the matter for a while. My guess is that they *have* changed the smell; they're always changing things. I walk back to the pharmacist. "I'm just not going to take the chance," I tell him through the window. "A tube of Unguentine lasts a long time, you know. If it weren't right it would be a constant annoyance every time I opened the medicine chest and saw it there. I'm just going to do without."

"As you wish," says the pharmacist. "It seems to be your problem, sir." He goes back to his own work.

The clerk and the pharmacist act as though I don't realize these are self-created problems. *Of course* I know that: if they *weren't* self-created I could solve them in a minute.

❦

Having Things to Do, as Against Getting Things Done

I'M SURE it scarcely needs pointing out that despite all this wild running around and scheduling and planning and all, nothing actually gets done, or very little, or very little that won't need doing again right away, or soon. The pane of glass that got fixed? In the house and outbuildings there are (not counting mirrors, medicine cabinets, picture glass, etc.) four hundred and seventeen (417!) panes of glass. I just counted them, as follows:

house downstairs (including porch)	116
house upstairs	57
boathouse	82
studio	58
garage	40
storage shed	40
tool shed	24
TOTAL	417

It really doesn't seem all that bright anywhere, either. People should *count* the panes of glass in their house every once in a while: it would give them a greater sense of the fragility that envelops human life. At any rate, I'm not saying that a pane of glass breaks every day; even I don't have a problem like that. It's just that you can't replace a pane of glass and say, "*There,* that's done," and feel you'll *never* have to do it again.

It's another of the paradoxes in the looking-glass world of retirement: You want the feeling of doing something all the time, of being busy and efficient, but you don't want to get too much done. It is an aspect of the working world, this emphasis on *getting things done.* In the no-work world, the idea is not necessarily to get things done, but to *have things to do.* Thus you may cut through the routines and the errands and chores and concentrate on getting a specific job done, but then you no longer have it to look forward to, you can no longer spend time wondering what's the best way to do it, and it's no longer on your list of things to do someday. It is true that if you don't get *anything* done, then you despair at your purposelessness and unproductivity–but you don't experience this so much if you are busy all day, quickly going from one thing to another.

❧

Maintaining a Country Place, as a Routine

INCREDIBLY HELPFUL (in fact almost indispensable) in achieving this balance between a sense of busyness and activity on the one hand, and a sense that there is always going to be something to do on the other, is the possession of either a house in the country or an old sailboat. Either of these is capable of solving the problems of even the most active man. (Always remember: a good deal of the problem lies in the solution!) And if a man were to possess *both*, then, by God, he could retire at *thirty*-one! This is one of the reasons rich people are more likely not to have jobs: they can afford things like country houses and yachts.

A place in the country is invaluable because it more or less automatically produces a variety and amount of work capable of filling even an infinity of available time. That's because the place actually *creates* more things for you to do, *even as you're doing them!* Undoubtedly, you can prune a bush faster than the bush can grow. But do you think that while you're pruning one bush all the others are just sitting there doing nothing? Even the bush you're working on is making new, more robust and determined plans for the future. Even as you're fixing something, other things elsewhere in the house are getting ready to break.

The "work" of a country place can run the whole gamut from simple contemplation (going to look at how the gutter is pulling loose on the north side of the house) to general maintenance (waxing the floors) to minor repairs (fixing doorknobs, towel racks) to projects (transplanting a rosebush) to giant projects (building a new porch). Whole seasons take care of themselves: snow shoveling, lawn mowing, lawn watering, leaf raking. Some tasks (painting or pruning, for instance) can be so prolonged or done so intermittently that they *always* need doing. *Always! Always* need *doing!* There's both consolation and terror in a thought like that. An infinity of time, seemingly, can be spent messing about with screens alone: painting them, washing them, wire-brushing them, mending them, replacing them, and of course taking them down and putting up the storm windows and then taking down the storm windows and putting up the screens again.

And it isn't at all necessary to try to do all these things oneself. Trying to hire somebody to mow lawns or put up storm windows and then trying to keep track of him – when he's coming, and then why he didn't come, and when does he think he will be able to come? – that can fill up the time nearly as well.

One of the things Montaigne meant, surely, when he said, "If you plan to withdraw into yourself, first prepare yourself a welcome," was, "Get a country place." He had one, of course, and that's where he went right away after he retired, and stayed there most of the rest of his life.

Maintaining an Old Sailboat, as a Routine

IT IS a truism that there is always something that needs to be done on (or to) a large sailing boat, especially if it is at all old (and hence wooden rather than plastic), and even if one were never to sail it. First of all, it always needs cleaning: getting the muck out of the bilges every so often, airing the bunk mattresses (nothing ever really dries), cleaning the galley stove, or simply the difficult business of cleaning up after a meal on board, endless swabbing and scrubbing the decks, and so on. And then there's maintenance: the brightwork to be sanded down and varnished, the deck to paint, the brass to polish, hauling it in and out to scrub or paint the bottom. There are always improvements to be made: a better way to rig the genoa leads, a better chart table to install on the centerboard trunk, more comfortable pipe bunks forward. But what really keeps one busy are the repairs: the tear in the leech of the mainsail; the third snap hook from the top on the jib doesn't close properly; the throttle cable on the auxiliary engine sticks; there are leaks in the cabin decking and leaks in the bottom planking; there's dry rot in the stem and regular rot in the deadwood in the stern; line ends always need whipping; blocks jam, stays fray, turnbuckles seize up, chain plates rust, propellers foul, ribs crack, sails mildew, portholes stick, pumps clog, winches won't work—sometimes it seems as though *everything* needs fixing! Then the garboards may go (the *garboards!*).

Anyone who has ever owned a largish, oldish wooden sailing boat must stand in awe of it as a time-consuming mechanism. All it lacks is a lawn to mow. It produces and consumes happy hours, days, weeks, months, *years* of work. God knows. It may in fact be God's supreme act of benefice to the man who retires early, for only a reasonably young man would have anything like the vigor and foolishness to take on an old boat in the first place.

During the halcyon, zealous early days of my retirement I owned

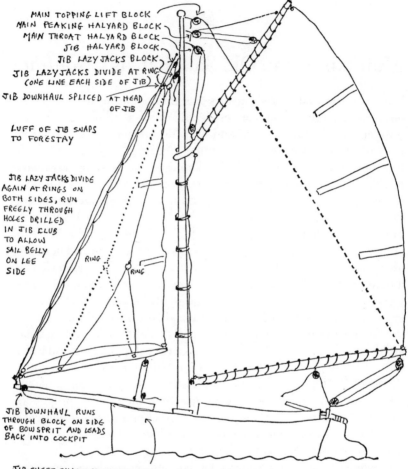

MAIN TOPPING LIFT BLOCK
MAIN PEAKING HALYARD BLOCK
MAIN THROAT HALYARD BLOCK
JIB HALYARD BLOCK
JIB LAZY JACKS BLOCK
JIB LAZYJACKS DIVIDE AT RING
(ONE LINE EACH SIDE OF JIB)
JIB DOWNHAUL SPLICED AT HEAD OF JIB

LUFF OF JIB SNAPS TO FORESTAY

JIB LAZY JACKS DIVIDE AGAIN AT RINGS ON BOTH SIDES, RUN FREELY THROUGH HOLES DRILLED IN JIB CLUB TO ALLOW SAIL BELLY ON LEE SIDE

RING

RING

JIB DOWNHAUL RUNS THROUGH BLOCK ON SIDE OF BOWSPRIT AND LEADS BACK INTO COCKPIT

JIB SHEET SHACKLES TO EYE BOLT PORT SIDE, RUNS THROUGH BLOCK LASHED UNDER CLUB, THROUGH BLOCK ON EYE BOLT STARBOARD SIDE, BACK AND THROUGH STARBOARD COMBING INTO COCKPIT.

(JIB IS LOOSE-FOOTED, SECURES TO CLUB AT CLEW AND TACK)

THE RIGGING OF TRUTH

such a boat, and of course I loved it in the despairing sort of way that fellow loved the waitress in *Of Human Bondage*. The sailboat fit absolutely perfectly into the boathouse. She came with no name, and I made no inquiries about it, simply called her "Truth."

"Truth" was only about fifteen feet long, but of course she seemed much larger, as old heavy wooden sailboats do. In fact, in a way, she was larger – a big wooden rudder stuck out aft, and a bowsprit stuck out four feet forward.

The first year I had her, I just slapped some paint on her and sailed her. But then I got into the grip of another of my looney dreams. I read about "Alerion," a sloop Nathaniel Herreschoff designed for himself in old age, the perfect single-handed day-sailer. Herreschoff could come tacking up to a yacht-club dock and drop all the sails, instantly and smoothly, without ever leaving the cockpit, barely even stirring himself. Before my eyes flashed the vision of me doing it too. I saw myself in "Truth," dressed in a white linen suit, with a necktie of course, and one of those floppy white sun hats Franklin Roosevelt wore sailing at Campobello. Over on elegant Fishers Island I'd sail "Truth" close by the DuPonts' big yawl, "Barlovento," and all the other fancy yachts, everyone in the harbor admiring how easily I handled her. Immediately I sent away to L.L. Bean for one of those hats.

But what I got into after that was an obsessive act, and it was the kind of thing you could only do if you were retired. Oh, I had a great time doing it! I rigged every line and sail so it could be handled right at the tiller, and I was going to do even more, until something finally made me hesitate: I'd already installed blocks and cleats all over the spars, deck, and cockpit, and I was beginning to get confused.

What if I had an accident? Who would figure it all out? Or suppose I got amnesia? Even if I didn't get amnesia, I wasn't sure I could remember how it all went. It was autumn when I did this, "Truth" safely in the boathouse where I could work on her, and the sails and spars spread out on the lawn while I rigged it all merrily, madly. I decided to make a diagram, called "The Rigging of Truth," which I know sounds like the way people in Washington manipulate the news, but isn't.

Finally I coiled all the lines neatly, neatly tied labeling tags to each of them, neatly lettered with what they were – main throat halyard, jib lazy jacks, main sheet, jib sheet, jib downhaul, main topping lift, jib halyard, main peaking halyard, main boom lashing line, gaff boom lashing line, and so on—then neatly tacked the diagram up on the boathouse wall and arranged all the lines on pegs around it. Off and on I'd go out to look at it, to see if I remembered, and of course to show it to people.

But then when spring came I was away, and when I confronted it all in midsummer it seemed far too complicated to set it up for just a few weeks' sailing.

Work Work, as Against Leisure Work

AN EARLY retirement provides an unparalleled opportunity to indulge in obsessive acts. You are young enough still to have the vitality to get your whole mind and body into a project and go at it full tilt (don't think of windmills). You think up the idea yourself; you don't have to talk anybody else into authorizing it. Whatever you decide to do—make a table, plant a huge vegetable garden, put up a fence, erect a flag pole, lay a terrace, add a porch, build a barbecue pit (or even a windmill)—whatever—you can draw up a plan for the project, approve it yourself, make a list of all the stuff you need, get to go to the hardware store or lumber yard and buy it, bring it all home on the roof of the car, and set to work, happy as a clam. Nothing beats this kind of activity: it's what *you* want to do, not what someone told you to do; the end result is going to be yours, not belong to someone else; you can do it really *right*, not cutting corners for economy of time or money; and you can go at the job just as long and as hard as you want.

Eventually you may have to come to the realization that your project was a dumb waste of time, that it was stupid to have got started on in the first place; but that's later, and anyway you get to make the evaluation yourself, because there are no subordinates or superiors to disappoint—just you yourself alone.

In all these respects, retirement activities are the opposite of regular office work. Most working jobs don't require, or even permit, anything like your full-time, full-steam effort. Every worker knows this, even though not everyone will admit it. Even the overworked executive, who works harder than most anyone else usually, who takes a briefcase of work home evenings and weekends, knows that during the week, during regular office hours, he's spent a lot of time in desultory chatting with people who stop in his office, leisurely lunching with a cohort or contact, or simply daydreaming behind his closed door.

Such a man or woman may gradually begin to realize that the job could be done just as well, or nearly as well, on a part-time basis. He may not even think of it as "semi-retirement," because he isn't really old enough to call it that; but what he wants to try is doing the same job working just in the mornings, or only three days a week. If the job doesn't really require more time than that, why should he spend it?

In some ways it's difficult to explain why the part-time job possibility doesn't work out, and in other ways it seems obvious on the face of it that it wouldn't. Employers and colleagues for the most part hate it, because it is an LCT that whatever day you're not in the office is the day everything happens, and you're never there when they want you, or think they do. No one else can quite figure out just what your on-off schedule *is,* or they pretend they can't. It disrupts them at the office and interrupts your endeavors at home. The part-time job demeans work: it thwarts involvement, denies any real achievement. A part-time job is a neurotic compromise between working and not working: it has the advantage of neither, such as they are.

Whatever activity you've gotten into in retirement, on the other hand, has a purity—an almost existential kind of purity (and whether it's a purity of purpose or a purity of purposelessness doesn't really matter), which simply cannot pertain to mundane workaday labors. Leisure work is uncontaminated by pay or directives or procedures or time-clocks or any other rigmarole of the workplace.

But the workplace concept of time is very difficult to escape. People don't realize until they've quit work how very basic, almost instinctual, the rhythms of the nine-to-five office working day have become. In the cities it's almost tidal: the regular ebb and flow of workers moving in and out, day after day. There's a sensitivity and accommodation to this workday routine, as if it were in the bloodstream or the metabolism of modern urban-bureaucratic-industrial man, the way primitive man was once attuned to the forces of Nature. And that totally arbitrary division of time, the week, which controls the activities and thinking of the rest of the world, pertains to you in retirement not at all.

You're busy, busy, busy, happy as can be, and suddenly the phone rings. It's a friend, calling from his office; he asks you to dinner, day after tomorrow. "That's Friday night," he says, "and boy am I looking forward to it!"

You feel a pang of nostalgia, a great wave of yearning. You remember how you all used to laugh together in the office: "Thank God it's Friday"—that sort of jolly, companionable anticipation of release from the busyness and tensions and boredom of the workweek.

After you've been retired for a few months, it's liable to hit you hard: no more weekends, no more Friday nights, no holidays or vacations ever again. No more "time-off" for you.

But when your life is *all* time-off, it's all "free time," and free time is the ultimate freedom. Because time is no longer divided in the conventional way—into workhours, workdays, workweeks—it may compress on you alarmingly or stretch excruciatingly, because it exists without regard to the time others are living by. It is *your* time, and yours alone. You can experience a scary exaltation, existing in a time that is utterly your own. Your daily destiny is unique and unpredictable, entirely in your own hands. You have transcended ordinary daily life! *C'est la vie quotidienne extraordinaire!*

This presents an enormous challenge: you must seize not just the day, but the hour, the week, the month, and the year as well, and elevate them all by the excellence of your leisure pursuits.

CHAPTER TWO

Life Among the Pursuits

The employments a man should choose for a life of
retirement should be neither hard nor displeasing;
otherwise there is no point in it.
—MONTAIGNE

❦

Training for Leisure Pursuits

WHAT IS needed for successful retirement is a kind of heroism—a
hero's body and a hero's mind. Unlikely as it seems, retirement and
heroism have a great deal in common. For instance, consider the
perfect model of a hero, Rudolf Rassendyll, hero of that textbook of
heroism, *The Prisoner of Zenda*. In the very opening line of that novel,
this hero of heroes is attacked for not working—

> "I wonder when in the world you're going to do anything,
> Rudolf?" said my brother's wife.

Now hear how Rudolf Rassendyll answers his busybody sister-in-
law:

> "My dear Rose," I answered, laying down my eggspoon, "why
> in the world should I do anything? My position is a comfortable
> one. I have an income nearly sufficient for my wants (no one's
> income is ever quite sufficient, you know). I enjoy an enviable
> position: I am brother to Lord Burlesdon, and brother-in-law to
> that charming lady his countess. Behold, it is enough!"

That is the elegant way retired people ought to talk, and how
unfortunate it is that so few of us do. Most of us don't even *have* an
eggspoon.

The thing is, that Rudolf is *equipped* to be retired, *trained* for it, *prepared* in both mind and body. How he describes it is:

> [My sister-in-law had been] pointing to the uselessness of the life I had led. Well, be that as it may, I had picked up a good deal of pleasure and a good deal of knowledge. I had been to a German school and a German university, and spoke German as readily and perfectly as English; I was thoroughly at home in French; I had a smattering of Italian, and enough Spanish to swear by. I was, I believe, a strong, though hardly a fine, swordsman and a good shot. I could ride anything that had a back to sit on; and my head was as cool a one as you could find, for all its flaming cover. If you say that I ought to have spent my time in useful labor I am out of court and have nothing to say, save that my parents had no business to leave me two thousand pounds a year and a roving disposition.

That business about the "flaming cover" of course refers to Rudolf's red hair, which makes him look exactly like the young King of Ruritania, who gets kidnapped, and Rudolf stands in for, and then rescues, and so on. Rudolf is a real hero, a real hero in the old-fashioned sense—not a modern nonhero and antihero or reluctant hero. Real heroes don't have jobs; they don't have hangups; they are socially and geographically mobile; they are skilled and vital and kindly. All the things it takes to be a hero are the same things it takes to be retired.

Ultimately, it's a question of vitality (most everything is, finally). And vitality comes from being used to doing a lot of things all the time, not hanging around. Energy expended creates energy available—that's an LCT if ever there was one: one of Life's most unfair and unpleasant Cruel Truths.

In retirement, in your choice of your pursuit to pursue, you pretty much have to go with what you've already got. At forty-one, you can't suddenly take up a new pursuit like polo or the piano, or suddenly start skiing. I mean, of course, you *can* do it, but it may be too hard, and you may very well find your first game of tennis, say, starting just from scratch, will fail to please you.

Again, this is another example of how the rich are so very different from the rest of us, even if they don't have more money: they have been prepared, *trained* from childhood in all the leisure pursuits. They had riding lessons and speak French. Very little in the American middle-class experience prepares the individual for leisure. Part of the trouble, of course, is the misemphasis in our educational institutions.

Perhaps the curriculum ought to be changed, or maybe just re-titling some of the courses would help. Instead of teaching Geography, for instance, we ought to teach "Travel." Botany and Geology could be called "Enjoying a Walk." Civics and Government courses would be renamed "Political Discussion" and teach us how to talk politics without boring one another to death. We shouldn't teach Composition, but "Writing the Amusing Letter"; not Literature, but rather "How to Get Engrossed in a Classic Novel," including such things as how to keep Russian names straight and posture control, so a youth could learn to sit erect in a wing chair by the fireplace, his legs elegantly crossed, like that man in the frontispiece of the Nelson Classics.

Our young people should learn how to play jolly, elegant tennis; an imaginative but superbly courteous game of chess; a snappy, audacious game of bridge, cutthroat hearts. They should learn how to play the piano—both how to pace a medley when everyone's gathered around to sing (Ivy League songs, World War II songs, Christmas Carols in season) and also how to express a melancholy mood, seated alone at the keyboard playing Chopin in the gathering twilight, Rachmaninoff while the surf crashes. They ought to take courses like "Painting Deft Watercolors" and "Courtly Ice Skating."

They should be taught all these elegant "leisure"-class things, but they should also be taught "working"-class skills as well. Everyone should know how to have the fun of tinkering with automobiles without making them worse. Everyone should be able to experience the joy of quickly fixing something (a faucet, say, or a light switch) instead of the chagrin of calling the plumber or electrician to repair what you spent frustrating hours on in your incompetence. We should all be taught carpentry and construction, landscaping and gardening.

The curriculum, in short, would be a combination of what used to be taught at elegant finishing schools on the one hand and the commercial-industrial-mechanical courses given at public high school on the other. The standard middle-class courses, in other words, would be reshaped toward either upper- or lower-class skills.

❦

Some Specific Pursuits Considered

Correspondence

SOME RETIRED people find that carrying on correspondence, with far-flung friends or with men and women whose interests are similar to theirs, is a pleasant way of consuming time. After I stopped work, I started writing letters to people, but all my friends were busy. I either got no answer at all, or brief, dictated, *efficient* replies—replying to just that part of my letter which I used as an excuse for writing. Or else they'd answer by phone, calling just when I'd found something to do. No one much writes letters any more, and I suppose there's no real reason to.

Anyway, I wrote a longish, rambling letter to Sears, Roebuck in Boston, for instance, about a power saw someone gave me years ago that seems to have some parts missing, and a letter to a friend who recently became editor of a periodical, asking how he liked it there, how things were going, and saying I hadn't seen the publication since he took over, as it wasn't available up here. Well, Sears, Roebuck wrote me that my inquiry was appreciated and that they would be glad to answer it immediately upon receipt of the information requested below. And below, a box was checked. "Please advise model number." Then they said:

> In sending in this information, please use the other side of this sheet, RETURNING YOUR ORIGINAL LETTER, WHICH IS EN-CLOSED. Your wishes shall then receive preferred attention.

Preferred attention is of course always nice to have, but the letter was mimeographed, so I suppose a number of us got it. Also, it was somewhat disconcerting to have my own letter sent back to me. I reread it, and it struck me as being from a nice sort of person, a little foolish and long-winded perhaps, but not without self-mockery and reasonably literate. I rather wished I could write back and forth with the person who wrote it. Sears, Roebuck, of course, did speak of my letter as "original," though, which was nice of them, I think. The same mail brought three issues of my friend's periodical, *with no letter at all.*

Crafts and Hobbies

The trouble with this sort of thing—stamp books and electric trains and making birdhouses and so on—is basically twofold, and then becomes threefold (making fivefold in all). First of all, most such activities are childish: although one can perhaps make a better wren house at age forty-one than he could in the second grade, the pursuit itself still feels sort of childish and foolish. This is akin to the second objection: it is so obviously a waste of time. Hobbies, almost by definition, are ways to waste time, and no one likes to feel he's quit work just to waste time. Hobbies are all right for the free time you have (evenings and weekends) when you're working, because they "help you to unwind" and "get your mind off your problems." Recaning the seats of chairs, weaving baskets, fitting flagstones—all that is great relaxation. But if you have to do it regularly you find: *first,* that soon all the chair seats are recaned, no one has any use for all the baskets you weave, and there isn't any more land left to put the flagstones on; *second,* that all this happens just when you were getting good at it; and *third,* you begin to realize that all this kind of work is more or less what you'd be doing in a prison or in a house of detention for the simple-minded—only there you wouldn't be expected to do it *all day.*

Outdoor Activities

Here I refer to such businesses as hunting trips, camping trips, fishing trips (salt-water or fresh), golf foursomes, serious ocean-racing, and other such getaway-from-it-all-for-a-while activities. All these have one great advantage and one great disadvantage.

The advantage is the amount of *equipment* such activities require. The available time consumed in actually doing these activities is often relatively small compared to the amount of time they use up by way of the equipment connected with them. The tackle's the best part. Fishing, for instance, provides an infinity of kinds of rods and lures and lines and reels and hooks and so on that can be fiddled over and discussed and compared endlessly. And fishing usually requires either specially rigged boats or some sort of elaborate garb for wading or whatever. Special garb is in fact essential and desirable and probably even inevitable in all these outdoor pursuits. Special shoes and special hats and special foul-weather stuff and lightweight this and heavy-duty that—all usually great-looking, very comfortable things to wear. Most all of the items of sporting equipment are neat to handle and heft and so on, and many many happy hours can be spent getting them out and polishing them and oiling them and interchanging their parts and making them better in some way, as well as debating about which whatever-it-is to use: whether to take this or that size or weight of gun or knapsack or golf club or spinnaker or fishing rod. And another great thing about equipment is that it has a mushrooming effect: much of it requires that it be kept in special cases or boxes or sheaths or bags or holsters—all of which must be carefully taken care of too.

The disadvantage of many of these sporting activities is the kind of *camaraderie* that they often entail. This may not be a disadvantage at all, if you can stand all the joshing and running jokes and especially all the talk about what happened last time.

Travel, as a Pursuit

Traveling is a marvelous time-filler. It takes an amount of time packing and unpacking, getting the necessary travel documents, the travel itself of course, deciding where to go, and reading up on it, discussing when to leave and when to return, greeting people and saying good-by, having to learn new languages and currencies. Leisured people have always liked to travel, and it is easy to see why.

Really to travel, to travel well, not just to be a tourist arguing with American Express (which can be plenty time-consuming too, of course), but to be a conscientious, competent traveler, requires discipline, scholarship, stamina—all kinds of hard things. You've got to be a connoisseur of everything from food to art, you've got to learn languages, study architecture and geology and history, memorize dates and the lines of succession of all the European kings, you must know the best hotels in each price range in all cities and, ideally, the name of the bartender (and, really ideally, somehow get him to know your name). Probably you ought to learn how to sketch architectural details and peasants working, but at least you have to know how to use a camera, not just so the pictures come out but so they aren't boring. There's not much pleasure in visiting Warwick and Kenilworth unless you know about them—even if it's only by having read Sir Walter Scott—and reading Sir Walter Scott after having retired at forty-one is no easier than it was in high school. Visiting Beaufort Cathedral you have to appreciate the quatrefoils in the spandrels of the clerestory arcade, if they have them, whatever they are. In the Uffizi, you gotta know your iconography.

Youthful adventurous travel—not necessarily anything really hard and dangerous like exploring jungles, crossing deserts, climbing mountains, and so on, but anything somewhat off the beaten tourist path—such travel tends to be *work*. And I mean work, not employment. You don't get paid for this hard physical labor. In fact, it is something you pay *for*. Everyone knows that the more rugged the "vacation," chances are the more expensive it is. The same's true of traveling as a retirement pursuit: the more it resembles work, and the harder work it in fact *is*, the more it is likely to cost you.

Social Life, as a Pursuit

Quitting a job is usually accompanied by a move to some form of "the country": seldom a really isolated backwoods, but more likely a semi-artistic exurb or a carefully chosen small town of some charm, where life will be cheaper, quieter, more tranquil. There either you get on the generalized dinner-party circuit (by giving them yourself), or you don't. Either you do or don't give a quarterly mop-up. Known locally here as "a Stonington stand-around," this averages as having fifty or a hundred people to drinks: you have one in the spring, so you'll get invited to everyone else's; one in the summer, which will be so crowded with EEHGs (Everyone Else's House Guests) that you'll hardly see anyone you know; one in the fall, to pay everyone back; and one very forlorn one in the winter ("we year-round people have to stick together"). If you *don't* give 'em, these awful parties everyone says they hate, then after a while you don't get *asked* to them.

In other words: either you deliberately set out to see the same people over and over, or after a while you end up not seeing anyone at all. Unless you deliberately arrange something you know in advance will be pretty dull, there is no reason for you (now that you don't go to work) to leave your home at all (except for your errand running, of course).

Thus, in retirement there's no easement of the three Cruel Rules of Social Life. They are in full force.

Social Cruel Rule #1

The first rule holds true both in direct statement:

(a) The only time you really feel like going out is when you don't have an invitation,

and in its converse:

(b) Whenever you are invited to go out, you feel like staying at home.

Now this seems to be a universal truth: an inevitable tragic irony of the human condition. It is just one of those sad-assed things: like the feeling you have when you're riding on a train at night and you pass through some nice, warm-lighted village, and you wish you were there, part of the village, knowing the people, at home with your family, and so on; yet when you lie in bed and you hear the marvelously lonesome wail of the train as it passes by, you wish you were on it, going somewhere.

Social Cruel Rule #2

The second rule also holds true both in direct statement:

(a) A party or anything like that that you look forward to is seldom as much fun as you expect,

and in its converse:

(b) The really good times somehow seem to come about by accident.

You get invited to what you anticipate will be a long, companionable dinner party, but it turns out not to be a nice sit-down dinner at all, but a buffet where you sit on a wobbly chair with your plate on your knee; or, if it *is* sit-down, you're at the wrong end of the table and can't hear what they're laughing about up at the right end. Cocktail parties, as is well known, get good not just *after* but *if* you've decided to leave early.

Social Cruel Rule #3

The third cruel truth of social life again has two parts, both functioning in direct statement or in converse:

(a) Uninteresting people invite you to their house; you do not invite them back.

(b) You invite interesting people to your house; they do not invite you back.

Social Rule #3 implies a concatenation of disaffection that makes one melancholy to contemplate. The dynamic structure of our social life seems to operate as a great sad chain of disappointment. For the interesting people who don't invite you back must know even more interesting people who don't invite *them* back, and those people never get invited by even *more* interesting people, and so on up the chain. Going the other way, the uninteresting people you don't invite back must know even more uninteresting people that *they* don't invite back, and so on. Somewhere down there it must be very dull indeed, and the person at the bottom is forced to give up.

❦

Pursuing "Interests," as a Pursuit

WHEN YOU'VE got a job you're always coming across something that interests you, and you wish you had time to "follow it up." But you'd be surprised just how passing a passing interest is. Things are really interesting only when you really get into them, and that takes specialization, *work*.

My father, after he retired, got interested in magnets and suchlike, tinkered with them for hours, for months. Then he decided he'd check the laws of probability. He made a sort of wire cage over a little platform with a crank to flip the whole thing over and then put five pennies in there; flipped them for months, thousands and thousands of *times*, keeping careful records of how many came up heads

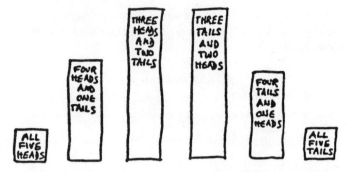

or tails. And he proved the normal curve of distribution, more or less.

You may ask what is the point of an "interest" like this? He only proved what everyone knows anyway, or would imagine. "Interests" usually operate at about this high-school level, and if a retired person is to keep his wits about him, is to seem sane and sensible not only to others but to himself, he must realize how foolish and futile his pursuit of them is.

But it is the very purposelessness of such labors that keeps them pure. If a retired man's pursuit of an interest actually led him into something interesting and substantive, it's likely he'd soon find himself landed in some whole new line of work. I mean, it can happen; there's always another newspaper feature about "mid-life career changes": an advertising copywriter quits the rat race, takes an interest in cataloging his books, and this leads into a new career as a librarian; or an engineer resigns his job, starts reading history, and becomes a history teacher at the local college; and so on, endlessly, for there are a million interchangeable possibilities. But there's no relevance to any of this. These people aren't retiring at all—they are just *switching*. A second line of work is like a second marriage, and it has as much relevance to the problems of retirement as remarriage does to the problems of the lonely divorced.

To preserve its integrity, the retirement interest must remain profitless; to remain a true passing interest, it must be transitory; and to be truly therapeutic, the interest must be truly obsessive. That all of this is true can be incontrovertibly confirmed in terms of a central episode in Samuel Beckett's novel *Molloy*.

Molloy is one of the great novels of our time, presenting an entirely modern hero with enough available time to feel the obligation to try to *get things right*. Molloy is a retired man, or at least he seems to be. Molloy makes great efforts to explain everything very carefully, and he is certainly to be admired for that, but there are a great many things (like who he is and what he's doing) that he isn't at all clear about. God knows he does the best he can. Most of the book consists of his travel reminiscences. (We mentioned before that retired people like to travel quite a bit.) He is going to visit his mother. He starts off to where he thinks the village where his mother might be may be, but either his right leg or his left leg stiffens and/or grows short. He can't remember which it was, because later they both stiffen. Eventually, of course, when the good leg stiffens and hurts worse than the bad leg (the hitherto bad leg, that is), but doesn't shorten, or doesn't shorten as much as the leg which had hitherto been worse has shortened, so that he still has to walk on the worse leg (the one that had been better before) because the crutches won't work properly unless it is the bad leg or the good leg, at any rate the *short* leg that is being supported—. Wait, as Molloy says:

> Let us try and get this dilemma clear. Follow me carefully. The stiff leg hurt me, admittedly, I mean the old stiff leg, and it was the other which I normally used as a pivot, or prop. But now this latter, as a result of its stiffening, I suppose, and the ensuing commotion among nerves and sinews, was beginning to hurt me even more than the other. What a story, God send I don't make a balls of it. For the old pain, do you follow me, I had got used to it, in a way, yes, in a kind of way. Whereas to the new pain, though of the same family exactly, I had not yet had time to adjust myself.

Anyway, because of all this (and he explains it as concisely as he can, endlessly over many unparagraphed pages), he finally ends up moving through the forest on his stomach, hooking his crutch onto something and then pulling himself forward. He covers fifteen paces a day regularly this way, "day in, day out," and it has the great advantage that "when you want to rest you stop and rest, without further ado."

Now there is an interlude in Molloy's journey, spent by the seaside, and while there Molloy keeps himself occupied with an "interest" very similar to my father's penny tossing—*so* similar, now I think of it, that it gives me some better sense of what my father may have thought he was up to all those months.

What Molloy does at the seaside, sitting out on a lonely strand of beach all by himself, is keep sixteen sucking stones in his pockets. "They were pebbles," he says, "but I call them stones"—perhaps in admiration for what Sisyphus did with a stone. His hope, his great dream, is to suck on those pebbles, those everlasting stones, one after another, *in order,* insofar as possible, without sucking the same one more often than he has to, or at least not until its proper turn to be sucked has come about. He tries to calculate how many stones he should keep in each of his four pockets, and how best to transfer them from pocket to pocket; he considers, one after another, what seems an infinitude of permutations; and his recounting of his efforts to approach the ideal he has his heart set on is beautiful and moving.

Clearly what Molloy does with those stones at the seaside is an effort to introduce some order into the random chaos of his life. But the point I want to make is that the period during which he is thus preoccupied, his time by the seaside, is far and away the happiest and healthiest period of his whole life. During this time he barely noticed that his good leg was growing worse than his bad leg. Only later does his asthma get really unbearable. As he says of his other weak points: "At the seaside they had developed normally, yes, I had noticed nothing abnormal." But he "had hardly left the shore . . . when they suddenly began to gallop," his weak points did.

Molloy shows what an interest can do for a man, if he puts his whole heart and soul into it and doesn't mind if the interest doesn't come to anything, doesn't even care if it couldn't possibly *ever* come to anything. This sort of interest correctly remains a *pre*-occupation rather than an occupation. I think we can agree that no matter what your original line of work might have been, a change to pebble sucking as your new occupation could scarcely be considered a successful mid-life career change.

Writing, as a Pursuit

MOLLOY DOES somehow make it to his mother's. At the beginning of the book he's back at where he thinks he came from:

> I am in my mother's room. . . . There's this man who comes every week. . . . He gives me money and takes away the pages.

So many pages, so much money. . . . The truth is I haven't much will left. When he comes for the fresh pages he brings back the previous week's. They are marked with signs I don't understand. Anyway I don't read them. When I've done nothing he gives me nothing, he scolds me. Yet I don't work for money. For what then? I don't know.

This seems to me to indicate either that he's in Hell or has become a free-lance writer. Poor Molloy: you'd think he'd deserve a better life when he's home from his travels.

Yet, you know, the same thing happened to Rudolf Rassendyll: when he got back from his exploits in Zenda he wrote down an account of all that had happened to him. Then:

> Since all these events whose history I have set down happened I have lived a very quiet life at a small house which I have taken in the country. The ordinary ambitions and aims of men in my position seem to me dull and unattractive. I have little fancy for the world of society, and none for the jostle of politics. Lady Burlesdon utterly despairs of me; my neighbors think me an indolent, dreamy, unsociable fellow. Yet I am a young man; and sometimes I have a fancy—the superstitious would call it a presentiment—that my part in life is not yet altogether played; that, somehow and some day, I shall mix again in great affairs, I shall again spin policies in a busy brain, match my wits against my enemies', brace my muscle to fight a good fight and strike stout blows.

In the sequel, called *Rupert of Henzau,* which is a botch and nothing like as good as *Zenda,* Rudolf goes back to Ruritania, gets into a peck of trouble, and dies at the end in the middle of an agonizing decision. He would have been *much better off* living his quiet life in his small house in the country. Even heroes have trouble retiring: like everyone else they start daydreaming about *getting back in it.*

Retired people almost always seem to get hung up on the idea of writing. This is perhaps inevitable, and for a number of reasons. There is superficially a good deal of resemblance between the life of the free-lance writer and the man who has retired at forty-one. They are virtually the only two kinds of men who are ever at home during the day during their middle years (except invalids), and as a consequence they share many of the same embarrassments and discomforts: worrying, for instance, what the postman thinks about them.

But a good deal of the writer's miseries stem from frustrations about his work. Being at home all the time is to him just a sideline disadvantage, an occupational hazard. The man who retires early, on the other hand, chooses this uncomfortable way of life (being at home all the time) deliberately: it is not part of his profession, but part of his avoidance of a profession—and not really just "part" of it, but actually the whole point, purpose, and result of his quitting work in the first place. A man retiring early who adds to these already difficult circumstances the miseries and frustrations of being a writer, or trying to be one, may seem to be straight out of his mind. But the temptations are many and great and very silky—and many poor retired souls succumb.

The sinister thing about writing is that it starts off seeming so easy and ends up being so hard.

You remember that we quoted Montaigne as saying:

> The employments a man should choose for a life of retirement should be neither hard nor displeasing; otherwise there is no point in it.

Yet Montagne himself perversely chose writing, the hardest and most difficult retirement pursuit of all. He says of his choice:

> It was a melancholy humor, very much an enemy to my natural disposition and born of the solitude in which I had taken refuge, that first put into my head this notion of writing.

Montaigne in his wisdom speaks of solitude and a melancholy humor as the causes of the writing urge, and he is right. Let us get some things straight about writing. Let us be as honest as we can. Advertisements for correspondence courses in writing, and for literary agents and others who make their money preying on the nonwriter's urge to be a writer, and also perhaps a few actual writers—three-name lady writers and old-magazine-hand hacks who grind it out like factories—such persons claim that writing is fun, a pleasure and a joy.

I once read an ad for a writing course written by someone named J. D. Ratcliff telling how great writing is as a way of life:

> It's a wonderful life. No commuter trains to catch, no office routine. Whether I'm abroad on assignment, at home on the Jersey Palisades or at our summer place off Cape Cod, I write from 8 A.M. to noon every day—no more, or less. My afternoons are my own.

Then, under a picture of a man and a dog, there was this caption:

> "Jack" Ratcliff on a typical afternoon strolls through the New Jersey woods, where he conceives many of the articles that prompted *Time* to name him "America's No. 1 craftsman in the field of non-fiction."

Time must know, of course; but I was in the magazine business for decades, off and on, and I never ever even heard of J. D. Ratcliff, until suddenly, in *The Reader's Digest*, I saw, "I am Joe's Man Gland," and it's by *him!*:

> I am Joe's left testis. Compared to other glands, I am not bad-looking at all: a glistening, pink-white oval. I weigh half an ounce and am $1\frac{1}{2}$ inches at my greatest diameter . . .

It was apparently part of a series Ratcliff had done about forty-seven-year-old Joe's organs for *The Reader's Digest*.

Anyway, in the writing school advertisement, Ratcliff says:

> I've earned a comfortable living for 25 years writing articles, and I've enjoyed every minute.

But I don't believe Ratcliff any more than I believe *Time*. Do *you* believe he's been writing from 8 A.M. to noon every day—no more, no less—for twenty-five years and enjoying every minute of it? Do you believe he *enjoyed* the moment he wrote that sentence "I am Joe's left testis"? Do you believe writing's "a wonderful life"? As an editor over those years, I met hundreds of writers, and I don't think I ever met one for whom writing wasn't some kind of misery.

Now that's of course when the writing isn't going well. But as long as we're going to try to state the real truth about writing, let's admit that by and large and on the whole it almost always isn't (is *not*) going well. Real writers know this. And for almost all of them it only adds to their torment to remember a time in the past when it did go well or to imagine a time in the future when it might go well again. Also, not only does writing *cause* misery, it is *born* of misery, as Montaigne said. Or melancholy, I guess he said. And solitude: the need to communicate with someone who isn't there. Just who is it anyway that wants to write? Lonely, miserable people are the ones who want to write, that's who.

Becoming a writer begins when you're a child and aren't chosen for games until the very end. That's why stories about kids who aren't chosen until the end are such clichés: it's part of every writer's experience. Also, lonely miserable adolescents want to write; they're the ones, not the happy ones who are having fun from age fourteen on. It's the "sensitive" ones who want to write—and no one would ever begin to think of himself as sensitive unless he was left out and lonely. That's what sensitive really means: unhappy. Happy people aren't sensitive, usually; that's what makes them such bores. And happy people don't feel the need to write—to "express themselves" or to "communicate with others" or whatever. And especially and certainly they don't feel the need to write in middle age all of a sudden, when they're busy working, or should be. The trouble is that switching from being a man who does nothing to being a writer seems as easy as taking a rest when you're pulling yourself along on your stomach: you can just go ahead and do it, without further ado.

Writing's no good as a retirement pursuit even if it were to start out as pleasure, just the way the nits and hacks and profiteers say. Even if at first it's done for enjoyment, for self-expression, for its own sake, after a while it gets all involved with ideas of publication and making money. Then a little later it gets somewhat disassociated from the money and publication ideas and gets hungry and demanding all on its own. It becomes an end in itself, a self-imposed duty, an obligation. Most writers are miserable unless they get at least a few pages written each day. Writing is a lot like heroin: it may start as a pleasure, shortly becomes an addiction, ends up as one hell of a big self-imposed monkey on your back. The retired man should avoid it as the plague. He has troubles enough of his own.

"Getting to Know Thyself," as a Pursuit

THOSE FEW oddballs who do retire young may not have a clear idea of what they're going to do, but they have a strong sense of being misfits (even when successful) in the striving commercial world. Quitting work young is no doubt a neurotic act: it is abnormal in the sense that it is different from the normal; and it is usually interpreted by others as either self-indulgent or self-punitive and certainly self-destructive.

The man who quits work, though, doesn't see it that way. He has the idea that his work, far from providing him with a sense of his self or identity, is actually consuming so much of his time, energy, and emotions, that nothing is left for himself. He feels that he is unable ever to know himself, to consider himself, to find out who he is, to come to terms with himself, and so on. He finds that while there are many ways of phrasing this feeling, they have an unfortunate way of always sounding like clichés.

The fact that this "search for the inner self" has become such a cliché suggests that it is becoming widespread. We have previously mentioned that leisure is something the upper class and the lower class have an emotional preparation for, that recently it is becoming a middle-class problem. But it is only *becoming* so: as of *now*, the middle-class man retiring at forty-one must expect to find himself very much alone.

But that is the way the man who is quitting work wants it. He is sick of so many people and so much activity: he *wants* time alone, he wants time to *think*. He wants time to observe, to study, to consider. He wants time to think things *through*, to contemplate, to sort out (he tries to explain) the *real* values from the phony pragmatism of the crass commercial rat race—and so on. He may even, after a while, begin to quote Thoreau:

> Most men . . . are so occupied with the factitious cares and superfluously coarse labors of life that its finer fruits cannot be plucked by them.

Or, if that was too hard to quote:

> . . . the laboring man has not leisure for a true integrity . . .

Or:

> The mass of men lead lives of quiet desperation. What is called resignation is confirmed desperation.

Every middle-class American has been exposed to *Walden* at some point in his life. Teachers in high school or college never seem able to convey how fascinating a book it is, and how funny it is; but I think it makes a sort of subliminal impression on young readers anyway, no matter how bored they are by it. The idea of going off into the woods, building a cabin, and then living there by yourself in great simplicity must appeal, in theory at least, to most everyone at some time or other. It is not perhaps so romantic a yearning as the one to buy an old schooner and sail to the South Seas and have adventures, but it is nearly so—and it seems more an actual thing one *could* do, not just a fanciful daydream, to go off to the country somewhere, after quitting work.

Thoreau is a hero to those who quit. He has great appeal for the disaffected. Some people admire him for his example of civil disobedience. But even more, surely, he is admired as being the prototypical American dropout. His is perhaps the only major voice in American literature that is so positively negative. As such, he is often confused with the sort of genuine-but-romanticized juvenile-delinquent figure—like Huck Finn or Holden Caulfield, straight thinkers who don't work.

We have already noticed how dangerously easy it is for a retired man to "decide" to "become" a writer. It is even easier, of course, and probably even more dangerous, for a retired man to "decide" or "realize" that he's something of a thinker or philosopher. It is one of the first illusions that besets one in retirement, that one is thinking clearly for the first time in one's life. What is actually happening, in fact, though, is that one is getting more and more out of touch with the way things are. More and more one substitutes opinion for information in one's thinking. One tends to begin to think in terms of ends or goals or absolutes or ideals rather than in terms of means. In retirement, the illusion that one has *thought things through* and has an opinion formed on his own is just fantastically difficult to avoid.

Perhaps the worst thing about all this thinking and this time to think, is that one tends soon to start turning it all on himself. Thus a man who says he's quitting work to get to know himself may find, somewhat to his surprise, that he's doing just that. It probably won't happen at all in the way he imagined it would. He may have some idea of pausing, early some morning while he's mowing the upper meadow, and having an insight about the true meaning of life. Or he may imagine that one afternoon, sailing alone in Long Island Sound, some revelation of an eternal verity is going to come to him. It doesn't work like that: there are too many rocks and squalls to worry about; and the modern mind isn't trained to think about eternal verities—they've all been thought of anyway.

But there does come over a person alone and in retirement a greater degree of self-consciousness, a greater awareness of self. There is more time to analyze and inspect one's behavior and to speculate about its motives. It may be so simple a thing as having the time to search for the answer to questions like: "Now why did I do that?" or "Why did I just think that?"

I believe that the first reaction of men who experience this is dismay: a hopeless disgust about the shallowness or banality or vulgarity of their preoccupations. Soon, however, this reaction may turn to amusement, or at least bemusement. With the time to track back for the reason, the source, for the vulgar daydream, one can afford to smile at the absurdity of it. If one has a trivial worrying preoccupation, one has time to discover what it is exactly, bring the matter up into consciousness, and either attend to it or laugh at oneself for being so concerned about such a matter. Soon one begins to see that what one felt was shallow is in fact just hopelessly natural, and that what one felt is vulgar is common enough. Increasingly it seems to me that the successful modern retirement consists of an extended process of self-forgiving: first forgiving the self for quitting work, then for not making some more profitable use of the freedom and time obtained, then finally forgiving the self for being the mess we discover it to be.

❦

Pursuing Montaigne, as Against Pursuing Thoreau

IT IS from Montaigne, much more than from Thoreau, that we can learn about the bemused, forgiving consideration of the self. He, perhaps more than any other writer, teaches us to be tolerant of the wretched *human*-ness of humanity. We left Montaigne, you remember, explaining how he had turned to the retirement pursuit of writing:

> . . . in a melancholy humor . . . born of the solitude in which
> I had taken refuge . . .

What could such a man, cut off from events and society, and in such a mood, find to write about?

> . . . and because I found I had nothing else to write about, I
> presented myself as subject.

And for most everyone the most interesting parts of Montaigne's *Essays* are those in which he does write directly about himself: where he tells us what he looks like, how he manages his chateau, how he's arranged his study in his tower room and how he works there, his various bad habits, what he likes to eat and drink, his illnesses, his laziness, and his plainness, his foolish thoughts and his fine thoughts. The more Montaigne tells us about himself, and the more detailed and more honest he is in his account, the more we realize that to know any one man is to know humanity, and that to know humanity is to know ourselves.

> Others fashion man, I repeat him; and represent a particular
> one, but ill made, and whom, were I to form anew, he should
> be far other than he is, but he is now made.

But by writing about "a particular one" so completely and so honestly he did in fact "fashion man," and readers through the ages have had the eerie, companionable sensation when reading Montaigne on the subject of Montaigne that they were somehow reading about themselves. Even Emerson, whom you mightn't at first think would've been one of Montaigne's big fans, had this experience. In his essay "Montaigne: or, The Skeptic," he describes his first reading of the *Essays:*

> I remember the delight and wonder in which I lived with it.
> It seemed to me as if I had myself written the book, in some
> former life, so sincerely it spoke to my thought and experience.

But then the tone of Emerson's essay changes, and he comes over all New England suddenly, as if he'd found this admission of identification somehow embarrassing. Montaigne, he says, is

> . . . the frankest and honestest of all writers. His French free-
> dom runs into grossness; but he has anticipated all censure by
> the bounty of his own confessions . . . He parades it: he makes
> the most of it: nobody can think or say worse of him than he
> does. He pretends to most of the vices; and if there be any virtue
> in him, he says, it got in by stealth.

Emerson makes this point:

> But, with [i.e., despite] all this really superfluous frankness,
> the opinion of an invincible probity grows into every reader's
> mind.

But that seems to me to miss the *real* point about Montaigne, after he once so obviously had it. Montaigne was admittedly (that is, I admit it, Montaigne never would have) a man of outstanding honesty and principled virtue in a more or less depraved age, but it still isn't his "invincible probity" that makes each of us feel that Montaigne has written our own book about our own selves. I mean, maybe it's the "invincible probity" of Montaigne that made *Emerson* feel that he himself had written the book in some former life, but for you and me it's more likely to be the "really superfluous frankness." And so, of course, the frankness isn't really superfluous at all, it's really the essential thing. What's essential is not Montaigne's wisdom, but his wise recognition of his foolishness; not his virtue, but his good cognizance of his vices; not his "honesty," but his *honesty*, his complete leveling with the reader.

What we could learn from Montaigne is how to live with ourselves as we are. What we could learn from Thoreau is a much better way to live. It is, I suppose, a matter of two kinds of pleasure. Thoreau distinguishes between pure pleasure and impure pleasure. Montaigne does not.

For pure pleasure, vitality's necessary; for impure pleasure, it isn't. Impure pleasure destroys vitality. Montaigne is somehow marvelously humanly indolent; Thoreau had an exceptional, almost inhuman, vitality. Thoreau kept in shape:

> Every man is the builder of a temple, called his body, to the
> God he worships, after a style purely his own . . . We are all
> sculptors . . . and our material is our own flesh and blood and
> bones. Any nobleness begins at once to refine a man's features,
> any meanness or sensuality to imbrute them.

"To imbrute them . . ." Well, one wonders. Thoreau's vitality seems almost animal; Montaigne's indolence and sensuality seem so thoroughly human. Thoreau did sculpt his own life and body with a fine aesthetic asceticism. In "Higher Laws" in *Walden* he explains why he never eats meat and seldom eats fish. And get this:

> I believe that water is the only drink for a wise man; wine is
> not so noble a liquor; and think of dashing the hopes of a morn-
> ing with a cup of warm coffee, or of an evening with a dish of
> tea! Ah, how low I fall when I am tempted by them!

Think of dashing the hopes of a morning (if you ever have any of them) *without* a cup of coffee! Montaigne loved his wine, and I'm sure he would've smoked too much and drunk too much coffee too, if they'd been available then, the weed and the bean.

A most companionable man, Montaigne was, even in retirement. You remember him saying, "I did not flee from men, but from affairs." There were often guests at his chateau, people from Paris, as well as local people. Even the King came, and Montaigne was proud of his household not needing to make special preparations:

> In 1584 the entire court was on my hands. The King of Navarre visited me at Montaigne, where he had never been before. For two days my people served him without the aid of any of his servants. He permitted no precautionary trial to be made of the food or the table appointments, and he slept in my own bed. The Prince of Conde, Messieurs de Rohan, de Touraine, de Bethune, de Haraucourt, the lieutenant of the company of the prince, his equerry, and about thirty-seven other gentlemen—besides the footmen, pages, and guards—were all lodged in my quarters. About as many more slept in the villages. On their departure I let loose a stag in my forest, which led His Majesty a two-day's chase.

It's a trickier business to get any kind of coherent line on Thoreau's social life. One tends to think of him living all alone out there like a hermit in his homemade shack by the lake. But in fact he only spent about a year at Walden, which was only a couple of miles out of town anyway. And people were always stopping out to see him, so many—as he records in the chapter "Visitors" in *Walden*—that

> One man proposed a book in which visitors should write their names, as at the White Mountains.

In the chapter just preceding "Visitors," one called "Solitude," Thoreau says he counts himself more fortunate than other men, "more favored by the gods," because

> I have never felt lonesome, or in the least oppressed by a sense of solitude—
> I find it wholesome to be alone the greater part of the time. To be in company, even with the best, is soon wearisome and

dissipating. I love to be alone, I never found the companion that was so companionable as solitude.

But Emerson said he felt that Thoreau's tendency toward solitude had somehow harmed him:

> The severity of his ideal interfered to deprive him of a healthy sufficiency of human society.

However then the next minute Emerson turns right around and says of Thoreau that he was

> . . . a very industrious man, and setting, like all highly organized men, a high value on his time, he seemed the only man of leisure in town, always ready for any excursion that promised well, or for conversation prolonged into late hours.

But we know from *Walden* that the best part of a winter's evening in town talking late, for Thoreau, was walking miles home alone in the snow afterward:

> It was very pleasant, when I stayed late in town, to launch myself into the night, especially if it was dark and tempestuous, and set sail from some bright village parlor or lecture room . . . for my snug harbor in the woods, having made all tight without and withdrawn under hatches with a merry crew of thoughts, leaving only my outer man at the helm . . . I had many a genial thought by the cabin fire "as I sailed." I was never cast away nor distressed in any weather, though I encountered some severe storms.

What kind of a man *is* this? What kind of a man can it be that *likes* the long walk home after staying in town late *especially* if it's dark and tempestuous? He goes on to explain how he gets home steering on automatic pilot this way, through areas where others are constantly getting lost despite the careful directions he gives them; and at the end of a long paragraph he finally brings his long and drawn-out nautical metaphor to harvest:

> Not till we are lost, in other words not till we have lost the world,
> do we begin to find ourselves, and realize where we are and the
> infinite extent of our relations.

"Not till we have lost the world, do we begin to find ourselves"—
surely there's a message there for the man who's retired at forty-one
so as to get to "know himself." The message is clearly *right there*;
just a question of figuring it out. It's mystic and Christian and yet
sort of Zen: through loss, gain—just the kind of paradoxical, enigmatic phrasing that we know contains a great truth. And it couldn't
be simpler either:

Step #1. Lose the world.
Step #2. Find yourself.

But that may be why I never learned to dance: people were always
trying to start me off with the two-step, which they said was simple
and easy, but which seemed to me much harder than some more
complicated dance would have been, one where you could actually
learn the steps and follow them. I tend to feel that to be really helpful,
directions on how to do anything ought to be explicit and detailed,
and perhaps not without circumlocutions to consider contingencies,
what to do if something goes wrong, and so on. Two-step methods
never have enough room for this.

Thoreau's two-step method for self-knowledge, it seems to me, for
instance, must have omitted something, some other step maybe,
either at the beginning or at the end or maybe in the middle. I mean,
you take the man who has quit work early in life so as to "find himself"; he has in fact already *done* Step #1—he *has* "lost the world,"
at least as he knows it: he's quit the workaday nine-to-five, he's
"given everything up." Okay, there he's *done* Step #1. Isn't there
some *other* step he has to make? Or does Step #2—finding himself—
just happen automatically? And what does he do if it doesn't?

Actually, in fact, Thoreau has a less abstract, although, as it turns
out, still a complicated and paradoxical "message" for us about man
and his work. Oddly enough, it turns out that Montaigne has more
or less the same bit of advice. They both reveal it obliquely, reluctantly and grudgingly, because, it seems to me, the advice either

presupposes or finally admits what they both want to stand against: the value of work, the virtue of personal busyness.

Briefly, let's turn first again to Montaigne, who knows so well the mess that self is you're so hoping to find. He says at one point:

> . . . we shall never rail enough against the disorder and un-ruliness of our minds.

And then in the essay, "Of Idleness,"* he says again:

> . . . so it is with our minds: unless you keep them busy with some definite subject that will bridle and control them, they throw themselves in disorder hither and yon in the vague field of imagination.

And he describes his own experience of idleness in retirement:

> . . . when I retired to my home, determined so far as possible to bother about nothing except spending the little time I have left in rest and seclusion, it seemed to me I could do my mind no greater favor than to let it entertain itself in full idleness and stay and settle in itself. . . . But I find . . . that, on the contrary, it gives itself a hundred times more trouble . . . and gives birth to so many chimeras and fantastic monsters, one after another, without order or purpose, that in order to contemplate their in-eptitude and strangeness at my pleasure, I have begun to put them in writing, hoping in time to make my mind ashamed of itself.

You must, Montaigne says, "bridle and control" the "disorder and unruliness" of your thoughts by keeping them "busy with some def-inite subject." The self being a mess, idleness makes it worse. "Rest and seclusion," idleness and solitude, "losing the world"—this *may* indeed be a first step toward "finding yourself," but it also leads through a chaotic sense of directionlessness that makes one feel he

---

*Now I find myself conscientiously quoting the *Essays* directly, but it's a pleasure because of the easygoing modern translation by Donald M. Frame, *The Complete Essays of Montaigne* (Stanford University Press, 1958).

may be going dead the wrong way. Something else, beyond idleness and solitude, seems to be needed: "some definite subject," a project or pursuit. Montaigne believed that every person possessed a *maîtresse forme*—an ideal of his given personality—which it was his duty to discover and develop. Thus the proper occupation for an individual in idleness would be to cultivate his own authenticity.

Listen to Thoreau, again extolling solitude:

> We are for the most part more lonely when we go abroad among men than when we stay in our chambers.

But now see what Thoreau really means by solitude:

> A man thinking or working is always alone, let him be where he will. Solitude is not measured by the miles of space that intervene between a man and his fellows.

What's this? Solitude is *work?* Can Thoreau (of all people) be saying that?

> The really diligent student in one of the crowded hives of Cambridge College is as solitary as the dervish in the desert.

It appears he is; he is saying solitude is work, and solitude is good. Hence, is he saying work is good? He compares that diligent student with the farmer:

> The farmer can work alone in the field or the woods all day, hoeing or chopping, and not feel lonesome, because he is employed; but when he comes home at night he cannot sit down in a room alone, at the mercy of his thoughts, but must be where he can "see the folks," and recreate, and, as he thinks, remunerate himself for his day's solitude; and hence he wonders how the student can sit alone in the house all night and most of the day without ennui and "the blues"; but he does not realize that the student, though in the house, is still at work in *his* field, and chopping in *his* woods, as the farmer in his . . .

Do you see what Thoreau's saying? Isn't he saying that no one gets lonesome until he's *stopped* work? Thus we conclude that for Thoreau: that solitude which is good is not so much *isolation* as it is *occupation*. This from a man who never really held down a job in his life (except in his family's pencil factory), much less ever *met a payroll?* Who fulminated against business and busyness. Who taught us that "most men lead lives of quiet desperation." Yet Emerson saw this paradox in Thoreau, said he was "a very industrious man" who set "a high value on his time" and still seemed "the only man of leisure in town."

Thoreau did in fact *do* a lot of work. He kept an elaborate and detailed journal most of his life. He had his studies as an amateur naturalist. He wrote books, gave some lectures, traveled and studied, and so on. Also, from time to time he did manual labor, acted as a sort of handyman and caretaker for Emerson and others. And in *Walden* he describes his labors in his bean field (marvelously funny) until he gives that up, finally, with the great realization: "What shall I learn of beans or beans of me?"

But the fact remains that Thoreau was "a man of leisure." And he was one of the most successful men of leisure the world has ever known. All this freedom, all this available time he had while others were working, never got to him. Thoreau had as little *need* for "something to do" as he had for "somebody to see," no more need for occupation than for companionship. In fact, we've seen that for him solitude in some way *was* occupation. How could this be? What in fact did he *do* when he was doing nothing?

Well, for instance, if you'll permit one more quote from *Walden* (and why shouldn't you?), let's take something like being laid out flat face-down on a sheet of ice, living death for most people. But see what Thoreau makes of it:

> The pond had in the meanwhile skimmed over in the shadiest and shallowest coves, some days or even weeks before the general freezing. The first ice is especially interesting and perfect, being hard, dark, and transparent, and affords the best opportunity that ever offers for examining the bottom where it is shallow; for you can lie at your length on ice only an inch thick, like a skater insect on the surface of the water, and study the bottom at your leisure, only two or three inches distant, like a picture behind a glass.

And he goes on to describe fascinatingly what he sees as he lies there. What he does, as he says, is "study" the bottom at his "leisure." No wonder he never gets lonesome. No wonder he never needs anything "to do." Thoreau tells us that no one ever feels the need for companionship as long as he is at work, and Thoreau is *always* at work, because his "work" is simple observation and thought. With his "merry crew of thoughts," he's *never* really alone. Thus his "occupation" is simple existence. "To be" is "to do." Lying on the ice, walking home at night, just leaning on a fence rail hour after hour, Thoreau is *working*. Whatever he does, even if he's doing nothing, he's working. *Being* Thoreau, being *himself*, is his occupation. He doesn't need *work*, when he has the twenty-four-hour-a-day occupation of being himself.

We're edging up now, I believe, somewhat closer to the real problem/solution of "leisure": it seems to have to do in some essential way with what is nowadays called "identity." Remember we quoted Montaigne as saying:

> The greatest thing in the world is to know how to belong to yourself.

And Thoreau recognizes the difficulty of this:

> How can we have a harvest of thought who have not had a seed-time of character?

Thoreau's two-step method,

> Step #1. Lose the world
> Step #2. Find yourself,

worked marvelously for him. But the rest of us may need "a seed-time of character."

Pursuits can help you in this. Obviously the retirement pursuits you choose will affect your character the way your occupation does now. But it is not just a question of activity. In Thoreau's words:

> With a little more deliberation in the choice of their pursuits, all men would perhaps become essentially students and observers.

Nor are pursuits the only means of establishing "a seed-time of character." Other seeds of the full-grown self must be sought, nourished, cultivated, harvested—uh, brought to home port. One's routines, roles, styles, manners, aspects, habits—all the qualities of the specific self must be experimented with, selected, developed. Thus, to Thoreau's two steps, which appear to be but beginning and end, we would add two intermediate steps:

> Step #1. Lose the world
> Step #2. Have "a seed-time of character" (Thoreau)
> Step #3. "Cultivate your authenticity" (Montaigne)
> Step #4. Find yourself.

In other words, most of us must grow our selves before we can know ourselves.

But this will all be amplified and clarified, I hope, in what follows; for this whole matter of "identity" and an early retirement raises many other problems.

CHAPTER THREE

Life Among the Other Problems

I wonder when in the world you're going
to do anything . . . ? —THE PRISONER OF ZENDA

Conversation with a Cleaning Lady

SOMETIMES I wonder whether there are lots and lots of other little problems, or if they're all just part of one giant one—like the whole matter of your existence and identity. How do you explain who and what you are, when you have to fill out a form for something, and you're faced with the "occupation" blank? How do you maintain your identity as a modern man even though you are living like an old-fashioned housewife? How do you explain to people who make deliveries, or to repairmen, say, how come you're home all day instead of at work? They all seem to look at you funny if you don't explain, and they look at you even funnier if you do.

Now the need to explain is clearly a self-created problem, and hence especially hard to solve. Finally, I had to invent a very special solution; and, improbably enough, the solution turned out to be an imaginary cleaning lady. This is an exceptionally odd achievement in problem solving, because we don't even *have* a cleaning lady, not an actual one, and never have. But I *imagined* how awkward it would be on the day of the week she arrived (say, on Wednesdays), with me home there, how she'd disapprove of my not being at work. Of course, I may have imagined this, too: but it always seemed to me she'd look at me funny. Talk about your self-created problem! And this one was invented as a *solution!*

Anyway, this cleaning lady was the one person I'd finally get to listen carefully while I explained *once and for all*. "Listen," I'd say. "Sit down. Put down that mop. Make yourself comfortable." Then I'd hand her a huge stack of hard books I'd collected for just this purpose. One must *plan ahead* even in his imaginings, for opportunities seldom recur. In the pile are a lot of old hard books like Hesiod's *Works and Days* and Seneca's *On Leisure*, most of which I've never read myself, on up through a lot of hard modern books, like David Riesman's *Individualism Reconsidered*, with a special marker by the essay "The Themes of Work and Play in the Structure of Freud's Thoughts" and de Grazia's *Of Time, Work, and Leisure*, most of which I've never read either, as well as copies of *The Prisoner of Zenda* and *Molloy*, which I've pretty nearly memorized.

"Thumb through the bibliographical footnotes at the end of the de Grazia, Cleaning Lady, and you'll get some idea just how much has been written on the relative values of work and leisure." She opens the book and looks at the notes in the back with apparent interest. "Historically," I run on, "work and leisure have seesawed in value in various cultures down through the centuries. The Greek word for work, 'ponos,' comes from a word meaning 'suffering' like our word 'punishment.'"

I pause to consider how to handle the big moment I've looked forward to for so long. I may have to provide a little sociological-historical-psychological orientation for her, but I don't want her to forget that the question in hand is a personal one. I remind her of it, with blunt simplicity—"Why do you feel disapproval and I feel guilt because I'm not at work?"—and she looks up at me: serious, thoughtful, no longer scornful, but truly involved and concerned.

Then I spring the answer, solemnly, suddenly: "Because we are all in the grip of the *Work Ethic!*" The cleaning lady looks a bit startled, and I smile at her kindly to reassure her. "These books will give you the history of this idea, how comparatively recent it is, but how it has its origins in earlier thought. A key thing in this is Max Weber's famous 'Protestant Ethic' thesis." I hand her sixty or eighty quality paperback books interpreting and criticizing this theory. "You might want to look into these—but you know basically what the idea is: that the rise of modern capitalism can be attributed to the influence of Protestantism, especially Calvinism. Or vice versa, maybe. We can't go into all that now. I just want to give you one example, one example of how passionately it came to be believed not just that industry is virtue, but that leisure is vice."

Then I pick up this really beautifully bound old book, *Holy Living and Dying* by Jeremy Taylor. "Why don't you read aloud from this, Cleaning Lady," I say, passing the book to her. She admires the marbled endpapers, takes out her cleaning rag and dusts the book carefully. "Read the part, right at the very beginning, 'The First General Instrument of Holy Living: Care of Our Time.' Read it aloud." So she stands up, and imitating the tones of her parish priest (as she later told me), she fulminates at me as follows:

> . . . An idle person [is] so useless to any purposes of God and man, that he is like one that is dead, unconcerned in the changes and necessities of the world; and he only lives to spend his time, and eat the fruits of the earth: like a vermin or a wolf, when their time comes they die and perish, and in the meantime do no good; they neither plough nor carry burdens; all that they do either is unprofitable or mischievous.

"That's how you feel, isn't it?" I challenge her. "You feel I'm so useless to any purposes of God or man that I'm like one that is dead. You think I only live to spend my time eating the fruits of the earth like a vermin or a wolf."

The cleaning lady shakes her head sadly, kindly, to deny this. She is sitting forward on her chair, her feet (in comfortable, worn shoes) planted far apart, her elbows on her knees. She is leaning forward; her left hand is kneading her right knee nervously. She keeps click-

HOW THE CLEANING LADY
SAT LOOKING AT ME

ing the thumbnail of her right hand against her upper teeth as she considers the problems of my early retirement.

"You know, sir," she says. "I probably ought to tell you that I usually read through your papers when you nervously leave the room because you think I'm looking at you funny Wednesday afternoons. In what you've written it seems to me that you *are* trying to be honest with yourself, but that whenever some subject comes too close to home, you turn the rhetoric to self-mockery. What *are* your answers to some of these questions?

"I think one problem is that you tend to compare yourself unfavorably with those who within the retired situation are able to be at peace with themselves: Montaigne, Rudolf Rassendyll, Molloy, Thoreau. They are your heroes, as well they might be. It's not for me, a cleaning lady, to say that they aren't great men. But none of them was ever expected to function within modern times. You have edged up to this question earlier, sir; but then you backed away. Do you really feel that it is possible in twentieth-century America, in as commercial and striving a society as has perhaps ever existed on this earth, for a middle-class, middle-aged male in reasonably good health to quit work and then go right on living in, or on the fringes of, the same society he dropped out of? And still be reasonably content and happy? At peace with himself?

"You've listed all the difficulties. You've shown how any potential solutions—whether routines or pursuits or whatever—become part of the problem. I know you constantly feel the need to *explain*. But perhaps you don't know the answer to your own question: How *does* a man retire at forty-one?"

"All right," I say to her. "Enough. Before your regular Wednesday hours here are up, you'll certainly want to give the upstairs bathroom floor a good scrubbing, won't you?"

Looking at me in amazed dismay, she gradually begins to disappear. But there is resentment in her eyes, and I realize she thinks of herself as more than just a cleaning lady. And *there*, I suddenly see, is the solution to my problem!

But her eyes haunt me as she fades. "*Wait!*" I say. "I can't save you. You are imagined entirely as a cleaning lady. You have no existence otherwise. You must disappear if I am to go forward."

For my sake, then, she vanishes instantly, willingly, a smile on her sweet face, for she recognizes that her own existence is simply a matter of occupational identity and that I am now prepared to go beyond that.

Beyond the Occupational Identity

REMEMBER THAT statement of Montaigne's that we began with, way back when:

> If you plan to withdraw into yourself, first prepare yourself a welcome.

We now see it isn't just a Comprehensive Day Plan you need, or a country place or an old time-consuming boat or an engrossing hobby or whatever (although these help, God knows); what's needed is some conception of yourself–of, that is, your *self*–now that you won't be working. You don't really realize, until you quit work, just how much of your conception of your self comes from your work– not just from *what* you do, but *how* you do it.

Your basic occupational identity–what you did, or "were"–permitted a lot of amplification by the *way* you did what you were. When you were working, you weren't (not in your own mind, anyway) just "an accountant" or "in fabrics" or "one of the salesmen" or "an insurance man" or whatever. You were also the way you did the work: you were the kindly boss, or the efficient second-in-command, or the talented idea-man, or the only one in the office who got along with the secretaries, or some such. Whatever you were, you had some sense of yourself doing it, some recognition of the role you'd chosen to play or the role you'd been forced into.

Let's take fishing, which can be either a work-for-pay occupation or a leisure-retirement pursuit. Say you were a fisherman when you worked, that's what you did, that's *who* you were, a fisherman. Okay, now there's also the style you used when you were a fisherman. A fisherman-by-trade can be, for instance, kindly like Manuel or whatever his name was (Spencer Tracy) in *Captains Courageous;* or he

can be surly like Ahab in *Moby Dick*. There are presumably an in-
finite number of ways to be a professional fisherman on this kindly-
surly scale, and kindly-surly is only one of many polarizations of
personality traits, as you know—although, admittedly, perhaps the
most important one.

But now, suppose that when you quit work you took up fishing as
a retirement pursuit. One assumes here that you weren't a fisherman-by-trade before, but something else; because you'd never retire
from being a fisherman at age forty-one and then take up fishing as
a retirement pursuit unless it was just to make fun of me. Say,
though, you were (used to be) an insurance salesman, and now at
forty-one you can quit work and live off your commissions from the
premiums we pay on the policies you sold us years and years ago.
You decide to take up fishing as a retirement pursuit. Now the *way*
you fish in retirement is the key thing. You can do it in a kind of
elegant, heroic, upper-classy, sportsman-type way—big-game fishing like Hemingway, or elegant dry-fly angling with delicate lightweight rods—that sort of way. Or you can take it up in a kind of
messy, kindly, puttery, lower-classish way—in an old rowboat or fishing off the bridge with the neighborhood kids.

You see what I'm saying? I'm saying that once the specific, defining, perhaps confining, at any rate *identifying* occupation is removed
from your life by your retirement from work, then your style or manner, your *"you*-ness," becomes the all-important thing, because
there isn't anything much else. The *way* you do things, the way in
fact you do *nothing* (now that there's nothing to do), that's now the
only self you have. If when you retire you do some fishing to fill your
time, you can sit out there in your rowboat all day long *with the pole
in your hands*, and they're still not going to say of you, "Oh, he's a
fisherman," because you *aren't* a fisherman. You *used to be* an insurance man. Now you're nothing. You're nothing except the *way*
you do nothing. Everyone thinks of you as nothing—unless you do
your nothing in a way that identifies you to people; unless, for instance, you do your fishing (or whatever) in a puttery, kindly sort of
way, say, in which case they'll say, "Oh, he's (you, that is, *are*) a
kindly soul, just as sweet and gentle as can be." Or maybe they'll
describe you, *identify* you, "Oh, he really stirs things up, a kind of
troublemaker, but fun to be around." Personality's a part of it, of

course, but it's more a matter of individuality, a kind of amplification of personality by consistency of style and manner.

With your occupational identity gone, you have to find another *existence* for yourself. Remember Thoreau leaning on the fence post, lying on the ice, and so on? Well, now imagine he's fishing. When he fishes, he fishes *as* Thoreau, not as a fisherman. He's *not* a fisherman, and he knows it. Like him, you have to be able to have the fishing (or whatever the specific nondefining, nonoccupational routine or pursuit you're up to) removed or replaced, and still be left with enough particularity of *how* it is done (not *what* is done) to provide a sufficient sense of self for yourself and others.

Beyond the occupational identity, that's all there is.

❦

"Leisure"-Class Leisure, as Against "Working"-Class Leisure

HOW THE occupational identity came to be so damned important in America is that in a democratically conceived, melting-pot-developed, fluid, expansionistic nation-society dominated from the first by the Protestant Work Ethic, it (the occupational identity) became a substitute for all the other, older, old-country ways of identifying people—by race, religion, country of origin, family, community, and so on. The more recent (last hundred years) developments in American life—the giant socioeconomic forces of Urbanization, Bureaucratization, and Industrialization, with their homogenizing, standardizing method-effects, like mass production, mass marketing, mass education, mass communications, and so on— they've all contributed further to the breakdown of the old orderings by which people identified themselves and others. It's simple enough. If someone asks you, "Who is so-and-so?" you wouldn't comfortably answer, "He's a Jew from Detroit" or, "He's one of the Lowells" or, "He's a Larchmont man, yon fellow." More likely you'd say, "He's a sociologist" or, "He's a poet" or, "He's the Simmons Mattress account exec at J.W.T." Even though they're always being told it's rude, few Americans can resist asking one another when they've just met, "What do you do?" It seems to be the best way to get a line on who the new person is. Asking "What are you?" is practically asking "Who are you?" Thus a person's occupational identity—the line of work he's in and the level at which he functions—substitutes, in the way we know ourselves and others, for that strange conglomeration of family, education, community, race, religion, money-and-how-long-you've-had-it, power, prestige, and whatnot that used to make up what used to be called one's "class."

The vexed, messy concept of class creeps into all this for this reason: until recently it was true that, while the upper and lower classes might or might not work, the middle class *always* did. Work was like the prime defining thing *about* the middle class. Going to work was how you got *into* the middle class from either the upper class or the lower class. The upper class was the "leisure class," so-called; the lower class was the poor unemployed. We now see in America what everyone should have realized all along: that the term "working class" should refer to the middle class; using "working class" to mean poor people has no more relevance to contemporary society than words like "vassal" or "serf." Most of us don't even know people who don't work: the upper class isolate themselves from us, doing nothing in their unvisitable resorts and residences; the lower class are off lazing around in their ghettos and poverty pockets. All the rest—from the executives to the factory workers—are essentially middle class *because* (and to the extent that) *they work.*

Both the lower class and the upper class have a tradition of leisure: there are certain social guidelines on how to act if you don't work; there is a certain social setup set up to receive you, even welcome you; there're others like you; and there're places for you to go, like the corner pool hall or the billiards room of your club, where you can just hang around doing nothing and not be too different from everyone else. But the middle class has no such tradition: the middle-class, middle-aged man is *supposed to be working.* When he quits, he'll find he has to tend either toward a lower-class pattern of life or an upper-class pattern of life. He also tends to become either younger or older, which is *not* a simple matter, but a complication we can't go into right now.

The direction you're going to go in is a key factor in developing your nonoccupational identity, your post-insurance-man-self, your "way" you do your nothing. To some extent it will depend on how much money you have and where you stand now in the middle muddle. It would seem that anyone, given the choice, would want to move up, rather than down, the social scale. But wait and see: upper-class life is pretty rigid, confining, boring—and the one thing to avoid when you're not working is anything boring. Your choice of your postretirement routines and pursuits will be key factors here too.

A lot of the specific pursuits of retirement tend toward the lower because they would be lower-middle as occupations in the working world. This is true of the whole do-it-yourself side of things—cabinet making, flagstone laying, vegetable gardening, and so on. The useless leisure pursuits, the ones that accomplish absolutely nothing—yachting, tennis, flower gardening, bridge, croquet, and so on—naturally have a more upper connotation. The more useful, the more lower-class; the more useless, the more upper-class—that's the rough rule—but with exceptions, of course, like handball.

❧

Two Sample Post-Occupational Identities

LET'S CONSIDER two sample post-occupational identities (or POIs, pronounced "poise"), one tending toward the upper direction, the other tending toward the lower. Both of these are well tried and tested, but if you try one, chances are you'll be testing it all over again. They both have associations with all our friendly role-models—Thoreau, Rudolf Rassendyll, the Cleaning Lady, Molloy, Montaigne—the whole old gang. The first of these POIs (the upper one) is that of "The Active Hero-Sportsman"; the second (the lower) is that of "The Kindly Putterer."

The Active Hero-Sportsman style of using up the available time requires a great deal of energy and probably a certain amount of money and some training. The idea here is that you actually do get out and *do things*. You *do* actually sail a schooner to the South Seas, perhaps as part of some oceanographic expedition, or perhaps just for the hell of it (and it probably would *be* some sort of hell). You actually *go* on skiing trips to Canada and Norway, and you hunt big game and discover tribes and things in Africa and up the Amazon and places like that. You're asked to cruise with yacht owners and to visit other people's country places and you wear your dinner jacket (an old one) a lot; but then you rough it a lot too and show courage and stamina when the going gets tough. You're a man's man and younger women really go for you and so on. Some of the Hemingway heroes are like this. You could probably even learn swordplay and try to find a king who looked like you somewhere, whom you could stand in for for a month or two and defend his kingdom and make his queen *really* love *you.*

Of course it doesn't have to be as romantic or as big-deal or as expensive as I've suggested, but the idea is that you're active and vital and that you get around a lot and know God's own amount of people and *do* a lot of things. People might say about you, if you chose this kind of role: "He doesn't have much money, God knows, but somehow he manages to lead The Good Life." The Active Hero-Sportsman is obviously one of the attractive POIs and doesn't need much arguing for it. If you've got the stamina to pull it off, more power to you.

What I think needs a little more consideration or understanding (not to say sympathy) is the second of these POIs, that of The Kindly Putterer. Here you don't get around so much, if at all, but you keep just as busy. You've got all your projects and your "things" that you putter with, and you've always got experiments and new ideas you're trying out with movie cameras or tape recorders or microscopes or magnets or canvas or sheets of plastic or whatever. Of course it's hard being kindly, especially if you aren't *naturally* kindly, and especially if kids and others keep coming into your workshop and messing things up. But that's the price you pay for not having to travel and show stamina and courage. Instead you get to stay home and mess about making things or melting things or growing things or taking up something new (a musical instrument, an interest in kite flying, designing a fishtrap—God knows, *anything!*), and then losing interest in it and having to clean up all the stuff left over from the old project before you start in on the new idea or contraption or enterprise or experiment or whatever it is you're going to start puttering with next. After Leonardo da Vinci retired (from being a painter), he spent most of his life puttering. You can even make drawings of your projects and keep notebooks about them the way he did; that fills a lot of time, especially if you don't draw well. I believe Jefferson puttered a great deal at Monticello too. It may not *sound* so grand to be a Kindly Putterer as to be an Active Hero-Sportsman, but it's in no less honorable a tradition.

There are some disadvantages, of course. The Kindly Putterer role may not require as much pretraining as the Active Hero-Sportsman; but unless you're reconciled to everything you putter with being a mess and a failure, you ought to have a certain minimal kind of competence with things like hammers and wrenches and glue. You can't be a complete clumsy boob *and* a Kindly Putterer successfully. You'd have to be *fantastically* kindly to be a kindly bungling putterer. It wouldn't be worth it. You'd do better to use one of the other good POIs, like The Avid Reader or The Semi-Invalid.

These POIs are admittedly poses, concocted life-styles, identities that are more or less deliberately cultivated. But adopted and adapted and worked over, the manner becomes the actual self, or very close to it.

❦

Toward the Leisure Ethic

THE ANSWER to "How to Retire at Forty-one?"—our title put as a question—thus becomes clear, all too clear.

It *can't* be done—not right, at least—is the answer; you *can't* retire at forty-one, *unless either* of two things: (a) society changes, or (2) you change.

The American social system is still hung up on an outmoded value concept that was once central to the development of the country, the idea that "Industry is Virtue." This idea consists of two parts: (1) that work is necessary for the good of the community or the nation or whatever; and (2) that work is also necessary for the good of the individual, keeps him out of trouble, and so on.

This dual value concept is eroding in America now, but the trouble is that we've found nothing to substitute for it.

We need another ethic to substitute for the Work Ethic; what we need to develop in our selves and in our society, in fact, is a commitment to the Leisure Ethic.

The tenets of the Leisure Ethic, to be proclaimed from platform and pulpit, not to say sold on television, would be:

(A) Work, as such, should no longer be considered beneficial to society. It should be recognized that most of what people do as work actually harms society.

(B) Thus it follows that individual industry should no longer be considered virtuous, nor individual idleness a vice.

(C) Hence work must be considered or evaluated only in terms that are individual, not societal—that is, in terms of whether work is desired by, or necessary to, or beneficial to, each individual.

Tenets A, B, and C thus unwind the twin premises of the Work Ethic that, gaining strength from being twined together for centuries, have stunted individual growth and misshaped the development of our culture. Tenets A, B, and C thus lead inexorably and joyously to Tenets D and E.

(D) Those who continue to work in a society whose moral/cultural values devolve from the Leisure Ethic rather than the Work Ethic would do so in open recognition by themselves and by others that it is by personal idiosyncratic preference. They work because of individual necessity—that is, by psychological rather than financial necessity, for in a society dominated by the Leisure Ethic those who indulge themselves in work would receive less money than those who remain pure and uninvolved. Work would be recognized as a sort of crutch-therapy: the fact of needing-wanting to work would indicate a certain failure of independence, a psychic inadequacy, a lack of strength of character. But with work still tolerated, there would always be more than enough of those who still wanted to work available to get what little is really needed to be done done. The worker, in terms of the Leisure Ethic, would have roughly the same sort of moral stigma associated with him—a kind of vague reproach from others, a kind of mild guilt about himself—that the man who does not work has now.

(E) Those who do not work in such a situation would be obliged to justify the Leisure Ethic by living lives that are demonstrably better than those who do work.

Everything depends on Tenet E. Tenet E should occur as the final stage, the ultimate flowering of the new society created according to the principles of the Leisure Ethic. But in point of fact, adoption of the Leisure Ethic fails to even begin to happen, despite the manifest failure of the Work Ethic, just because Tenet E – providing demonstrable examples of the successful life of leisure – seems to be beyond us. Give unionized workers shorter hours, they moonlight – and studies show it's not just for money. The more powerful an executive, the less he utilizes his opportunities for leisure. Sons of "the leisure class," so-called, are on tight schedules running for office or administering family foundations. The lack of successful examples of the life of leisure is a great part of what's blocking acceptance of the Leisure Ethic.

To live by an ethic presupposes an idea of what is moral. Under the old Work Ethic, what was clearly moral was industry. If we are going to substitute the Leisure Ethic for the Work Ethic, with its idea that "Industry Is Virtue," it is not sufficient simply to say, "Idleness Is Virtue." It used to be the use that was made of work that made it seem to have value and hence be virtuous. Now we see clearly that work has no real use, hence no value, and hence no virtue. But idleness doesn't seem to have much use either. What we've got to do, if we want the Leisure Ethic, is not just show that work has no value, but that idleness, despite appearances, in fact does.

In recent times (America in the 1960s and 1970s), the young people of the middle class seemed to recognize the uselessness and hence the valuelessness of work. But they established no Leisure Ethic to substitute for the Work Ethic. In fact, many of them lived a slatternly life in their urban crash pads and rural communes. Getting stoned or tripping were perhaps part of the search for a successful leisure self, but they seemed to search more than they found, and drugs, anyway, seem scarcely a better way of filling the available time than the boozing of the idle rich and the idle poor.

Modern medicine prolonging life expectancy and bureaucratic regulations specifying that workers must retire at a certain early age have created a horde of retired "senior citizens" in their "sunset years" who spoil some of the prettiest, warmest parts of our country – Florida, California, and Arizona, for example. With their shuffling and shuffleboard, gossiping, pestering their middle-aged children with grievances – they could scarcely present a worse case for not working. There are exceptions, of course, but by and large old people have also made a botch of leisure.

So the idle rich, the idle poor, the idle young, and the idle old have all failed to demonstrate the use, hence the value, and hence the virtue of idleness.

The middle class has traditionally been the bastion of morality. Middle age has always been the age of responsibility. It is up to those who retire at forty-one to point the way for America to develop the Leisure Ethic.

A middle-class, middle-aged man who quits work, as we've repeatedly said, has no traditional social patterns to guide him, the way the rich and the poor do. That's what makes it so difficult for him. But it is also what gives him the vital, unique opportunity to select his own individual routines and pursuits, make his *own* pattern of life, to so devise the use he makes of his leisure as to demonstrate its virtue. There's no exclusive club's snobby billiard room or loafer's pool hall to entrap him; no vile tradition of philandering, drink, drugs, shuffleboard, or other Foul Vice.

It is all up to us—us middle-class, middle-aged men and women who *have* worked, who traditionally and historically as a group *always* worked—to show that we can do better than the idle rich, the idle poor, the idle young, and the idle old. They've made a balls-up of it historically, and they're doing little better now. We must show that our POIs (our Post-Occupational Identities, remember?) are the SLSs (the Successful Leisure Selfs) they've so long sought in vain. If it's just a few of us who quit work now, we must point the way—the *right* way—as "Frontiersmen of the New Leisure" and try to take this role seriously when people look at us funny.

EPILOGUE

What Finally Happened to Me

What a story, God send I don't make a balls of it.
—MOLLOY

I NEVER really found a satisfactory Post-Occupational Identity for myself. Do as I say, I keep telling you, not as I do. Against all my own best advice I fell into the leisure pursuit of writing, but I was never able to think of myself as being really "a writer"–perhaps because I had been for too long an editor. Worse, I began to write out of an identity–that of the so-called Fussy Man–that was not quite exactly my own, yet seemed to those who knew me (and to myself at times) to be a direct representation of my own speech and manner. That is: personal and individual and recognizable as the Fussy Man's voice may seem (for better or worse), it is not *me*. I'm not even fussy. I like things to be nice, of course; but then, who doesn't?

It's true that as a joke–well, perhaps maybe somewhat more than a joke, but still in something less than full seriousness–signs went up in our kitchen, like:

> **CLEANING UP AS YOU GO ALONG**
> **IS HALF THE FUN**

and:

> **ONE OF LIFE'S GREATEST PLEASURES**
> **IS PUTTING SOMETHING BACK**
> **WHERE IT BELONGS**

Maybe I did get to be sort of a sign freak for a while, but I knew it and fought it. Copying a good idea of my father's, I once hung a tennis ball on a string from a rafter of the garage. The ball hung just where it would hit the windshield of the station wagon when it was far enough in so you could shut the garage doors behind it. Good idea, no? No. *No!* When the car was out of the garage, no one knew what the ball was for, and a tennis ball hanging on a string in the middle of an empty garage gets bopped and yanked at by every visiting kid who's big enough to reach it, even if he has to jump. The string was always breaking, and it was complicated to retie it, because you had to drive the car in, make sure it was just right with the garage doors, not too far in, but still so they could close, then climb up on the car, being careful not to scratch the finish, and get the wretched ball adjusted just right touching the windshield again. So finally what I did was get one of those labeling tags that, needless to say, I have a whole lot of, wrote on one side:

> Please see other side.

and *on* the other side:

> Please do not play with this
> ball or interfere with it in any
> way, as it serves a useful or
> fairly useful purpose. And
> please, God, don't let me start
> putting signs up everywhere.

Friends would stop by with friends of theirs—people I'd never met—and ask if they could take their friends out to the garage and show them the ball with the sign on it that they'd been telling them about. I'd follow them out, explaining it all. What would *they* do about a problem like this, I'd ask them.

People were always stopping by at Coveside, on their way from New York to Cape Cod, to break the journey, or from Boston to Long Island, waiting for the ferry from New London to Orient Point, or invited up for the weekend, or having invited themselves up for the weekend. There was a companionable network of friends who were almost like relatives, to one another as well as to ourselves; and as close friends took houses for the summer in Stonington, and then friends of theirs arrived and became our friends, there were summer weekends so crowded with tennis, sailing, picnics, and cocktails— huge gangs gathering the next morning for brunch or merging several dinner parties into a spur-of-the-moment dance later, or whatever—that one was always late for something. Everyone had kids. Coveside became really quite like "the grandfather place" I'd imagined. There'd sometimes be twelve or fourteen for lunch, say, at the long table I'd made, all ages, eating snapper blues we'd caught that morning. It was pure idyll or pure chaos, depending on how you looked at it. The kids would get up from the table, restless, and while their parents sat drinking white wine, they'd go yank at my tennis ball or scatter Frisbees and croquet balls all over the lawn and lose the horseshoes. I was always picking stuff up and repairing things. No doubt I often lost my temper: orderly people do. Summer weekends would sometimes seem to last all week, but then there were lonely pockets too, when it seemed no one was around. These were mostly in the winter, when all the New York people would go back to New York.

What I was writing used all this as material. I began by writing short self-mocking pieces that I hoped were funny, playing the normal chaos of family life off against my orderly attitudes, the Fussy Man persona. "How to Organize a Family Picnic (and Keep It That Way)," "How to Eat an Ice-Cream Cone," "How to Be Kindly," and so on—were all composed in this mood, along with the longer essay, "Delight in Order." Most of these were printed sooner or later in magazines, but they were all conceived as part of a book, and the book kept growing. Two pieces in the book, especially, grew unconscionably: "How to Retire at Forty-One" threatened to become book-length in itself; "How to Be Good" stood about six-hundred manuscript pages with no end in sight. Soon I was in that most discouraging of positions: writing more stuff all the time, when you know that what you ought to be doing is cutting what you've already done. My beloved Fussy Man Book became more and more unpublishable as this obsessive-compulsive nonwriter within me scribbled, scribbled, scribbled. The editor, also within me, and filled with dismay, was somehow powerless.

Of course a real writer, a "professional" writer, would never have allowed this to happen, would have crafted one little marketable book after another, gained strength from the acceptance and publication of one to go on to the next. It's clear to me that I've written an amateur's work in an amateurish way. I don't mean that too slightingly, actually. Many fascinating books seem the work of amateur authors (not that this is one of them), and professional writers seem often by contrast to just knock things out in a shape that's marketable, not in the shape, or lack of shape, to which the material naturally grows. Be that as it may, the amateur writer, like the amateur scholar (one not connected with a university), can get himself into what seems like an endless, hopeless project. Facing it all alone, *with too much work already done to be able to abandon it,* he may still feel *he just can't go on.* It's a very painful situation, partially (and *particularly*) just because it has to be faced alone.

I was getting lonely anyway. The wife and stepchildren and companionable network of friends-who-were-almost-like-relatives tended to come and go, and to be away most when I was writing. Whether that was because I was so irascible when I was writing that they had to go away, or because I was only able to get organized to write when they weren't there, or because I was so irascible about not being able to get organized to write when they were there that they had to go away so I could, or because they simply had things of their own to do—never became clear. It's just clear that they often weren't there when I was writing.

And so, gradually, or suddenly—what I'm describing covers years, and while things happen gradually our realization of them is often sudden, and vice versa—it appeared that Coveside was empty. I'd go away myself from time to time, often return to find it vacant. Gradually—or suddenly—wife and stepchildren had found other things they had to do more and more. The Real Ones, as I began to call them, would reappear, of course, from time to time, but less and less. The dog was mostly there, yapping. Always nervous, he was now hopelessly confused by all these comings and goings (which became mostly goings), but confident (the way dogs are) that the family would all be back soon, a confidence that he must finally have realized was misplaced, after he'd been given away.

It was after a couple of months of being more or less entirely alone at Coveside that whatever Post-Occupational Identity I'd achieved for myself (and, as I've said, it wasn't much) began to come apart entirely. The Real Ones were replaced (gradually, suddenly) by a trio of characters I reluctantly recognized as aspects of myself, like the brothers that I, an only child, never had. Nor were they friendly and devoted like the brothers in *Beau Geste*, but irritable and at odds, like the Karamazovs.

The first, the oldest in a way, certainly the most "grown up," was of course the Fussy Man. He'd been around a long time, was almost a father to us, but a dithering, ineffective, faggoty-uncle sort of father. Then there was Larry Placebound, in control sometimes. Then there emerged LOMLIC, whose dominance of us at a certain period was complete and terrible. And also there sometimes—sometimes with the others somehow, some other times just watching somehow—there was me.

LOMLIC is an acronym, short for LOMLICDAT OF QUIAMBAUG (Lonely Old Man, Lives In Country, Drives Ancient Truck—Quiambaug Cove being the gloomy waterside by his battered, haunted old house). Some of you will find it appropriate, I guess, that LOMLIC rhymes with MOM-DICK. We realized later that LOMLIC had probably always been there, lumbering around the grounds, doing the Chores & Maintenance like a surly hired hand, picking up things, muttering as he'd retie the tennis ball. He used to live, maybe, in the garden-tool shed. But after The Real Ones left, he came out of the shed and moved into the house, and took over. No longer a simple surly caretaker, he began to think of himself as some Dark Ages minor manor-lord whose tenants had all deserted the land because of his black moods. His left hand was in a cast for a month. I slipped playing tennis on a wet asphalt court at the Community Center and fractured the hand, but LOMLIC imagined he broke it in some deep Heathcliffean rage, too abominable to allow to the surface of memory. And, in fact, he did break our other hand, the right one, in just such a way, a month later.

Some evenings LOMLIC would drive the rest of us away and sit alone at the head of the long table, watching television as he ate and drank. We'd sneak back and watch him through the window. "LOMLIC eats now," we'd say. "LOMLIC is watching his television as he eats." It's the Lawrence Welk Show; LOMLIC chews stolidly as he watches all the golden oldsters having a jolly time dancing down in sunny Florida. Sometimes, if he'd had too much to drink, LOMLIC would grab the dog by the forepaws and make him dance with him in the kitchen, the way I often did when the Lawrence Welk Show was on Saturday nights. Then we'd watch LOMLIC put the dishes in the sink for the Fussy Man to clean up in the morning, turn off the lights one by one, and keeping his balance as best he could, slowly climb the stairs. "LOMLIC goes toward slumber now," we'd say to ourselves as we did it.

The next morning the phone rings.

"Abode of LOMLIC," I say, all business.

"Rust?" says someone, tentatively.

"Yes," I say slowly, as if annoyed. "I am also known as Rust Hills."

"What's all this LOMLIC stuff?"

"Just a joke," I say. "Did you want to invite me to dinner or a party or something?" The caller is part of a network of friends-like-relatives.

"No," they say. "I was just wondering if you knew how I could reach ———." They name one of The Real Ones who are gone.

LOMLIC dominated us with his loneliness and black despair, except when Larry Placebound managed to get us away from Coveside. Larry, like the rest of us, was once a fiction editor, but then he went over to the enemy, the New Journalism. The Fussy Man said Larry was deliberately trying to disgrace us by becoming that saddest of all things, a free-lance magazine-article writer. Larry continued to call himself "Placebound," perhaps out of some *nouveau* "ancestral pride," but the rest of us thought of him as "Lawrence Gadabout," for he was always bopping off somewhere or other. He took us to Florida once on an impetuous and ill-conceived bus trip that became a nightmare when it turned out he had no money, just a Master-charge card with a faulty number. He embarrassed the Fussy Man by spending two weeks at a Club Méditerrané resort on Guadeloupe. He took us to Chicago, to Hugh Hefner's *Playboy* mansion, of all places. Also to Barbados, where he freeloaded disgracefully on a friend of ours. Two winters in a row he dragged us off to a depraved mountain town in Mexico called San Miguel, an "artist's paradise" we nearly got kicked out of. We spent two months each at three writers' funny farms—The MacDowell Colony in New Hampshire, Wavertree Hall in Virginia, and Yaddo in upstate New York. Once he even went to the Bread Loaf Writers' Conference in Vermont. Our then sister-in-law was always forwarding his mail.

He got a lot of mail, too; for he was once supposed to be doing book reviews and got copies of new novels and was on publishers' promotion lists; he worked as *Audience*'s fiction editor, and manuscripts and other correspondence were always arriving from them; there were lots of bills, too, for when we were at Coveside we ran at least a dozen charge accounts around the area. Someone once told Larry, "You can tell how important a man is by how much mail he gets," so he'd delight in it, walking back up the driveway from the mailbox, flipping through a big pile of stuff. The Fussy Man would go right to the secretary and immediately pay the bills; Larry would sit at the long empty table reading all the publishers' announcements and personal letters; L O M L I C watched disgustedly, but hung around, because if there were any "Sexually Oriented Advertisements," Larry would let him have them.

It occurred to me often, during this time, that I was playing dangerous games with myself, inventing these argumentative companions as aspects of myself. I couldn't figure out if it was some solitary vice—a kind of psychological masturbation—or some crazy kind of therapy—interior psychodrama, say, or single-person "group." Was it self-abuse or self-help? Sick self-pity or healthful self-mockery? I'm going crackers, sure, I'd say to myself, but like Saul Bellow's Moses Herzog, I'd add: if so, I might as well enjoy it. It did not escape me, finally—or perhaps I should say that well after these characters had appeared and established themselves, I suddenly saw (or gradually realized)—that they partake of the classic Freudian trinity of the self. That is, of course: the Fussy Man was some sort of parental or avuncular Superego, proper and moral and trying to do things right; Larry Placebound was the Ego, still functioning, moving around, getting the work done, dealing with people, and so on; and L O M L I C was the Id. Most people get a fun-loving Id. It didn't seem right we'd get such a mean, angry, dour son-of-a-bitch, but maybe that's just what was there in the tool shed, and sooner or later he had to come out. In any event, the whole bunch seemed a far cry from the "merry crew of thoughts" that used to keep Thoreau company when he'd walk back from town late at night. Clearly there was some sort of identity crisis occurring. Clearly ego reinforcement was needed because of this alternating domination of the Superego and the Id; but none of us really liked Larry Gadabout enough to *want* to help him. He seemed kind of a jerk.

At one point, in our continuing quest for our identity, we became obsessed with finding the secret message in my name. Larry got sent

How to Retire at Forty-One

W. H. Auden's marvelous commonplace book, *A Certain World*, and the Fussy Man got to reading it. Under "Anagrams," the first entry is from D. A. Borgmann:

> Almost any name with a good distribution of alphabet letters can be turned into either a flattering or an unflattering anagram of itself. Thus the full name of the author of this book, DMITRI ALFRED BORGMANN, lends itself to the flattering anagram, GRAND MIND, MORTAL FIBRE!, as well as the negative anagram, DAMN MAD BORING TRIFLER!

The only comment Auden made on this was WHY SHUN A NUDE TAG?, which is of course an anagram of HUGH WYSTAN AUDEN; but whether he thought that was flattering or unflattering, none of us could guess.

Of course nothing would do but we had to try it for ourselves. The Fussy Man said the rule was that we had to use *all* the letters of my full name, LAWRENCE RUST HILLS. We cut up a manila folder into small cardboard squares; Fussy carefully printed on each of the letters; then we laid them out on the long table, and set to work.

LUNCHER RATES SWILL is what we got right away.

We soon found a couple of unflattering anagrams, ALL SIN RULES WRETCH and WASTREL, SIN, CUR—HELL!. Also WRITER'S CALLEN LUSH—"Whosa callen' us a lush?" joked Larry. But we kept looking for the flattering one Borgmann had said would be there somewhere, and meanwhile we came up with some oddities, which we'd explain to one another.

> WHALE SLURS TRINCLE—Trincle is a lovable dolphin. . . .
>
> LESSER CHAT WILL RUN—There were these two brothers named Chat, both of them in politics, one not as important as the other. . . .
>
> REAL STEW CHILLS RUN—Downhill racer eats too much for lunch. . . .
>
> A man who has a terrible case of poison ivy goes to see his doctor (named Sell), who tells him he must stop scratching it. . . . "RULE ITCH!" WARNS SELL.

≈ 164

I *am* losing my mind, I thought, as we played this game with my name and the weeks went by. We were sort of enjoying it, laughing at some of the crazy things we found, until LOMLIC came across ALL WIT HURLS SCREEN, which he said meant that all this joking was part of a barrier of humor we were throwing up so as to keep ourselves from finding the real secret message. Thereafter it became less fun, and we were about to give up, when the Fussy Man discovered WILLS SEARCH LET RUN, so we decided to keep looking a while longer. It was only when Fuss came across WRITERS SHALL UNCLE that we decided to give it up for a while and paint the cars.

After LOMLIC moved in and took over, Coveside became somewhat like the house of that poor soul Usher in the Edgar Allan Poe story. The Fussy Man would try to keep it neat, but everything was gradually wearing out. When Larry Placebound would go away on his jaunts he'd either rent or lend the place, and that never did it any good. In the Coveside living room, the worn comfortable brown-velvet chairs gradually (or suddenly) became uncleanable and unrepairable. Sitting in them, Larry would restlessly start plucking out soft down feathers, like Kleenex, from the corners of the cushions. The springs bulged gravidly underneath the sofa, then finally settled right down on the floor—not really uncomfortable if you knew in advance how low you were going to sink. There's a certain coziness when things get this run-down, perhaps an aspect of the security implicit in knowing you've touched bottom.

But it distressed us too. Oil paintings flaked; the Fussy Man claimed he could no longer see what they represented, only the patches of bare canvas; even to glance at them, he said, stabbed him with guilt at how they'd deteriorated under what he called his "trusteeship." We all felt guilty about the beloved sailboat, "Truth," which remained in her cradle in the boathouse. We hadn't the time to put her into commission (much less go sailing!) but we knew that her planks were shrinking from not soaking up in the water. The stone dock was gradually becoming a stone breakwater, the effect of each winter's ice, each summer's neglect. Gangplank gone, the big heavy float I'd built was sort of half-tied, half-moored just offshore, where it came to rest in the mud at low tide; the drums on one side sank, that side went slightly underwater, mallards used it as a slide to sun on. In the studio, rain rusted the Franklin stove, leaked through the skylight so that sections of the plasterboard around it hung from the ceiling.

Get busy and fix these things, you say. I would, I would. In spasms, at least. Too often I'd spend hours trying to fix something (a wall light, say, or a leak under the kitchen sink) only to find I couldn't fix it after all. Just as often I'd mend something (a broken chair leg, the fan belt of the tractor lawn mower, the screen door), only to have it break again a week later, or something enough like it not to make any difference. I *did* fix things, I did, I did. *Constantly.* Well, maybe not constantly, but certainly continually—that is, constantly when I wasn't intermittently in the sloth that accompanies melancholy. There was just too much of it all. Too *many* things, too many *things.*

With all that desperately needed doing, God only knows why we ever started painting the cars. None of us later would ever admit it was his idea, but we all wanted to do it—when we started at least. Neither vehicle was, strictly speaking, a car. I'd bought the two of them for a package price of $1,000 from Don Fisher, a local used-car dealer, about two years earlier. One was a battered blue snub-nosed Chevy truck, and the other was a pale-green Toyota station wagon. Both cars were always breaking down, being well past their prime, not to say on their last legs, and we were always jump-starting one from the other, or using one to tow the other to the garage—that is, when they weren't both out of commission at the same time, which was not infrequent.

We started off by taking all the rust spots down to bare metal with an electric sander, then undercoating them with Rustoleum. Then we hand-sanded the original finish lightly so that the paint would stick. Then we lovingly painted both these big cars, inside and out, *with a paint brush.* Two full weeks it took us. Everyone said we did a marvelous, careful job; it was one of the few things we did that came out really right. Unfortunately, though, we chose a sort of flesh color, called on the Pittsburgh Paints chart "Harvest Tan," but referred to by those who came to watch as "Liver Brown" or "Ca-Ca Yellow."

After that, we spent another two weeks futilely attempting to install automobile radios. Still the cars broke down. Briefly we had a membership in the Allstate Auto Club, but after the third tow-in in two months, they canceled our membership. The Fussy Man wrote them a letter saying he didn't blame them, but he just wanted them to know that all the breakdowns really happened, we weren't trying to swindle them or anything. We got a nice letter back from Allstate saying that they couldn't renew the membership, but that they understood, which of course they didn't. They couldn't possibly have had any idea. When Larry Placebound, who was still fiddling with the anagrams of LAWRENCE RUST HILLS, came across LET HIS CARS RUN WELL, we all burst out laughing. Even LOMLIC shook his head, snorted through his nose, and stamped his foot. "LET HIS CARS RUN WELL! *That's* a good one all right," he said.

One Saturday morning during this time I awakened at 5:30 with an absolutely unaccountable but just as absolutely overwhelming desire to hear the original-cast recording of *South Pacific*. So I put it on the record player—at full blast, which is one of the very few advantages of living more or less alone in a fairly remote spot. Somehow it animated us all. "Younger than springtime am I," we all sang at the top of our lungs, "Gayer than laughter am I," Larry carrying the melody, Fussy Man the tenor, and LOMLIC with his bass-baritone, which can be quite rich and lovely on some of those songs. I can't carry a tune, but I joined in as best I could.

"This is what I need, this is what I've longed for," sang LOMLIC, "someone young and smiling, lighting up my years." I played the record through twice and the second time through, Larry Placebound nearly broke down right in the middle of singing, "Once you have found her, never let her go." "I've got to get *out* of here," he kept saying. It was lost on none of us that we were very like Ezio Pinza as Emile de Becque or whatever his name was, living alone on his plantation high on a hillside above the sea, getting older. We were sad, but still full of hope that morning, for we knew that eventually he'd found that bouncy little nurse, Nellie Forbush (Mary Martin), and had never ever let her go.

And then, as if conjured by these idiot dreams, at 8:30 that very same morning into our driveway came a girl in a gray Volvo station wagon. I remember it so vividly! I went immediately to the car and leaned in the window. "This is what I need, this is what I've longed for," I said to her. Then I explained how lonely I was now that The Real Ones had left, how she could lighten up my years, could become for me what the young Mary Martin had been for Pinza, what Marie de Gournay (age twenty-five) had been for Montaigne (age fifty-nine), a "covenant daughter" and a "cherished reward." I really poured it on, but she was nice about it—nervous at first, then amused, then getting nervous again. Freckled and pretty, she really was "someone young and smiling." She'd entered our driveway entirely by error: she lived in Mystic with her husband and kids, was looking for the Burdicks', who live further upcove, where she was arranging a Tupperware party. Certainly we had found her (or she had found us), but after about twenty minutes we had to let her go.

Occasionally in his travels Larry Placebound would meet a woman, and some of them would come to visit at Coveside. The Fussy Man could scarcely stand some of them, but LOMLIC liked them all. Then, too, Larry would be on the phone with some publisher's assistant, first doing business, then trying to sweet-talk her into coming up for the weekend. We'd all listen as he made the arrangements: we'd meet her train at 7:21 Friday night in New London; we'd recognize her by her green hat; she should look for our butterscotch-colored station wagon, in case we missed her on the platform. Listening in pure amazement at the way Larry operated, LOMLIC would sit there, running his tongue over his lips nervously, *imagining* the girl. He knew all the rest of us said it was his fault Miss Tupperware had been scared away, and he was determined to play it cooler this time if he could. The Fussy Man was also listening, but he'd pretend to put his hands over his ears. Such scandalous goings-on! A girl we'd never even met coming up for the weekend! What was the world coming to? What were *we* coming to?

During a lot of all this—for at least three months—I was going to church secretly. Every Sunday I'd get all shaved and dressed nice. I couldn't go to the Episcopal church in Stonington because people would know me there, and turning up alone at church would strike everyone as even more forlorn than turning up alone at cocktail parties. So I went to a Congregational church, The Road Church, so-called, a couple of miles inland, on the Pequot Trail, just off Flander's Road. It was a frame building on a hillside, tall stone foundations at one end—quite lovely, and rather old, I think. Inside, it was all painted the pleasantest yellow and white, with handsome big windows.

The first time I went, I was a little late, and the eighteen or twenty people in the congregation looked up startled at this stranger in their midst. I walked down the aisle and sat in a pew all by myself behind everyone else, although they were all scattered around toward the rear. Aside from an occasional wedding or funeral, I hadn't been in a church for twenty, maybe thirty, years. God knows what I was doing there now. Ah, I thought to myself, that's just it: *God* knows.

It was Fourth of July weekend, and the minister gave a sermon about freedom. He was all for political freedom, but he was against the contemporary excess in personal freedom that leads to immorality, directionlessness, irresponsibility, and unhappiness. The totally isolated person is totally free, but to what end, if he be lonely and guided not by purpose in his life? Ah, that spoke to me! And the sermon was neatly ordered in three parts, related to the readings he'd chosen from the *Bible;* even the hymns seemed to tie in.

I thought I ought to try to pray or something, now I was in church, but all I could find to pray for was some sort of increase in strength in myself to continue in this situation if necessary, and that the situation itself would somehow soon pass away. I didn't know what to pray for myself to "do" or for what to have "happen."

After the service, people introduced themselves and welcomed me, shaking hands heartily. Virtually everyone in the congregation seemed to have some official capacity. The men wore green business suits, their hair close-cropped; the women were buxom in below-the-knee flowered dresses. I never saw a pretty girl there the whole time I went—what a thing to be thinking of. Later, when my left hand was in a splint, they commiserated over my tennis accident, said how they appreciated my coming each week anyway. They were just awfully kind, as if I were a first tourist and they really wanted me to like their country.

The minister gave some pretty good sermons during the first month, although none so good as the Fourth of July one. Then he went away to some church meetings somewhere, and the man who took his place was nothing like as good. And when the first minister came back, he gave a series of sermons on what role the church could play in modern life, which sounded like notes he'd taken at the meetings and was pretty boring. I still kept going, though, except for the Sunday after the Saturday night LOMLIC broke our other hand in his rage. Both hands were completely wrapped up for about six days and I was pretty helpless. "Pathetic" is the precise word I used, thinking about myself that week.

But the Sunday after that I took off both bandages and went. I tried to get away from people right after the service, because I guess I knew what was coming. But no, they wanted to greet me. "Where *were* you last week?" "How *are* you?" "Good to *see* you again!" All the men emphasized their words with good firm handshakes. When the fourth man, a short wiry fellow, came down on the "*missed*" in the sentence, "We really *missed* you!" I felt the broken bone move. Pain swam into my eyes, and I nearly fainted.

The wiry man looked up at me, great concern in his narrow features.

"It's just . . . just my hand," I gasped.

"Oh," he said, horrified at what he'd done. "Everyone always says I shake hands too hard. I'm so sorry." Then he looked puzzled. "But I thought it was the *other* hand you broke, the *left* hand."

"No, no," I said. "It's this one. But that's all right."

"Are you *sure?*" he said, really puzzled now. "I could have sworn . . ."

"Of course I'm sure which *hand* I broke," I said. "How could I not be '*sure*' about a thing like that? Excuse me, I have to go now."

I fled and never went back.

I've got a thick folder, labeled "The LOMLIC Papers," full of memorabilia of this period in my life that I most want to forget. Some of it is copies of my long letters, alternately whiny and reasonable, sometimes demanding a divorce, sometimes beseeching a reconciliation; all carefully interfiled chronologically with the far-fewer, far-shorter answers that came in. But the biggest part of the folder is the accumulated "Lists" from the clipboard. God knows why I kept them in the first place, much less keep them now.

This clipboard was the center of my life during this period. Everything I thought or did revolved around and in some way depended on the clipboard. It was always either with me or on the long table. I was always consulting it for what to do next, adding things to do, scratching off something that had been done, changing the order to do things in, jotting down notes and comments. It was different from the orderly, scheduled "Comprehensive Day Plan" I'd made anew each day during the happy early days of my retirement—no less pathetic, but far more emotional and desperate. Every several days I'd make a new list, clinging to the old one as long as I could, for it showed how much I'd already done. I'd transfer the (usually few) things that remained up onto a fresh sheet of paper I'd clamp on top, saving the old ones underneath on the clipboard until it grew thick—not so much with achievement, God knows, as with effort spent.

Some of these pages have dozens and dozens—perhaps nearly a hundred—items on them, most all crossed off, often with different-colored pens and pencils. The lists were not neat, but sometimes they were somehow pretty. Once or twice a visitor would ask me if he could *have* a list he particularly admired, and I'd give it to him, freely, gladly. Groceries and other shopping might be in one corner, a small calendar in another; lists of people to phone, with notes on what to say; letters that needed to be written, manuscripts to be read, things to tell so-and-so, what needed typing or xeroxing, the order of an errand-running trip to Westerly or Mystic, household chores, boat chores, auto chores—*everything* went on the clipboard.

We were all actually very busy during this period, is part of it. Larry had his *Audience* editing, plus setting up a series of "Conversations" between authors that came to very little, plus fiction reviewing for *Harper's* that came to nothing at all—half of what one does comes to nothing, but that doesn't mean you still don't have to do it if they ask you—plus that trip to Bread Loaf to write an article on the writers' conference for *Audience.* The Fussy Man was finally arranging to have his monstrous manuscript published in three volumes by Doubleday, trying to get the contract transferred from The Macmillan Company, getting the manuscript of the first book in order and trying to sell parts of it to magazines, and at the same time cooking nourishing meals for us (cleaning up as he went along, of course) and keeping a neat house. Meanwhile LOMLIC would be messing around outdoors, getting into too-big projects like transplanting small apple trees and cleaning out down by the boathouse, carting stuff off to the dump in the ancient but freshly painted truck. The rest of us might want to read of an evening, but LOMLIC would come in at twilight exhausted and just want to get drunk and go to bed early. We kept getting up earlier and earlier. Sometimes I awakened sweating, heart pounding, in the middle of the night, and thought I was having a heart attack. It was just anxiety and all this trivia on my mind. I often thought each of us should have had a separate list of his own, but I never got into that, thank God.

On the clipboard lists occasionally are snatches of dialogue between us, as if a tape recorder had accidentally been left on. At the top of one list, for instance:

> FUSSY MAN: "Even seen in *advance*, your activities are more or less pointless, aren't they?"
>
> LOMLIC: "So is complaining about them. Unless perhaps you have an alternative?"
>
> LARRY PLACEBOUND: "I consider us all martyrs to The New Leisure."
>
> LOMLIC: "You talk a lot of crap, too. Why don't you get off your ass and either start writing or do some work around here?"

We were always soliciting advice, from any of the network of friends-like-relatives who would visit, about what I should do. Many of them wouldn't say anything, feeling it would have been "taking sides." "Why don't you want to take sides?" I'd ask them. "Don't you want to be on the *right* side?" We got a lot of advice anyway, and sometimes it seemed that our situation was like some sort of psychological projective test: everyone advised doing either what he himself had done or wished he could do. Often this advice would get onto the clipboard. I have a three-page "Analysis of the Situation and Solution to It as of Sunday Night March 20," which lists a lot of this. And in one friend's late-night handwriting, I have *his* solution for me:

> Recap (Steps to Take):
> (1) Stop making lists
> (2) Get out of here
> (3) Get a girl
> (4) *Do* something

Good advice, clearly. But it's in the nature of steps, *as steps*, that they have to be taken one at a time and in order; and I knew I couldn't manage to leave Coveside unless I first made a big list of all the things I would have to do before I could get away. Finally I was given some convincing advice about advice itself: "If you could take it, you wouldn't need it."

Sometimes we'd get to quarreling amongst ourselves about whose fault it was that The Real Ones had left. Often we'd blame the Fussy Man for his picky, annoying way. But he'd say it was LOMLIC's bad temper that had driven them away. Then they'd both claim it was Larry Placebound's obsession with getting some writing done and his going away on trips all the time, especially in the winter. I'd reassure each of them as best I could: tell the Fussy Man that The Real Ones were actually somewhat untidy people and that his reputation for fussiness was much exaggerated and mostly an act anyway; tell LOMLIC that there really was far too much to do around Coveside and no wonder he got discouraged and irritable sometimes; tell Larry that his work *was* important and that if he hadn't taken trips now and then he wouldn't have been able to work at all. But then the question just hung there—well, then, whose fault was it?—and they all started blaming *me*. I could absolve only aspects of myself, not the whole.

It was lonesomest for me when I was at Coveside, most haunted with how it had been, so I'd always be leaving, and it would be better for a while somewhere else. Then I'd start hitting what I'd call "lonely pockets," and I'd go back to Coveside to see if I wasn't better off there. I was always being told to "wait," and I'd conscientiously pass that advice along to myself. "Wait," I'd say to myself when I got anxious. "Just wait." And I *did* wait, too—thinking I ought to, and not knowing anyway what else to do if I *didn't* wait. Dropped into a lonely pocket after hours of work, I'd lie on a bed, whether at Coveside, or in Virginia, or in New York, or even in that dreadful cold house I rented for $90 one month in San Miguel—like living at the bottom of a well it was, the hot bright sun would pass over the central patio in an hour and a half each day, around noon, while I had the lights on and a fire going inside. "Wait," I'd say, lying there. I began to get an almost physical reaction to the word after a while—a squirm not just of distaste but something very near horror.

"Wait," I'd say to myself.

All this was wretched, not to say ridiculous excess, I grant you, carrying on this way about having to spend just a year or so more or less alone. But when a part of you is screaming at you to do something and all the other part can do is just keep saying "wait" over and over, it does more harm than good. "If you tell yourself 'wait' one more time," I said to myself at one point toward the end, "I'm going to crack you wide open, I really am."

It ended, of course–finally. Everything has to end, although it sure seemed there for a while that this was going to be the first thing ever that wouldn't ever. And it ended, again of course, as any conflict in character always ends, not in a resolution of the conflict, but in a dissolution of it. The *deus ex machina* is unsatisfactory as a device to provide a solution only on stage, not in life. In life it is only some God-sent event or person that can release us from the prisons we put ourselves in. The self-made prison is like the self-created problem: just as in any self-created problem worth its salt, you've anticipated all the possible solutions; so with any self-made prison that isn't just a botched job, you've made sure you don't secretly know of an open door somewhere. *No known exit*, that's of the essence in your successful self-made prison.

Larry met her first, of course, but when she came to Coveside it was immediately clear to each of us that she'd been sent to us all. Everything was suddenly different, nothing gradual about this: a miracle of change.

Something *had* finally "happened." We were able to "do something" again. With her help and with LOMLIC and Fussy working together instead of against one another, the house at Coveside was not just restored to order, but renewed and made available for summer rental. Larry, revitalized, worked hard; among the things he did was invite the whole network of friends-like-relatives, plus the same 180 people in publishing he still knew, to a publication party he gave in New York to celebrate the first volume of the Fussy Man's book.

Our separate identities gradually faded. Each of us–the Fussy Man, Larry Placebound, and LOMLIC–had been unhappy in his own way; in happiness we could scarcely tell ourselves apart. It was some kind of unbelievable miracle of transformation, how with joy we three once again became one.

❧ **Book Three** ❧

How to Be Good

OR,

The Somewhat Tricky Business
of Attaining Moral Virtue in a Society
That's Not Just Corrupt but Corrupting,
Without Being Completely Out-of-It

CHAPTER ONE

A Modern Good Man

Telling Good from Bad

THERE'S BEEN an amount of consideration given, down through the centuries, as to where virtue resides, what it is, how it's acquired, and so on. Now we have every hope and intention of finally getting to the bottom of all these matters in this discussion, at least I do (have hope); but we don't want to get involved in all the centuries' previous theories, since it's clear no one's yet solved the problem. We want to deal with the question, not a lot of wrong answers. Problems, anyway, have always interested me far more than solutions.

How to tell good from bad? One of the simplest and most famous wrong answers to this question was Ernest Hemingway's. Hemingway always liked simple, famous wrong answers. You remember, for instance, when Fitzgerald was wondering how come it was the rich are so different from the rest of us, Hemingway said the only difference is "they have more money." That's a simple, famous wrong answer if ever there was one. Then, as to the question of virtue Hemingway said, "What's good is what makes you feel good afterward; what's bad is what makes you feel bad afterward."

Simple, famous wrong answers are usually just a way of making fun of a problem, instead of relishing and refining it. This kind of affective answer reduces the whole question of morality to such basic terms that the question itself suddenly seems as simple as the answer. Hemingway's concept bears the same relation to ethics that the statement "What's good is what I like" bears to aesthetics. "There's no disputing taste," they say, meaning that there are no absolute principles as to what's good in art. Similarly, it is thought that morality is all culturally determined or personally determined or determined by the situation. It's pretty much agreed: there are no absolute principles of right and wrong.

Sometimes bad behavior is "excused" on either (or both) of two grounds:

(1) it didn't do anyone any harm,

and/or

(2) everyone else was doing it.

Now, these two statements embody the two "principles"—if they can be called that—that modern America substitutes for an ethics. The first is a pragmatic kind of concept of right and wrong: you judge an act by its effect, and if its effect is to harm people it's bad, but if it doesn't hurt anyone then it's okay to go ahead and do it. This "morality" derives from a sort of "Do-unto-others" idea that must be as old as time; but unless I'm mistaken, John Dewey's systematizing and popularizing of the pragmatism of Mill and others, plus the down-to-earth American-ness of the concept, has made it into the foremost, primary, and perhaps *only* ethical principle of most Americans today.

The trouble with the idea is that it's often immensely difficult in application. Anyone can think of a lot of dilemma-type situations in which harming two people may help two hundred and all that, but more consequently one is never fully aware of the ramifications of any act, especially "questionable" acts, which of course are the very ones that are brought into question, aren't they? Even if what you do doesn't demonstrably destroy someone else—financially or socially or emotionally or however—each and every one of these "questionable" acts of yours contributes to the moral smog that pollutes our culture.

And simply because "everyone else is doing it" doesn't mean a thing. Everyone else is *always* doing it. That doesn't make any difference, or certainly *shouldn't* make any difference, and *most* certainly it (going by the behavior of others) shouldn't be built into a kind of principle according to which you will or won't do something right or wrong just because everyone else is and you don't want to be different. The concept of being *normal* is ultimately what's in question here, and with its dual emphasis on conformity and statistics it's another view of the matter that has a particular appeal to Americans. The psychoanalysts tell us to go ahead and do whatever the sociologists tell us everyone else is doing and stop feeling so guilty about it. No one wants to do anything that's *ab*normal, right *or* wrong. In cases where immorality pervades the society, then conforming to the society is demonstrably *not* right. At the farthest fringes of such societies, men are given orders that we're all sure we would never follow—send Jews to the gas chambers, shoot women and children at point-blank range, break into someone's doctor's office in search of information to discredit him—but as we get closer to home, what we are expected or required to do (what we might "normally" do, conforming to what everyone else does) becomes progressively more ambiguous—destroy an enemy village from a bomber high in the air, take an interesting, high-paying job in the "defense" industry, even (as law-abiding citizens) pay the taxes that make all the rest possible. Any really virtuous man would refuse to participate at all and simply go to jail. We should *all* have been in jail *long* ago. But few of us have got *that* much virtue. And what good would it do? And isn't something very backward when the good people feel guilty about not being in jail?

Something is indeed very backward. But something is always backward. Things were all backward when Thoreau went to jail for civil disobedience in Concord that summer night in 1846. Something's *always* backward, and everyone else is *always* doing it: you can count on both those things. Sometimes it's the laws of the land that actually enforce conforming in wrong acts; sometimes it is "idealism" or "overzealism"; sometimes it is merely (merely!) pressures from family, community, business, the national temper as a whole. It isn't just that everyone else is doing it; it's that hardly anyone else *isn't* doing it—and the ones that aren't are perceived as cranks and outsiders and defectors.

❦

The Scruple and You

IF YOU'RE good in a bad society, ethically good, then you lose, true or false? Well, the answer is "true," by and large and on the whole and all; but it is a little more complicated than that. Sometimes being conspicuously good and getting the reputation for it does pay off. Your average employer doesn't usually want entirely right-minded men of integrity: they don't seem to understand how things work; they seem "difficult"; unwilling to compromise, they rock the boat; often they are too slow or meticulous. But sometimes for some specific purpose or reason, government or industry will really want an honest man. Sometimes the attitude of doing-what-is-really-right-regardless can carry the day, can influence people, can affect policy and so on. A man of principle is seldom wanted, but when he is, he is hard enough to find, so he can command good wages and occasionally gain some power. It costs a little more, sometimes, to buy a man of integrity.

But the real reason for being completely correct about financial matters at least, even though you usually lose, is that finally and somewhat paradoxically it is simply uneconomical to be otherwise. There are already too many things—not our fault, most of them—that make us feel uneasy and guilty: vague life-long remorse about things done or not done or worry about how one has had to neglect someone or something—parents, children, wife, old friends, mistress, work, or even the dog. There are so many things one feels bad about anyway, things that seem to be unavoidable, that it is simply and finally *not worth it* to add to this in-built guilt-burden any uneasiness (however slight) about some minor, semi-unethical, sleazy half-cheating about money matters.

I mean, you wouldn't take a newspaper from one of those honor-system stands without paying, would you? It isn't worth it. It isn't worth the money saved to go through one of the automatic toll lanes on the freeway without paying, even if you know the police don't bother to chase you. If not paying your parking tickets bothers you, it's silly not to pay them; they don't cost much if you don't let them accumulate, and you know yourself that parking violations are half the problem with traffic in the city. If a sales clerk or a waitress makes a mistake in your favor, a dollar or so, in your change, it's just not worth it not to point it out.

You have scruples.

The word scruple derives from the Latin *scrupulus*, which meant, significantly enough, "a small sharp stone." A scruple in Roman times was the smallest unit of weight, $1/288$ of an *as*, and an *as* was the Roman pound (*libra*), a bronze coin originally weighing about a pound, but then reduced to about half an ounce. I think a basic mistake was made back there somewhere, when the poor people let the rich people reduce the weight of money. It didn't really cut down on the burdens of wealth at all, but it made it seem as if it did. I mean, it would be obvious that there's not all that much point in having millions if you had to keep it stored in shedsful of one-pound bronze coins. As I say, it was a very basic mistake, but there's not much we can do about it now.

A scruple, anyway, was $\frac{1}{288}$ of one of those pounds, about $\frac{1}{24}$ of an ounce. During the Republic (says my *Webster's Collegiate*, where I get all this stuff), it was worth about seventy-five cents. It is now used as a unit of weight, but "used only by apothecaries"–used, that is, only by your overcharging druggist or by the ethical (hah!) drug companies for their pharmaceutical price-fixing. A scruple is denoted by this symbol: Ə. If you have one scruple, it is noted thus: Əi. Half a scruple is Əiss. Two scruples–a great many in this day and age–is Əij. You can't have more than two scruples, because three is a dram. You get the idea: a scruple is *a very small thing*.

It should be distinguished from a qualm, which is defined by the dictionary as a sudden, uneasy scruple. In trying to distinguish between a scruple, a qualm, and a misgiving, *Webster's Collegiate* goes a bit wrong, it seems to me, in failing to emphasize what they mention in their primary definition of scruple, that it is "hesitation as to action or decision *from the difficulty of determining what is right or fitting*." The idea that you *care* about "what is right or fitting" seems to me what's involved in having a scruple. If you have a qualm or a misgiving, what's involved is that suddenly you've got that sinking feeling that somehow or other someone or other is going to find out what you're doing. "Scrupulous implies the utmost nicety or exactness." It is just too bad the way it sounds like "scrofulous"; it is, in fact, exactly the opposite, and it is the best way to be.

You remember Sir Thomas More, and Robert Bolt's play about him, *A Man for All Seasons?* More is presented there, as indeed he must have been, as a man of scruples. He is also, of course, presented as a man of principle: but as I intend to show, principles are really just somewhat codified scruples. Anyway, More gives up his power, his position, his family's welfare, his fortune, and eventually his life for some insane scruple about not being willing to approve of the King's eighty-eighth divorce or something. All he had to do was say that he didn't *dis*approve. The point is that he wouldn't do this thing they wanted him to, out of some sense that it wasn't *right and fitting* for him to do it. Now, God, he's a *saint.* That's what scruples can do for you. He'd be dead now anyway, and meanwhile he's a saint. I don't say that paying your parking tickets is going to get you made a saint, but it's *the same sort of thing.*

Anyway if you are scrupulous today, people don't think of you as a hero or a saint but as a crank or a fool. Modern society is so set up to deal with the dishonest man that it punishes the honest one. Insurance companies practically demand the false claim: someone I know had an old brooch stolen and was told by the insurance agent that if she wanted the true value she'd have to double the claim, as they always cut the estimate in half. So do the income tax regulations: find a loophole or you're foolish. My income tax man always wanted to put down things that were wrong—wanted to give a wrong reason why the return would be delayed when we were applying for an extension, for instance, when the right (true) reason was just as good. "What's the difference? They don't care," he'd say to me. "*I* care!" I'd shout at him, finally. "One's the truth, the other's a lie." Eventually he says, "Oh, all right," but you could tell he didn't much like it: it wasn't according to form. The form is a plausible lie. On expense accounts, you're just cheating yourself if you don't add a little under "transportation expenses" to make up for what you feel they'll think excessive under "entertainment expenses," even though you really spent it. You're expected to establish "fairness" yourself by "adjusting" to *un*fair bureaucratic regulations set up to prevent the dishonesty of "most people." You're *expected* to do this. You're encouraged to *falsify* so as to achieve an *honest* judgment. If you don't, you're foolish. If you do, you're as dishonest as "most people." How can you be good in a society like this and not go broke? What kind of a society *is* this anyway?!

Well, calm down. It does seem to be a commercial society, and it does seem to be a somewhat corrupt one. But perhaps there's some consolation in the fact that it does now also seem possible to draw up this neat equation representing the formula for Modern American Life: MAL = Ǝ vs. $.

Morality: Public, Private, and Personal

A LOT OF our confusion in thinking about virtue occurs because of the idea that there is some big difference between public morality and private morality. People make this distinction in either of two ways.

You hear someone say, "So what he cheats a little on his expense account? What's it matter the stuff he sells is junk? He's doing it for his wife and children. He loves them dearly and he'd do *anything* for them." Or you hear someone say, "I hear he sleeps around a lot and has a whole slew of girl friends; they say Marilyn Monroe was trying to get him on the phone when she died; he finally got the divorce, just married the new one, and now I hear he's got *another* new one, up in Seal Harbor, Maine; I heard three reporters saw him escorting this blonde out of his room at the Carlisle—well, what difference does that all make, he's still a good president, governor, senator, isn't he?"

What happens is that people use morality in public life to justify immorality in private life, and they use morality in private life to justify immorality in public life. They use the argument both ways! So anxious are we, these days, to judge not. It isn't that we judge not lest we be judged; it's just that we judge not lest we be thought square.

It really isn't any kind of sufficient justification for immorality in either public or private life to refer to the morality of the other (the aspect that *wasn't* immoral). Businessmen have always used love for their families to justify what they do in business. How his family lives in the suburbs justifies what the adman does in the city—*requires it,* he says. This is an old story and fools no one. It certainly doesn't fool the kids.

Of course, no one *asks* the kids. Daddy never says, "Now, Sonny, listen. Daddy wants to send you to this expensive prep school so you can get into Yale so you can become a lawyer so you can make lots of money so you can have all the advantages Daddy didn't have. To do this, Daddy may have to cheat a little on his income tax; maybe the airplane parts Daddy makes won't be quite what they'd be otherwise; Daddy may have to use his insider's information to make a killing on his company's stock; Daddy may finagle prices a little with the friendly competitors; Daddy may have to back-stab just a little to get his promotions up the corporate-bureaucratic ladder; Daddy may have to make something a little worse and write a little copy to say it's a lot better. Daddy is willing to do all this because he *loves* Sonny so much—and Mommy and Sissy, too. He is doing it all for *you.* Aren't you grateful? You want Daddy to, don't you?"

Daddy never asks. Daddy never dares to. He knows the answer would be what he doesn't want to hear: his kid's answer would destroy his big excuse. It seems to me that men who say they're doing bad things "for" their kids are committing some dreadful kind of double desecration. To use some sentimental warped sense of morality in one's private life—devotion to wife and children, one's "love" for them—as an excuse for shaded morality in one's public doings is to compound the original immorality, not to justify it.

And it works the other way, too—or rather, it doesn't work that way either. What I mean is, you can't justify a man's private immorality on the grounds of what a good honest job he does in public life. You may hear that the stress of an active political life requires the "release" of adultery; or that the strain of a busy business situation requires "unwinding" in some way that's clearly immoral, if not in fact unlawful—illegal use of drugs, or abuse of alcohol. Who cares, it is asked, so long as the work he's doing is in a good cause?

The fact is that morality is morality. Whether it is public or private makes no difference, it's still personal. If a person isn't personally moral publicly and personally moral privately, then he isn't personally moral period. A man can love his wife and kids, but if he cheats on his income tax, then he isn't moral personally. A man can be meticulously scrupulous in all his business dealings, but if he cheats on his wife, then he isn't moral personally. Perhaps it isn't all that important to be moral personally; perhaps it isn't even possible these days. But the fact remains that personal morality is the only *kind* of morality we've got; it's the only kind there is, ultimately. A good man—if you could find him—would be a good man in public *and* in private, not one or the other.

CHAPTER TWO

Some Uses and Misuses of Virtue

Is Virtue Its Own Reward, or Isn't It?

BENJAMIN FRANKLIN was an interesting man, no doubt about it; but his *Autobiography* is a big bore, I don't care what they say, except for one fascinating little part of it in which he tells how he devised a method for how to be good.

He was about twenty years old when, as he says, he "conceiv'd the bold and arduous project of arriving at moral perfection." As he felt he knew what was right and what was wrong, he didn't see any reason he "might not always do the one and avoid the other." It's like the way he didn't see why there shouldn't be a public library in Philadelphia, so he started one; no reason there shouldn't be an academy, so he founded the University of Pennsylvania; no reason there shouldn't be a first American magazine, so he started *The Saturday Evening Post;* no reason Philadelphia's streets shouldn't be paved, so he got them paved; no reason lightning rods and bifocals shouldn't be invented, so he invented them. He thought it would be just as easy to be good as it was to do all those other things.

"But I soon found," he says, "I had undertaken a task of more difficulty than I had imagined." The main trouble was that bad habits "took advantage of inattention." His theory was that good habits would have to be formed to break the "contrary" ones, and he "for this purpose therefore contrived" *a method.*

The method involved, to begin with, purchasing "a little book"— and it ought to be remarked here that one of the few pleasures in a project like this is being able to go into a stationery store where they have all those marvelous ruled account books and actually have some reason to buy one. Franklin listed the virtues he sought down the left of the book, with a column for each day of the week, where he would "mark, by a little black spot, every fault . . . committed respecting that virtue upon that day." He gives this sample page:

	SUN	MON	TUES	WED	THURS	FRI	SAT
TEMPERANCE							
SILENCE	•	•		•		•	
ORDER	•	•			•	•	•
RESOLUTION		•				•	
FRUGALITY		•				•	
INDUSTRY							
SINCERITY							
JUSTICE							
MODERATION							
CLEANLINESS							
TRANQUILITY							
CHARITY							
HUMILITY							

The order in which the virtues are listed is according to his falling domino theory of moral reform. Since "the previous acquisition of some might facilitate the acquisition of certain others," he says, "I arranged them with that in view, as they stand above." Temperance, for instance, comes first because "it tends to procure that coolness and clearness of head" that guards against the "unremitting attraction of ancient habits, and the force of perpetual temptations." It's easier to stay good if you're not drunk, in other words; we all know *that*, don't we? Also, Temperance would help Franklin maintain Silence, which was a big thing with him because he wanted to break the habit of "prattling, punning, and joking," which he says made him acceptable only to "trifling" company. His plan was to "give a week's strict attention to each of the virtues successively . . . leaving the other virtues to their ordinary chance, only marking every evening the faults of the day." After thirteen weeks, if it all worked, the page was to have been completely free of spots, and he should have achieved virtue.

The plan, surely, is marvelously simple and sensible and ingenious—characteristic of Franklin in every way. How did it work, though? Well, it didn't work like the lightning rod or the University of Pennsylvania. More like those smoky Franklin stoves. When he found he couldn't achieve it, moral perfection finally seemed to Franklin as not all that great anyway, like the fox and the sour grapes, or like his own marvelous story of the man and the speckled ax:

> . . . like the man who, in buying an ax of a smith, my neighbor, desired to have the whole of its surface as bright as the edge. The smith consented to grind it bright for him if he would turn the wheel; he turn'd, while the smith press'd the broad face of the ax hard and heavily on the stone, which made the turning of it very fatiguing. The man came every now and then from the wheel to see how the work went on, and at length would take his ax as it was, without further grinding. "No," said the smith, "turn on, turn on: we shall have it bright by-and-by; as yet, it is only speckled." "Yes," said the man, *"but I think I like a speckled ax best."*

Franklin finally settled for a speckled morality because, as he says, among other reasons, "a benevolent man should allow a few faults in himself, to keep his friends in countenance."

It was Industry, anyway, that was really always the big virtue with Franklin. Even though he puts Industry in the middle of his list, all that comes before and after really points to it. "Lose no time," he says; "be always employed in something useful; cut off all unnecessary actions." All the rest of the virtues really figure as helpful timesavers, methods for avoiding waste of time. Even his Comprehensive Day Plan is called his "Scheme of Employment."

I have to admire that 6 P.M. line, "Put things in their places," but

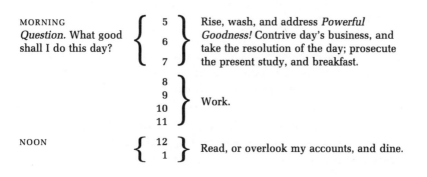

MORNING
Question. What good shall I do this day?
{ 5 6 7 } Rise, wash, and address *Powerful Goodness!* Contrive day's business, and take the resolution of the day; prosecute the present study, and breakfast.

{ 8 9 10 11 } Work.

NOON
{ 12 1 } Read, or overlook my accounts, and dine.

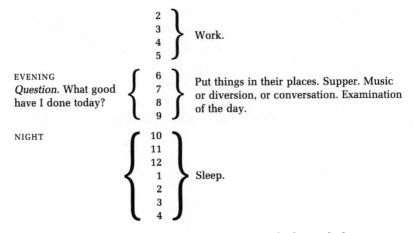

	2		
	3		
	4	}	Work.
	5		

EVENING
Question. What good
have I done today?

6
7
8
9

} Put things in their places. Supper. Music or diversion, or conversation. Examination of the day.

NIGHT

10
11
12
1
2
3
4

} Sleep.

my own idea of a good schedule isn't so much that it helps you *get things done* as it is to help you know *what to do next,* and Franklin's day plan wouldn't help me one bit. Besides, all those hours marked with such sinister simplicity, "Work," would be a real moral question mark for many of us today: just what is this good "work" that we're supposed to do?

The irony is that Franklin was apparently the most sociable and companionable of men. This is not to say he didn't get things done— he obviously did, more than most people could in several lifetimes. Of course he lived to be eighty-four, which *was* several lifetimes in those days. But he fought this continual battle with himself that he ought to get *more* done. In his "Dialogue Between Franklin and Gout," written at midnight, October 22, 1780, when he was seventy-four, his gout keeps stabbing him and reproaching him for overeating and overdrinking and for never taking any exercise, but just sitting around playing chess. Says the Gout to Franklin between stabs at midnight:

> "Wrapt in the speculations of this wretched game, you destroy your constitution. What can be expected from such a course of living, but a body replete with stagnant humors . . . ?"

And it was not until he was eighty that he contrived a method to be a little easier with himself. Writing a friend about the time he wastes playing cards, he says:

I have indeed now and then a little compunction in reflecting that I spend time so idly; but another reflection comes to relieve me, whispering, *"You know that the soul is immortal; why then should you be such a niggard of a little time, when you have a whole eternity before you?"*

The method he'd devised here is a marvelous sort of reverse *carpe diem:* that is, it doesn't say you should go ahead and drink and play cards and be merry now because tomorrow you may die and your whole chance to enjoy these things will be over; what it says instead is that it's okay to waste a little time and enjoy yourself now, because soon you'll have a whole eternity to get some work done. It imagines an afterlife, a Paradise, in which Work has a central place.

And as a young man, Franklin was a tiger for work. Of course he himself retired when he was forty or so, left his printing business to conduct his experiments with electricity, eventually becoming our first ambassador to France and whatnot. But he was always very big for everyone else working hard and long. The *Autobiography* is full of it, and he says that when he was publishing *Poor Richard's Almanack* he had filled "all the little spaces" with "proverbial sentences, chiefly such as inculcated industry and frugality as the means of procuring wealth, and thereby securing virtue." The "thereby" in that sentence is purely extraordinary! In the last issue of the *Almanack,* as a kind of preface, often reprinted as "The Way to Wealth," he strung together all these sayings, proverbs, maxims, adages—*platitudes* is what I'd like to call them—into a sort of lecture on how great industriousness is. You must have read "The Way to Wealth" somewhere, unless you were luckier than most everybody; it is full of things like:

God helps them that helps themselves

and

Early to bed and early to rise
Makes a man healthy, wealthy, and wise

and

> Then plow deep while sluggards sleep,
> And you shall have corn to sell and to keep.

The dreadful moralizing of "The Way to Wealth" and of a lot of the *Autobiography* has always seemed to me difficult to reconcile with the rest of Franklin's writing—cogent political argument, facetious hoaxes, charming letters, and so on. He is a very puzzling man. Mark Twain says that he was twins; he just says this as a joke, to account for there being two Franklin birthplaces in Boston, but maybe he had something. The way Franklin lived his life, half in America and half in Europe, seems to have had something to do with it. When he was relishing Paris, flirting with all the elegant and extravagant ladies, he wrote a blistering letter back to his daughter in America lighting into her for wanting a new fancy gown to wear to a ball where George Washington was to appear. Franklin seems always to have been somewhat more uptight in America, somewhat more loose and easy in Europe; this was true from his first trip to London when he was eighteen to his last years in Paris.

Anyway, toward the end of his time in Paris Franklin hung out a lot at the salon of one Madame Helvetius. It was a crazy household: three acres adjacent to the Bois de Boulogne, full of pet animals and birds, inside and out; Madame Helvetius was a philosopher's widow, and two ex-abbés and a young doctor lived with her, in a friendly way with a lot of running jokes between them; famous people were always dropping in, Franklin among them, and he was made part of the family; Madame Helvetius was then about fifty, I think, no longer so beautiful as she'd been, and she came on "careless and jaunty," in the words of Abigail Adams, who was shocked by her ways; and descriptions of the informal, relaxed place made it easy to see why Franklin liked to go there so much, and thought toward the end that he might move right in with them all and stay there too. Anyway, the name of the young doctor who lived there was Cabanis, and Franklin was always telling Cabanis stories about his early days—how he left Boston as a boy and went to Philadelphia and made his way there through thrift and industry and frugality and so on, all the stuff that's in the *Autobiography*—and for some reason Cabanis liked to hear him tell all this, and remembered what he said, and after Franklin's death published some of it. One of the things Cabanis remembered Franklin saying was this:

"If the rascals only knew all the advantages of virtue, they would become honest through sheer rascality!"

Which brings me to my question, to why I brought Ben Franklin up in the first place: Is virtue its own reward, or isn't it? Do you get anything *else* out of it, or not? And what does it mean anyway for virtue to be its *own* reward? There seems to be some sort of *reproach* implicit in the saying, as if you'd be wrong to expect to get anything out of doing right except the sheer satisfaction of the act itself.

Mark Twain blames Franklin (or Poor Richard) for the idea that virtue *is* its own reward, but my Stevenson's *Quotations* doesn't show it, and it isn't in "The Way to Wealth" or any other list of Poor Richard's sayings I can find. And anyway "Virtue is its own reward" is not really what Franklin believed. He believed virtue had a *lot* of rewards; he believed what he told Cabanis, that if the rascals only knew all the rewards of virtue, they'd *be* virtuous just to get the advantages.

We have agreed that if you're good, you lose—nowadays. But in Franklin's time it was possible for him to believe the opposite: that if you were good, you succeeded. It was possible for him to believe this because to a great extent for Franklin virtue was really nothing more than industriousness.

There were a lot of reasons for Franklin to feel that industry and virtue were the same and that they (it) got you ahead and that to get ahead was good. In the first place, *he'd* worked hard and *he'd* got ahead; that proved something to him, for when something happens to *you*, it's hard to realize it's just one example. This is what makes most self-made men so mentally monolithic and so politically Neanderthal.

And in the second place there seemed to be, incredibly enough, then, a *need*, a *real* need, for a lot of things to be *done*. It's hard for us to imagine it now, when there really isn't much that needs to be done at all, when most everything that *is* done is pretty bad, and when we'd be better off if everybody did a lot *less*. But back then it was good when people did things, or at least they thought it was, which makes it amount to more or less the same thing as far as industry-being-virtue goes.

For instance, there was this whole great continent with only a few people and a lot of woods. It sounds great now, and what they had in mind doing to America in Franklin's time—populating it and paving it and civilizing it and so on—was obviously a great mistake, and we can scarcely imagine, now that the country is crowded and noisy and in danger of becoming one vast parking lot, how so many apparently smart and virtuous people could ever have been so terribly wrong. But there was general agreement then: it was good to work hard and get all these bad things done. All that unpaved wilderness out there was why the "work ethic" idea of industry being made into virtually a religion by the Protestants in cahoots with the businessmen has had such a tenacious grip on the American mind.

The work ethic was fine as an ethic so long as there was work to be done and it still seemed worth doing. Even getting ahead must have seemed like a first-rate thing to do if you believed that what gets you ahead gets others ahead, gets your family and your community, your country, and even the world as a whole ahead with you. Nowadays, though, we don't even know if *ahead* is even the way we want to go; it doesn't look all that good up ahead there to some of us; *back* looks better in a lot of ways. "Ahead" sounds suspiciously like "progress," which we're all beginning to realize is just another word for "wrong way."

The Righteousness of Busyness

ONE REASON the idea that industry is virtue persists so, even in the face of the growing realization that work as such is no longer necessary and hence of no value and hence of no virtue, is that the state of being busy creates a kind of euphoria that makes a person feel he's actually *in* a state of virtue. Some very busy people, possessed or *seized* by busyness, seem to think they're not just virtuous but just about divine—a busy doctor, for instance, in my experience, thinks he is God Himself—and to the rest of us, lolling there, pulling in our feet to get out of the way, wondering what to do next, they sometimes do *seem* divine, such people, or at least scary. Being busy, I'm afraid, is a little like being drunk: there's the same insane certainty that what one is doing is right. And being *very* busy can be like some wonder drug (misprescribed by one of those busy arrogant doctors) that gets ahold of you and makes you feel about ten feet tall; and because, as everyone knows, energy expended creates energy available, a terrible synergetic momentum can get going that'll turn even nice unconvinced Dr. Jekylls like you and me into awful Mr. Hydes, full of passionate intensity. It is an awesome state, busyness is, all on its own, no matter what you're busy doing.

The dreadful righteousness of busyness is akin to the dreadful righteousness of do-goodism, but it is different from it in this respect: that it is the busyness itself, basically, that causes the righteousness, not the specific activity.

> Now it came to pass, as they went, that he entered into a certain village: and a certain woman named Martha received him into her house.
>
> And she had a sister called Mary, which also sat at Jesus' feet, and heard his word.
>
> But Martha was cumbered about much serving, and came to him, and said, Lord, dost thou not care that my sister hath left me to serve alone? bid her therefore that she help me.
>
> And Jesus answered and said unto her, Martha, Martha, thou art careful and troubled about many things:
>
> But one thing is needful: and Mary hath chosen that good part, which shall not be taken away from her.
>
> LUKE 10:38–42

Now, surely it would have been clear to Martha, if you could have got her to sit down and just be still a minute and think about it, that to hear the Lord's word, actually to have the chance to hear Jesus say some of those enigmatic and provocative things he was always saying, right there *in person*, is actually a lot "better" a thing to be doing than running around banging pots and pans in the kitchen, fussing and fuming, cumbered about with much serving, and being careful and troubled about many things that don't matter. But she was too busy, too full of the righteousness of busyness, to realize this.

"*Someone* has to do the dirty work" is what busy people say when we remonstrate about their bustling, and one's tempted to ask them why, if the work is dirty, they do it. But they don't usually mean that the work is dirty—in the sense of being bad or evil—just that it's not much fun, but has to be done. The truth of the matter is, though, that busy people bustle most, *not* when they're doing work that needs to be done—there's never really much of that—but when they're doing *extra* work, something special, making a special fuss. And this extra work is done—nine and a half chances out of ten—because they *want* to do it. There is nothing wrong in all this, of course, until it leads to resentment of others who don't help, like Martha's resentment of Mary.

Kipling wrote a whole long resentful poem about this, called "The Sons of Martha," often read as a paean to the working people of the world, but actually just one long slam at people of leisure. The image throughout seems to be of men building a railroad (it is much murkier than Kipling's usual stuff) and how the blood of the sons of Martha and the sweat of the sons of Martha and even the lives of the sons of Martha go to building this railroad just so the sons of Mary can ride on it. But what's the point of building a railroad if you don't want anyone to ride on it? Kipling seems to think there's been some *burden* laid on the sons of Martha to do all these things for the sons of Mary. But that's just as absurd as the so-called white man's burden toward the black man. Who is it lays these burdens on the sons of Martha? God? But God's son said in effect: "Take it easy, Martha. If you don't want to do all that, sit down and get the word, like Mary here."

Busy people have been blessed with energy, stamina, willpower, enterprise, good old-fashioned get-up-and-go, motivation, and God's own amount of other gifts. What do they want besides, our gratitude?—when half the time we wish they'd sit down and the other half envy them their energy? Do they wish they *didn't* have this energy?

You remember the Little Red Hen? Maybe you missed her in your childhood—I wish I had. I've always hated everything about her, even that her name has the same initials as mine. The Little Red Hen lives in this house with a Fox and a Mouse, and she gets up one morning and decides she's going to bake a cake. "*Well,*" she says cheerfully, you know how she sounds. "Well, now, *who*'ll help me gather some grain?"

"*I* shan't," says the Fox.

"*I* shan't," says the Mouse.

"Well, then, I'll do it myself," says the Little Red Hen.

So off she goes and gathers some grain and comes bustling and

clucking back and says, "Well, now, *who*'ll help me grind the grain
to make some flour?"

"*I* shan't," says the Fox.

"*I* shan't," says the Mouse.

"Then I'll do it myself," says the Little Red Hen. And off she goes
to grind the grain. And so on: she keeps asking them to do one thing
after another, but of course they never will, until she gets the cake
all made; then she asks them, "Well, now, who'll help me *eat* the
cake?"

"*I* will," says the Fox.

"*I* will," says the Mouse.

"No. I'll eat it myself!" said the Little Red Hen.

Eat a whole cake!? All by herself!? She'll be *sick*, for heaven's sake.
I have always thought that of all the extraordinary things that happen
in those childhood stories—frogs turning into princes, people climbing up one another's hair, tigers going around a tree until they turn
to butter, and so on—that the most extraordinary story of all is this
one of the Little Red Hen. What could have been in her *mind* that
morning to decide to bake a cake? There wasn't even any *flour;* she
had to start from scratch. She lived with those people or whatever
you want to call them, the Fox and the Mouse—and she must have
known they weren't in the mood for cake-making that morning. Why
on earth did she go on asking them, when she knew they weren't
going to help? Why ask them if they want some cake if she isn't going
to give it to them? And what kind of a lesson did she think she was
teaching them by eating the cake all by herself and making herself
sick?

Why build a railroad if you don't want anyone to ride on it? Why
bake a cake if you don't want anyone to eat it? It's not that easy on
the rest of us, you know, all that banging and clanging. My heart's
with the sons of Mary, riding that railroad through the lines of workers glaring at them; and with all those housewives who don't make
public martyrs out of themselves serving supper to unexpected enigmatic and provocative guests, nor baked a cake either, probably, because if you're the kind who doesn't get around to doing one thing,
you're the kind who doesn't get around to doing another; and I'm
with the Fox and the Mouse, who must've hated it, hearing her get
started:

"Oh no, not again," says the Fox under his breath.

"I'm afraid so," mutters the Mouse.

"I'll do it myself," says the Fox, imitating her.

"*Shush,*" giggles the Mouse.

But she overhears them. "You two shut up. I'll do it myself," says the Little Red Hen. "*Someone* has to do it, you know."

And they both burst out laughing at her.

❦

Doing Good, as Against Being Good

DOING GOOD for others, it seems to me, can hardly be underestimated as a way of being good. Judged pragmatically, actively-doing-good-for-others always seems to cause a great deal of trouble to everyone involved—both the doer and the done-to—and this is true on an individual-to-individual basis, on a family or a community basis, and even on the international level. Judged motivationally, doing good for others—whether as an act of "love" or "charity" or "duty" or whatever—is a kind of displaced stage of growth. Love comes in all sizes and shapes, but it always seems to have something to do with food and sex, the emphasis being on one or the other depending on the maturational stage: first we love our mothers (they feed us); then we love our sweethearts (they give us sex); then we love our children (we feed them); thwarted in any and/or all of these, thou then starts loving thy neighbor, or thy neighbor's wife, or "the poor" or "the underprivileged" or (if thou art a rich nation) the underdeveloped nations of the world (we give them surplus food and at the same time screw them).

On the east porch of my house there's an open space in under the eaves where birds nest in the spring right by the window and make a lot of noise and a big mess. It's not nice cute little wrens who nest there either, but great big messy, noisy, ugly grackles. But boy do they love their young! Or at any rate, do they ever feed them! The mommy and the daddy bird are flying in and out, in and out, all spring with a lot of bugs and worms, and the little ones (they're really huge little ones) set up a great caterwauling and have these great insatiable open yellow gaping beaks, pushing and shoving and squawking at one another to be the one who gets the worm. It is really disgusting, and if I were the mommy bird I wouldn't have anything to do with them; but she does, and keeps coming back and back. That's love, *love properly placed.* If the mommy grackle came and tried to put a worm in *your* mouth, you'd quite rightly feel that's *love improperly placed.*

Of course it isn't really love at all, what the mommy bird does; it's just instinct–and that's my point about it. It's just a maturational stage. It never occurs to one of those selfish little birds that he ought to feed a worm to his sibling nest-mates, but the mommy bird knocks herself out gathering food for the wretched greedy creatures. You can call her behavior selfless or altruistic or something, say "wonderful"–which is what a lot of people *do* call it, spring after spring. But you can't for one moment believe it's really anything she doesn't *have* to do. She can't *not* do it, any more than she could help being hungry herself when she was young. It's stages, then: sometimes it's the hunger to eat, later it's the hunger to screw, then it's the hunger to feed. It's entirely a human–that is, a not-natural–perversion to sentimentalize this as "love," and a kind of additional, double perversion to exalt as "charity" the already plenty perverted instinct to go around putting worms in the mouths of strangers. Even a grackle has sense enough to keep the worms where they belong.

Parentalism in all its forms–"love," "charity," "duty to others"– should be kept just as close to home as possible. What we need in this country, this world, is a New Parochialism, a new more limited and at the same time more exalted sense of family and community– more limited in scope, deeper in meaning. As a nation we're probably still stuck in our phase of marauding paternalism, and there's not much we two hundred million individuals can do about that. The dreadful national "development" and the appalling economic "growth" bring nasty national maturational stages as inevitably as Nature's own. But as individuals we can separate ourselves from this terribly dangerous assumption that we have a "responsibility" to the whole world. It's all part of the most characteristic American vice: meddlesomeness.

Professional Ethics, as Against the Morality of an Occupation

BUT SUPPOSE, for the moment, that at some substantial financial sacrifice, you decide to go into a line of work that is demonstrably "good." You can almost *tell* it's good work, simply because it *is* so underpaid. I'm thinking of something like teaching or what used to be called "social work"—helping the blind or the poor or the homeless—something "worthwhile" like that.

Here you'd think you'd be able to do your work well and take pride in it because it clearly is *good* work. But a strange thing happens: another false turning on the road to virtue. What happens is that the professional ethics of men and women working in various occupations seem to be in inverse ratio to the morality of the occupation itself.

The ethics of the criminal underworld, for instance, are said to be very rigid, although this may of course be over-remarked-on simply because it is so remarkable. Also it's romantic—the "honor among thieves" conception. But it does appear to be the case, for example, that a professional gambler's handshake is his bond. Of course, if you lose and don't pay him, he may have your knees broken, but that's not the point. The point is that if you *win* he'll pay you without a trace of bad feeling, entirely "professionally"; *you* won't have to get after *him* about the debt. According to this inverse-ratio theory, mafiosos are the most trustworthy people of all.

All this seems crazy on the face of it but logical enough when you think about it. In a world that operates outside the law this way, you'd almost have to have some other sort of honor system going or things couldn't function at all.

On the other hand, and at the other extreme of occupational morality, it is said that the most unscrupulous and unethical professional behavior is to be found in the most altruistic professions, in such fields as social work and charity fund raising and poverty-program funding. Again this is less inexplicable than it might at first seem. It's understandable that those involved in what they consider good works would feel justified in some slipperiness in their own personal-professional behavior on several counts. First, they are usually in this sort of work at some sacrifice or disadvantage to themselves, in terms of money or ambition or whatever, and thus they are only too likely to feel that it may be necessary (read: "it's only fair") that others be sacrificed or taken advantage of. Second, just because the work *is* so "good" (by their thinking) everybody in the office is working practically to the *tune* of "the end justifies the means," the way the dwarfs in "Snow White" whistled while they worked. Third, the "idealists" who go into this line of work believe so earnestly in some dream or scheme of their own that they'll "do anything" to get *their* dream scheme funded instead of someone else's dream scheme, which they don't believe in *half* so much. And, fourth, there's a kind of incorrigible amateurism in the do-good mentality that fancies it is somehow "professional" to be slick and ruthless – almost an *envy* of "toughness." You see the same amateurish admiration for roughness in every political "reform" movement.

Once I heard Rose Kennedy being interviewed on television. "Being in government is the crowning glory of a career," she said. "Politics is the most honorable profession." You can see why she'd say that, why she'd almost *have* to feel that way. But the rest of us don't feel that way, do we? We look at the way actual politicians actually act, and it seems almost ludicrous to us to say, "Politics is the most honorable profession."

It *could* be, though. Politics would seem to provide the greatest potential *opportunity* to be of public service, to do something for the nation and for your fellow man and so on. It *seems* as if, if *anything* meaningful and really worthwhile could *ever* be accomplished, then it could best be made to happen by taking leadership in government.

But we know, we know through so much experience that now we very nearly know it in theory, that far from being the most "honorable" profession, politics may very well be the most *corrupt,* and in fact the most *corrupting* of all the professions. It doesn't seem to be just what running for office does to a man – the deceptions and compromises required of him to win election. Some candidates seem to improve in character during a campaign and during their term in office, while others seem to have been just as tricky and deceitful *before* they were even elected. Nor does it seem that it is the fact of *being* in office – that it is the power and the eminence that corrupt, although they must certainly help. Aides and assistants seem as vulnerable to character deterioration as the men they work for, perhaps even more so, for they have more justifications for doing bad things:

they're doing them "for someone else," for someone they "believe in," and they're acting "under orders," even though (as they say later, after they've been caught) they may have disapproved of the action "privately" or "personally."

Rather I think what it is that is most likely to corrupt a man in politics is the sense that what he is doing is "important." The *more* important you think whatever you're doing is, the more all-out and anything-goes and corrupt you'll be in the way you do it.

In this the "idealistic" political activist is at a great disadvantage morally-ethically as compared with, say, the "cynical" advertising men, to turn to those other major shapers-and-movers of our society. People in advertising perforce take a very dim view of the ultimate end of their work. The ultimate end of advertising that everyone uses as an example is selling dog food, but there are worse ones, ends that are both more futile and more harmful. But just because the end result of their work *is* so dopey or dreadful, their commitment is to real expertise and excellence in the means itself—good design in the art work, good clever copy, high "quality" in the television commercials, and so on—and to relatively scrupulous behavior in their personal-professional dealings with their colleagues and competition and clients. In other words, they take out their virtue not in the *kind* of work they do, but in the *way* they do it. They perceive their professionalism as a virtue in and of itself.

❦

"Professionalism" as a Machismo Con

SUPPOSE YOU accidentally overhear the women in the office talking about you (they do all the time, you know). Which would you rather they were saying?—

> "He's a selfish, inconsiderate son of a bitch, and I hate his guts. But you have to hand it to him: he's a real pro at his job."

as against—

"He's a kind, good, honorable man, and I love him dearly.
But let's face it: he can't handle the work."

Of course it's nice to hear them say they love you dearly, but you don't want it in quite that tone of voice, do you? To be called good, kind, and honorable should please you a lot. But how do you feel about hearing you can't handle the work?

It's absurd, of course, but true, that your average man would rather overhear *anything* about himself than that he's bad at his work. That he's not "up to" the job he's got is perhaps the most destroying realization a man could have, if he were capable of realizing it, which of course he isn't, because the realization would be so terrible.

As Americans, we're expected to "grow" in or into our jobs. Harry Truman did it, why can't you? But sometimes it's hard to tell just what your job *is*. The nature of most enterprise is now no longer simple and individual, but complex and corporate: your work is integrated with the activities of others into organizations, which organizations have, beyond their various time-consuming internal functionings, an overall purpose, which purpose is presumably something you believe in and you can't expect to change. What I mean is, if you thought to involve yourself in, say, the medical profession, you couldn't expect to change the profession's basic purpose, which is to heal people. Presumably you wouldn't even want to change it: you'd make some kind of scary doctor if you did. Similarly, presumably, theoretically, if you joined General Motors, you'd be interested in making and selling automobiles; otherwise you'd join the National Biscuit Company because you were interested in crackers, or Lever Brothers because you liked soap.

In fact, of course, none of this is the case, or little of it, anyway. Young men or women take to these occupations or join these organizations (money aside, for the moment) because they want to do research, or write and design, or become executives or whatever. They expect to follow their interests or develop their expertise or practice their skills within the organization, and as long as they do a good job it doesn't matter to their employers or (more importantly) even to themselves whether or not they believe in what the organization as a whole is up to. It is possible for them to take pride in their work, in the skill with which they do their jobs—in their speed, their meticulousness, their "know-how," the way they manage their staffs, their resourcefulness, their coolness under pressure, general efficiency, knowing how to keep costs down, stamina, ability to meet deadlines, and so on—in a way that is so separate from whatever else is going on in the big organization that it very nearly does restore individualism of enterprise to the American system. This attitude, representing somewhat of a modification in the Work Ethic, considers "professionalism," rather than work itself, to be a virtue.

This tendency is in contradistinction to some older, pejorative uses of the word "professional." We used to feel that a professional— when we weren't referring to a doctor or lawyer or minister, to someone "in the professions," as they were called—was a person who was only in it for the money. When we said, "He's an old pro," of a writer, say, it meant he was a hack, grinding out magazine articles or books more or less to order, without much regard to excellence or imagination. When we said it of a politician, it means he was just interested in getting his party elected, with no pretense of idealism or any intention of doing anything worthwhile. Even then, though, it meant he could win elections, get out the votes, could in a word, *produce*.

The professional is of course always contrasted with the amateur; but, again of course, we use the word "amateur" in two, or maybe three, ways. First, there's the idea that an amateur does what he does not for money, not as his occupation, however devoted he may be to it. This is related to the second way, as when we speak of "a true amateur," one who is a connoisseur or expert in a certain area. But then we also speak of someone being "a rank amateur," using *rank* here not as meaning dank and rancid, the way it sounds, but as utter or absolute, and referring to someone who's just a beginner and not very good at what he does.

As this use of the word "amateur," meaning an unskillful bungler, has become more general, it is only natural that the word "professional," first as considered the opposite of amateur and later all on its own, has come to refer simply to someone who is good at his work.

A really good professional scarcely ever worries about money, he gets it anyway—although, of course, one should never underestimate the importance of money. What talented expert professionals look for in an organization is opportunity—the power and free hand to do the job the way they want, or the equipment or the staff—whatever it takes to let them do whatever it is they do *right*. It practically never occurs to them to question what use the company's making of what they're doing so conscientiously.

For instance, during the years I worked at *Esquire,* I could never figure out whether the purpose of the magazine was to sell clothes or publish fiction. Maybe it was just to make money. But there I was as a professional fiction editor (at least I became one there) and I took a professional pride in my work, procuring and editing short stories for the magazine. I looked on the clothing ads with the same baleful eye the space salesmen had for the fiction, but presumably they took a professional pride in their work too—"Boy, did I get a *great* clothing ad yesterday," one of them might say to another, for all I know. The point is that even when an organization isn't diversified (as most companies are these days), there are still people working in it efficiently at divergent purposes, maybe even working skillfully at *cross*-purposes, who still somehow serve the organization-as-a-whole's purpose, which nobody quite knows what that is anyway, interpreting it only in terms of his own aspect of the work, and you never really care, either, what the over-all purpose is, so long as you get to do your job the way you want.

The highly placed executive's pleasure in exercising his organizational and managerial techniques, the skilled scientist's satisfaction in demonstrating his imaginative or intellectual capacities—"on the job," no matter what the job *is*—their professional pride is basically no less absurd than that of some extraordinarily simple-minded, perhaps necessarily even demented, assembly-line worker who may take no pride in the finished product—a shoddily made mass-produced washing machine, say—but does take *great* pride in the real good way he does *his* part of the job: screwing down one particular nut, hard and firm and true each and every time. No less ludicrous, ultimately, is the young copywriter who feels professional pride in a great piece of ad-copy he's just turned out—well before deadline, clever, fluid, getting in all the points he was told to make, exactly to the character count the art director allotted—even though it may be written about that same shoddy machine. The chemist in his laboratory, the fiction editor in his cubicle, the space salesman making his calls, the executive at the boardroom conference table—they're all no less absurd in the pride they take in the excellence of their work, so long as they consider it just as "professionalism" as such, without reference to the final use this good work is put to.

One cannot of course take exception to a man wanting to do his work well, or to his taking pride in his work when he *has* done it well. What one can take exception to—and should protest against and protect oneself against—is having this natural pride taken advantage of. When a man is persuaded to do something he really wouldn't want to do if he thought about it, simply by the opportunity to do it *well,* when one's vanity about one's expertise or efficiency obscures from him the bad use made of his good work, when you start taking satisfaction in the *way* the job is done rather than in what the work itself *is,* when the means don't just justify the ends to you, but in this backwardness, the means *become* the ends—then you *and* your work are being corrupted by flattery.

It's the ultimate absurd American masculine vanity, this vulnerability we feel about our work. It seems to be as basic to us as the Latin's fears about his courage and his pride in his virility. "Professionalism" is the North American machismo.

It's part of being a professional not to question the job, but just buckle down and do it, "like a man." If you get all emotional about your work, somebody might say to you, "Try to take a more professional attitude, for God's sake, and don't be so damn amateurish about it." What's implied here is that if you are professional you're cool, calm, collected, and *manly*—especially when things go wrong. If you're acting "amateurishly," then you're getting upset: if the work doesn't go right, you blow up on the job or act petulantly, "like a child"; or you take criticism of your work personally, "like a woman."

The idea is that to be a real pro at your work, you've got to be a *man.* Not too young: "Don't send a boy to do a man's job." And not too old: "He just can't cut the mustard on the job anymore."

Even if you are a woman in business today, you may be expected to *act* like a man. You don't want to overhear the men say—

> "She's a sweet girl, kind-hearted and good-natured, but she's hopeless at the work."

You'd prefer, maybe?—

> "She's an ambitious cold-hearted bitch, and I can't stand her. But you have to give her credit: she's a professional who gets the job done."

What it all means is that to be really professional at your work you have to be *tough*—you gotta be tough on others, to get everything you can outa them. "Professionalism" is thus used as a justification for ruthlessness, the way "efficiency" always is.

The worst of it is that by exploiting this absurd personal pride in professionalism, impersonal organizations use the good work of millions to bad avail. All that individual energy and skill and conscientiousness get used collectively to produce something dopey or dreadful. All our best individual efforts are converted into all our society's worst things. Professionalism is the latest bureaucratic con, in a long series of them. They *use* our professional pride, is what they do—just as they've always used our pride in our patriotism or our bravery to send us to war. Pride is always the most manipulatable of the vices, and a man who takes pride in his masculinity is especially and absurdly vulnerable to use by others.

Pride almost always cometh before exploitation, and to take pride in one's "professionalism" proves once again what we are all beginning to realize is true: that a man can't preen himself on being "a man" unless he's also willing to be something of a jerk.

❦

Indifference, Considered as a Virtue

TAKE CARE, I say to you, but *don't* care. Take as good care as you can, in everything you do; but care as little as you can about anyone or anything that is not very close to you. Caring is the cause of most everything that is bad. Certainly the worst things are done by people who care deeply.

I don't say this just to say something provoking: I mean it entirely. The people who cared most in Northern Ireland, for instance, are the ones who set off the explosions in crowded shopping districts at Christmastime. It's the strong believers who kidnap and hijack. A terrorist by nature is a completely committed person. You don't find people who are "indifferent" setting off bombs downtown or even ordering them to be dropped on native villages thousands of miles away. It's only the believers who can do that.

It's excited, dedicated people, not indifferent people, who menace us all. People who care about race, one way or the other, are capable of doing terrible things. People who care about religion, one way or the other, are capable of doing terrible things. People who *don't* care about race and religion, one way or the other, aren't (are simply *not*) capable of doing terrible things – at least not in the name of race or religion.

People who care enough to do terrible things are always doing them "in the name of" something that sounds wonderful. In fact what they care so about almost always *is* something wonderful – "freedom," or "liberation," or "independence," or "reform," or "equality," or whatever. There's probably no truly valuable thing that people who care haven't done terrible things in the name of.

It's not the fault of the value. There is of course nothing wrong with freedom, equality, liberation, independence, and all the rest. It's *caring* about them that's wrong. Terrible things have been done in the name of "Christianity." Terrible things have been done for "brotherhood." Oddly it seems sometimes that the *better* the value, the *worse* the acts. And it's also oddly true that the only justification anyone has ever offered for evil acts was that he cared – too much! – for something good.

It's not ideology I'm against. It's fine to believe something, or even okay to believe *in* something. But don't *care* about it. That's when the trouble starts, just as soon as people start believing something matters, *really* matters. That's when they begin to feel they have to "do something" about it. If you care too much, finally you either do something about it or get a terrible ulcer. That's when the shooting starts. Once you feel you *have* to do something, that's when you are committed and hence dangerous to the rest of us. If I had my way, we'd commit committed people.

It's the people who care, who *really* care, who *get things done*. And most everything that *is* done, we see now, would be better left un-done. It takes men of heroic commitment to build great empires, and it takes heroically dedicated men to mount revolutions against those empires. We've known for a long time that we never really wanted the empires, but now we're beginning to see that even the revolutions we could do without, for every revolution seems to go through two stages: at first they are vengeful and savage; then they become repressive and corrupt. Both the empires and the revolutions began in the name of some ideal, of course, the ideal of someone who really cared.

But it's not just the caring of the heroes and the leaders that causes all the trouble. They couldn't do so much harm without the stirred-up emotions of the rest of us: our public outrage, our national pride, our religious righteousness, our racial consciousness, or whatever other nonprivate emotion we've allowed to become inflamed. Indignation is the root of so much evil. Indifference is the root of none.

Indifference as a life attitude seems far from an ideal, but it's the ideals we care about that cause so much harm. To be indifferent may in fact be the most virtuous way to be when you're involved in a bad society. It's hard *not* to care, I know, when you see so much that's wrong all about you. But if you don't ever care *much* about anyone or anything that's not very close to you, then I can almost guarantee you'll never do anything really bad. There is really nothing worth caring *about*, once you realize that caring almost always causes harm.

Indifference is a great help in remembering what it is so easy to forget when you're involved in work that seems "worthwhile" or "important": that the end never does justify the means when the means mean that you yourself do something wrong. And indifference has at least this over caring: that it may be used as an excuse for doing things badly, but not for doing bad things.

CHAPTER THREE

The Somewhat Separate Question of Sexual Morality

The Ugly Head of Sex

SUPPOSE YOU'VE been working late, at the office or somewhere, with a group of people or with just someone, and this woman, who is known to you and is not especially attractive or anything, asks you if you want to stop by on the way home and have a drink, or a beer, say, and a sandwich, or some eggs and bacon. You have every reason to believe that her husband, who you rather like and seldom see, will be there and will be glad to see you; and restaurants are closed now and your wife is away or something, and anyway it seems like a pretty good idea to have a drink and unwind and have a chat with them and all. So you get there, and the husband of course isn't there.

I say "of course" because you knew of course the husband wasn't going to be there when you read this, but you *didn't* know it when you went. In fact, when you went in you didn't even realize for a while he wasn't there. You think he is in another room or something and will be out in a minute. So you sit down, and this woman, a medium-good acquaintance and, as I say, not good-looking or anything, maybe even somewhat older than you but maybe not, at any rate not necessarily older, but not really attractive to you, or sexy or anything like that, she goes chattering about and brings you a drink and makes one for herself and then starts frying bacon for your bacon and eggs out in the kitchen and talking back and forth with you in the living room, or maybe you're sitting in the kitchen watching her work and talk. After a while she makes you another drink and hands it to you.

"Where's so-and-so?" you say, mentioning the husband's name.

"Oh, he's out of town tonight," she says, or: "I thought you knew; we're separated."

Scruple? Qualm? Misgiving?

What do you do? There's the bacon, done more or less the way you like it (not crisp, I hope, but somewhat underdone, as that way it has more flavor, but not *too* underdone, of course), on top of the stove on neatly spread paper toweling, and she's just putting the eggs in. Just at that moment the pop-up toaster pops up the toast. But it doesn't seem well done enough for her, so she pushes it down again, firmly. What do you do? Do you get up and leave right then? Isn't that fantastically rude and insulting? Doesn't it imply she's trying to put the make on you or something, instead of just being friendly and giving you something to eat? I think you had better stay, and eat, and act as though nothing were wrong.

So you do that, and you talk along and things are all right and in the middle of the meal she gets up and makes you a third drink before you realize what she's doing, but she's making coffee too, so it seems all right. Meanwhile she's talking interestingly and admiringly of you and your work and it is pleasant enough, and she's not really *un*attractive and she leans toward you as she talks and has a pretty good figure and occasionally touches you to emphasize certain things she's talking about and it gets later and you decide you'd better go.

"Well," you say, pushing back your chair if you are at the kitchen table, or leaning forward to get up if you are in the living room. "I guess I better go."

"Oh, don't rush off," she says. "It's nice to talk to somebody."

"No, but it's getting late. I'd better get along." You stand up.

She leans back and eyes you. Then she says: "You know . . . ?"

"Know what?" you say, and in retrospect it may seem to you that here was where you made your mistake.

"You know I'd like to go to bed with you."

It may not be only qualms, misgivings, and scruples, but also just plain reluctance. Maybe the brazenness of this excites you a little, or maybe the aggressiveness puts you off. No matter, it isn't anything you really want, and certainly not something you need.

But what do you *say?*

Her eyes are challenging, so you look away. Making it as casual as possible, you might say, for instance. "Oh, I don't think that would be a very good idea somehow."

"*Why* not?"

Abandoned woman!

What are you to tell her? Do you say it's because of so-and-so? He's not here, would never know, and probably wouldn't care anyway. Do you say it's because of your own wife? It's obvious that she'd never know either. Do you say it's because you don't *want* to sleep with her? You can't say that and you know it. Do you say it's because you don't *believe* in sleeping around, that you're against promiscuity in modern life? Come off it: that's an outrageously pompous thing to say, and it's quite out of the question at a time like this. You try to joke about it, but she remains serious and wants an answer: Why not?

You are about to commit adultery. It's either that or hurt her feelings.

Now I ask you this: Is it better to break one of the Ten Commandments, commit one of the Seven Deadly Sins, violate one of society's and religion's oldest and most established strictures? Or is it better to hurt someone's feelings?

No matter how you load the question, the answer is inescapable: You can't just deliberately hurt someone's feelings. So you can't help it. You relax, as they say, and enjoy it—or try to. You forlornly, or cheerfully, or at any rate dutifully follow her into the bedroom. And you sin.

❦

History and Theory of the Mercy-F**k

YOU CAN console yourself that there's considered to be a big difference between, on the one hand, sexual promiscuity and common adultery, and on the other, an occasional mercy-f**k. I'll admit there's one big similarity too, but let's put that aside and concentrate on the differences. There's a sort of basic righteousness, a kind of functional hypocrisy, to the mercy-f**k concept; and to emphasize this quality of it, mercy-f**k should always be spelled with the asterisks—how you pronounce such a nasty notion is your problem. One thing that may make the mercy-f**k less of a sin than common adultery is the presumption that there is substantially less joy in it. Sin is supposed to be fun, you know. So if you don't *enjoy* it very much, maybe you're not *sinning* very much. Following this theory, you'd try as hard as you *can* not to enjoy it. Sinning-without-enjoying-it is admittedly a cool, modern existential kind of behavior, but it seems to provide none of the real benefits of either morality or immorality. Anyway, the mercy-f**k is also, almost by definition, an act of mixed motives—that is, kindliness mixed up with lechery, another example of how sex makes strange bedfellows—and clearly an act of mixed motives is better than an act of purely bad ones. Then, too, the situation of the mercy-f**k—the temptress woman undoing the virtuous man—is one of the real old standards of literature and legend, and it's perhaps a bit nicer to have the feeling that one's doing one's sinning within a well-established tradition—although, in truth, it would probably be hard to find any sin that doesn't have a certain amount of tradition behind it, and if there were, it probably wouldn't be worth perpetrating.

There's plenty of examples of the situation in all the literatures—Hippolytus and Theseus' wife Phaedra, Sir Gawain and the Green Knight's wife, Captain Horatio Hornblower and his French host's wife, and so on—but the archetypal case of the mercy-f**k withheld, is the story of Joseph and Potiphar's wife:

> And it came to pass . . . that his master's wife cast her eyes
> upon Joseph; and she said, Lie with me. But he refused. . . .
>
> GENESIS 39:7–8

Joseph reveals his reason inadvertently in his answer:

> But he refused, and said unto his master's wife, Behold, my
> master wotteth not what is with me in the house, and he hath
> committed all that he hath to my hand;
> There is none greater in this house than I; neither hath he
> kept back any thing from me but thee, because thou art his wife:
> how then can I do this great wickedness, and sin against God?
>
> GENESIS 39:8–9

The last of this strikes me as kind of a pious afterthought on his part, but the rest reveals what he was really worried about: his position in the household and how well he was doing. You've got to remember that from the beginning Joseph felt that the sun and the moon and the eleven stars made obeisance to him. He told his brothers he dreamed that, and that he dreamed that their sheaves bent down to his upright sheaf. Hoping to get rid of him, they threw him in a pit, but he got out and got carted off to Egypt. Now he's developed a real sense of purpose: he's going to become a big success in this strange land, save Israel, and make his brothers' sheaves bend. You remember how lovingly he torments them when he's in control and they don't know who he is. He's in charge of all the grain in Egypt, and Egypt is the only place there *is* any grain. His father, Jacob, tells his brothers to take money and go to Egypt: "Buy us a little food," he says, his exact words (Gen. 43:2). Joseph first accuses his brothers of being spies, and locks them up. Then he lets them out, sells them some grain, but puts their money back in their sacks to confuse them. Then when they have to come back for more he makes them bring beloved youngest brother Benjamin, hides his silver cup in Benjamin's sack, so it appears he's a thief, then sends his steward out to accuse them—and so on, a very long-drawn-out, complicated, *knowing* kind of revenge. Bewildered, frightened, they always refer to him as "the man" before he lets them know he's Joseph. He really finally does make all their sheaves bend down to his upright sheaf, and he knows he's not going to get to do *any* of this if he starts playing around with Potiphar's wife.

So he can't throw her the mercy-f**k because he's afraid it'll mess up his position in the household and his role in history. He doesn't want to mix business with pleasure. Specifically: he doesn't want *her* pleasure to interfere with *his* business, which of course is really Potiphar's business, Potiphar having turned all his business over to Joseph and wotting nothing of what goes on. Joseph is just the kind of young-man-on-the-make who is only too ready to take over someone else's business, and he was always running into men who were too lazy to do their own work. When Potiphar's wife gets him thrown in the prison, it takes him about three lines to take over all the warden's responsibilities; then when he gets out, he takes over all the Pharaoh's business, and soon he's running all Egypt. Joseph is just too involved, too busy getting things done and getting ahead, too busy *making it*. He can't spend long, lazy afternoons balling Potiphar's wife.

The instructive contrast to an obnoxious get-ahead fellow like Joseph is the noblest Roman, Mark Antony, a really great loser. Remember the title of Dryden's play about him and Cleopatra: *All for Love; or, The World Well Lost.* I don't mean a good sport or anything silly like that when I refer to a good loser. I mean a man who makes some kind of art out of losing. Hamlet was another real good loser, but he got so involved in worrying about not doing what it seemed to him he ought to be doing (murdering his uncle the King to revenge his father's death) that he refused to mercy-f**k Ophelia, poor little creature, when she needed it.

Business—whether it be murdering your uncle, bringing about famines, or whatever kind of ultimately not-really-very-worthwhile enterprise you're up to—business shouldn't interfere with pleasure. Specifically: *your* business shouldn't interfere with *another's* pleasure. In history, legend, or life, those who so determinedly set themselves against the mercy-f**k have just too big a sense of their own importance to enlist our sympathy. Clearly, in these peculiar cases, chaste is chintzy.

You say: Yes, okay, but wouldn't Potiphar's wife have expected Joseph to keep it up once he'd started? I say: Watch the dirty way you talk, but okay, we'll discuss that. For it is in fact true that the real trouble with this kind of behavior—whether merciful or otherwise, but most especially otherwise—is that it does lead on to involvement.

Involvement and Disorder, as we know, are the evil enemies of the most basic virtues, Extrication and Order. Chastity, Continence, even Moderation—these aren't the real virtues. The real virtue is Not Getting Involved. It is probably true that no matter how carefully you choose your friends, no matter how carefully you behave yourself, no matter how upright and correct and high-minded and scrupulous you are in all other kinds of dealings, there is bound to be a time, sooner or later, modern society being what modern society is, when you will have to commit adultery. Maybe *more* than one time. But then you should get along home where you belong and stay there. Don't answer the telephone for a few days. Don't go to the office. Take a vacation. Stop doing whatever it was got you into this situation. Potiphar's wife got the incriminating garment off of Joseph when he "went into the house to do his business; and there was none of the men of the house there within" (Gen. 39:11), everybody else having quit work and gone home. She'd never have noticed him in the first place if he hadn't been pushing ahead so. If you hadn't been working nights late, your friend's wife might never have cast her eye upon you.

If you are really involved and busy and get to be important, a lot of temptation's going to be thrown across your path. If you go on working late nights, and it just "happens" to you, you can't help it, night after night, one girl after another, *over and over,* then you're getting into the *habit* of mercy-f**king. You're falling into common adultery and appalling promiscuity, falling like a glittering rock star among the groupies.

Well, is adultery really so bad? Everyone else is doing it. Apparently no one is harmed by it. What's the big fuss about?

❦

What's Wrong with Adultery

IN A CURIOUS little book called *Good Behavior,* Harold Nicolson quotes Montaigne as saying, "I'd rather commit adultery than tell a lie." I've never been able to find this in the *Essays* myself, but I've always thought it was a really great line, a perfect example of the funny stuff you can get off when you have a principled morality. But what I've never been able to understand about it is how Montaigne could manage to commit adultery *without* telling a lie. Lying and adultery seem to me to go hand in hand, in fact arm in arm *grappling* each other right into the motel room. Maybe adultery was simpler in Montaigne's time, in sixteenth-century France, and easier for him, a charming man and a nobleman. But for most of us now, even in these permissive times, adultery is often a pretty complicated business, and that's of course what's wrong with it—all the rigmarole.

What I mean by rigmarole is definitely not the old-fashioned courtship or pursuit, the wooing and seduction that a woman might put a man through, or vice versa, for nobody seems to mess around with that sort of thing anymore. The rigmarole I mean is all the *arrangements* nonsense you have to go through, even after both people involved are not only consenting, but maybe even anxious. The trouble is that everything in modern life is already fantastically complicated and involved. When you add to all your normal involvements the involvement of being involved with someone *extra*—someone you're not even *supposed* to be involved with—it can all get to be purely too much. People are always having to make complicated arrangements and plans in their normal, nonadulterous life, and it fantastically compounds the complicatedness of everything (both the normal *and* the adulterous) when these two kinds of life get mixed up together.

The worst of it is that all these sinister, essentially superfluous adulterous arrangements have to be made in secret, without the advice and participation of the person you'd normally be planning how to spend the afternoon or evening or weekend in question with—your spouse, that is, of course. But the adulterous arrangements have to be made to *fit in with* all the already complicated normal arrangements. And they have to fit in *secretly!* Thus the secret plans often have a very irregular and ill-planned shape—invisible adulterous secret plans shaped to fit secretly and invisibly between all sorts of maybe already odd normal nonadulterous plans.

It all doesn't work out most of the time anyway. Split-second timing is required of the sort of people who may not even wear a watch. It might work out more often if you could do it the way they do in the movies: hand-pick ex-underground people and tough convicts, glib and resourceful types who're already well schooled in commando cunning and precision; then discipline them and train them and rehearse them for the mission for months; clock their routes, synchronize their watches, then send them off to make the rendezvous. Even then it's a scary business. And anyway, who wants to have an affair with a tough convict?

The difficulty with secret plans is inherent in the very point of them: the people they're secret from don't know about them and are always liable to do something unexpected to mess them up. Adulterous secret plans are always contingent on the often tentative plans of at least two other parties—her husband and your wife. The poor little invisible secret contingent adulterous plans that try to nestle into the crevices between these open-but-tentative spouse-dominated nonadulterous plans have only the remotest chance of ever coming to fruition; they can be *crushed* instantly by the slightest shift in regular planning. They are *so* contingent, most of them, that they're really just hypothetical, sheer wishful thinking and fantasy, nine times out of ten a bloody incredible waste of time. Complicated arrangements are made to meet precisely at such and such a place at exactly such and such a time *if* so-and-so does go here or there *and if* so-and-so doesn't come back, *and if* this thing or that thing does or doesn't happen, and if a million other *and ifs*. All this ingenuity and carefulness and organization and contingency-planning wasted on something that usually doesn't come off and even if it did is something you shouldn't be doing in the first place!

Phone calls, for instance—what a mess *they* are! There doesn't seem to be any other way to arrange anything these days, and adultery just makes them, like everything else, more complicated. It's bad enough at the office, where your secretary or your boss always seems to take the calls. But what about phoning one another's home? Whenever she phones you, she gets your wife. Whenever you phone her, her husband answers. "Well, how are you?" you say to him, real warm and friendly. "I thought I'd just phone and see how things are going." Are they puzzled? Of course they're *puzzled. How* puzzled are they, that's the real question. Puzzled enough so they suspect? When you're home alone and *could* receive a phone call from her, she never phones. She said she'd phone Wednesday afternoon, so you spend all Wednesday afternoon waiting by the phone. You can dial their number, let it ring just once, or just start to ring, then hang up quick, as a kind of signal *you're* free to get a call. But what does her husband think when the phone goes "ping" all the time and when he answers there's no one there and then right afterward she goes out? Does he *believe* she's just going to get an extra carton of milk? Does he realize she's gone to phone you, or is he just puzzled? *How* puzzled? You can do it just so often.

Then suppose there's a question of long toll calls that appear on the bill. She can phone you collect so as to get the charge on your phone bill, which your wife doesn't see, instead of on their phone bill, which her husband does see. But then suppose through some balls-up your wife's there and *gets* this collect call from her, what in the world does she think? *That* would puzzle her enough, I'd think—more than enough. And even if she (not your wife, the other one) has been real clever and has put through the collect call in some fake name, there's a limit to how many collect calls "for anybody from Ms. Lila Ovington"—or some other outrageous fake name—"in Garden City" that your wife will suspicion-free get and politely refuse: "I'm afraid we don't know anybody by that name, operator; you must have the wrong number." What if by some *real* balls-up, confused, she accepted the call anyway, even if she'd never heard of any Lila Ovington? She can hang up quick (the other one). But you can do it just so often.

And phoning from a public phone booth, either the one on the corner near your apartment or one of the ones down on the parking area of the shopping center, is no help—in fact, the opposite. Just being *seen* in one of those glass booths is enough to give you away. You figure that if people see you they'll just think you forgot the grocery list and are phoning home. But that *isn't* what *anyone* thinks. What everyone thinks is just what's the case "*Uh*-oh," is what everyone thinks. "What's he doing in that phone booth? Must be some call he can't make from home." Being seen in a phone booth is like having a giant scarlet letter "A" *drip-painted* on you, front and back. And the phone booth can't do you much good anyway: at least one of you has to be at home. To think you could phone her from one phone booth and have her answer in another phone booth is to hope for a fortuitous kind of connivance on God's part that you really oughtn't expect of Him, considering what you're up to.

Surreptitious phone calls, mail drops, confidants, borrowed apartments and rooms rented for an afternoon, lame excuses for not being where you're supposed to be, neglected work, extra baby-sitters and special dog-walkers, asking old friends to cover for you, secret codes and double meanings, obviously significant glances that you aren't quite sure what they mean—everything and everybody involved in an affair of this sort is just as complicated and unpleasant as can be. And all this is not to speak of what a mess it would be if you fell in love with the other person, which of course isn't likely but would lead to that sure sign of disorder and sorrow: lawyers. Remember the saw—

> Oh, what a tangled web we weave,
> When first we practise to deceive—

and a tangled web is clearly a mess. A nice neat web might be okay, especially if one has a tendency to be devious and a talent for organization—but not even a *spider* likes a tangled web. Everything involved in adultery militates more or less directly against one's ideal of a simple orderly life.

And adultery is ultimately wrong, too, because it separates you from the very person you ought to be close to and planning carefully with (your spouse, for heaven's sake, *not* the other one). There she is, poor soul, trying to work something out with you and you're trying to figure out how it will "fit in" with something she doesn't even know about. Or she's doing that to you, being maddeningly difficult and contrary, and you, poor soul, haven't the foggiest idea why.

The plans that emerge, needless to say, are often very bad plans indeed, from everyone's point of view. Knowing this secret reason, and remarking how much bad planning there is in this country, we've got to be alarmed at all that must be going on.

CHAPTER FOUR

The Extricated Life, as Against the Involved Life

❦

The Rationale of Involvement

WITH THE desire to be good, and faced with a bad society, you've got two choices: one, you can avoid the society, to the extent that's possible; or, two, you can get out there and try to do something to improve things. The second course of action leads you into what I call "the involved life"—a life of commitment and caring, and quite possibly a way to be good in a bad time.

Living the involved life you are engaged with others and with events. You're *in* on things. And because you know these things, people tell you other things. Information attracts more information (LCT). And working hard and late and getting around a lot you meet a lot of new people and are always bumping into people you already know and getting to know them better and they're all impressed at all you're doing and at all the people you know and they ask you to do other things and to come to dinner and meet other new people and you ask the new people to come to dinner at your house and they ask you to meet someone else and do something more and gradually or swiftly you get more and more involved with more and more things and more and more people. The nature of the life is self-perpetuating, accelerating and cumulative.

People who are involved complain a lot about how busy they are—how their office is always crowded with people and the phone is always ringing and how they have to fly straight from Chicago to Washington and won't be able to get to Easthampton for the weekend—but I think you'll agree, unless the involved people you know are entirely different from the involved people I know, that they really wouldn't have it any other way. We see them, some of the most harried men we know, answering a ringing phone themselves—if there's something new coming in, they don't want to miss it. We see them sympathetically listening to the most long-winded people—for they are basically open and curious and sympathetic, these busy people. They are the people that other people are always turning to for help or for advice, for counsel or information. If you want something done, ask a busy person (LCT). Involved people, then, usually are in fact reasonably happy, although most of them are reluctant to admit it.

Thus it is thought by many that the complex, active, participating, involved life may be a possible model of the good life itself—in the same way that in other lands in other times the life of, say, solitary contemplation was considered a model of the good life. The busy happy helpful housewife and the busy happy efficient man of affairs are both American ideals. And this kind of involvement with the lives and concerns of others and with "causes" and the idea of "being of service" and of "doing something" for "someone else" or for mankind-as-a-whole is often spoken of in a way that goes beyond the idea of an American ideal to a kind of American religion, a non-religious religion, a way to believe in something now that God's dead, a way of implementing Christianity without Christ.

An involvement with others is considered a value not only because of the good you may do these others, but because of the good it will do *you*. The end of being involved with others is thus seen also as a means to a kind of personal salvation.

Involvement must then be taken quite seriously as a possible answer to the question of how to be good.

❦

Moral Choice in Modern Life

THE ONLY problem with Involvement in Modern Life as a path to Virtue is the nature of the modern life you'd have to involve yourself *in*. For the sad fact of the matter is that every modern bureaucrat and every modern businessman every hour, or every *minute* possibly if he is particularly busy and efficient, *does* something, quite routinely takes some action, that a man of sensitivity and scruple would agonize the pros and cons of for months or years on end. This is not to say that bureaucrats and businessmen are necessarily not men of sensitivity and scruple (in fact, of course, usually they aren't, however); it's just that for various reasons (we'll go into them) the implications of most of the actions they take are obscured from them, and anyway they've established a kind of rationale, a kind of business anti-ethic that seems to them to justify any appalling thing they do.

Let's take the rationale first. It's naturally in the nature of business life—it's in fact the whole point and purpose of commerce—to buy things cheap and sell them expensive and hence make a profit. You have to make some profit even to stay in the game: if you make a lot, you win; if you don't make any, you lose. This is a commercial society, hence this is the real-life game of our lives, and those are the rules—or rather, that's how it's played, for there really aren't any rules as such, or they're always changing, as we'll see. The basic idea is to take advantage of someone else. You buy something as cheap as you can, and if it is at a price that is ruinous to the seller of it, then that is his worry. He screwed up somehow: he didn't keep up with modern methods of manufacturing or marketing or merchandising; perhaps he got greedy, tried to make a killing and didn't keep a sufficient cash reserve; or perhaps he was too cautious, didn't commit himself enough and take advantage of the opportunity when it was there. You've played Monopoly: you know how business works.

Competition—ruthless or otherwise—was the "nature" of things, we were told when this was a nation of competing small businesses. The fact that this do-or-die competition was "natural" was supposed to be a justification for it. I refer to so-called "Economic Darwinism" and all that, which emphasized the naturalness (the like-Nature quality) of the dog-eat-dog, survival-of-the-fitter "nature" of commercial life. The individual consumer was supposed to benefit ultimately from the more efficient methods and organizations that "evolved."

Things have changed now in American business, but of course not for the better, even though they were so bad before. Now, instead of the dog-eat-dog analogy, we have that other unpleasant truth about Nature: the big fish eat the little fish. The idea that competition between small businesses makes for efficiency has given way to the idea that only giant industry is efficient. The whole concept of "efficiency"—insofar as it isn't just a myth anyway in a world controlled by SNAFU and FUBAR—always functions as a justification for ruthlessness. Modern mass production methods require the modern methods of mass distribution and mass marketing. Chain stores buy more and hence buy cheaper, sell more and hence sell cheaper; the two factors interact to give large outlets an immense advantage and the small stores skitter away or get gulped down like a school of minnows. Competition is now rather more vertical than it is horizontal, for the truly big fish, the giant corporate whales, don't really compete but rather cavort together in playful mock battle, in price-fixing fair-trading cahoots with one another and in industry-wide lobbying and special-interest collusion with the government in a more or less managed and planned economy.

Let us deplore. In many ways the appalling bureaucratization of America is even more appalling than the appalling urbanization of America and the appalling industrialization of America. The appalling systems and techniques, the appalling procedures and regulations, the appalling pre-established methods and impersonal personnel directives, all these appalling structures and workings of our bureaucratic society seem almost deliberately designed to make possible, to make routine, in fact to make inevitable the perpetration and perpetuation of everything senseless and wrong.

The big institutions have developed a sort of purpose and direction of their own. Within these corporations and agencies it is getting less and less clear to any one person just what's happening. Not only do people as a whole have less and less power over what these complex organizations do, but also each man—and each man is what I'm interested in—has less and less realization of the implications and consequences of any action he takes.

All the way up and down—not just up and down the assembly line from beginning to end, but also up and down the hierarchy from top to bottom—no one is responsible for the consequences of an action taken. That's because the action is so divided up. Say the stockholders complain about poor dividends; a board chairman says the company must increase profits; an executive sends out the word to each division to cut costs by a certain percentage; a division head directs his team to cut down; a designer moderates his specifications; a purchasing agent pays less for something, say steel; a steel pourer pours less steel in, say, a car fender; a welder on an assembly line welds on the fender with less steel; the distributor sends the car out to his

salesmen; the ad agency works up a sexy-young-rebellious campaign; the salesman pretends to give you a good deal on your old car
and sells you the new one. Whose fault is it that the car fender has
less steel and more steal? Who takes responsibility for the consequences of this action, or series of actions, that had the result of further decreasing the quality of one more thing in this world of already
shoddy things? That probably isn't why we have less steel in our auto
fenders at all; I'm sure it's all much more complicated than that, you
could ask Ralph Nader. But once again that's the whole point: it is
so complicated, everything is, that no one (no one person) ever really
knows what's going on. Everyone involved in a thing like this—board
chairman, welder, salesman—should have scruples and compunc-
tions about what he's doing, should in fact be slapped right in his
complacent face with a good old-fashioned fat moral dilemma. But:
"Who, me?" they can each say. "What'd I do?" My point is: responsibility diffused is responsibility evaded.

Every day every man who is actively involved in modern commercial life compromises the quality of something (a magazine, a
line of frozen goods, a car fender, whatever) so as to make more
money for himself or for his firm (and even then it's for himself, for
if his division of the company makes more profit, he gets more salary). Either he lowers the standards of something so as to make more
profit selling it at the same price, or he inflates its value with promotion and advertising. Either he does these things himself, or he
directs someone else to do them.

He does this all routinely, according to "the book," the standard
procedures of his company, or the familiarity with the methods of
the industry that comprise his "know-how." He has been hired as
suitable for his job level by a system of bureaucratic personnel pro-
curement procedures. The organization won't hire the man, unless
it knows in advance that he will do what the organization wants in
the way the organization wants it done. And what the organization
wants is to increase its size and make money; or if it is a government
organization, to increase its size and get more money, by appropri-
ation or whatever. Everybody *in* the organization of course wants
more money too: all the agency heads, board chairmen, stockholders, horny young execs, drab clerks, sexy secretaries, overweight
welders, fast-talking salesmen—all want more money. And because

the organization controls what they do and how they do it, they don't have to contemplate one single minute about the implications and consequences of whatever it is they're doing to get it.

The Rationale of Extrication

BECAUSE INVOLVEMENT in a bad society would require the choice between two evils–collaboration or subversion–and because virtue is, among other things, the refusal to choose evil, virtuous behavior requires inaction now, commands disengagement, necessitates in fact the morose extrication of the self from the society.

What I mean by "extrication" is dropping back, not dropping out. If you are an adult, you can't drop completely out of society without becoming either some kind of bum or some kind of hermit. I have no advice for bums; I understand there are elaborate codes for their behavior anyway–to be drunk most of the time is the main idea, I think. Nor have I advice for a hermit, even one with a family. If you decide to drop right out–take your family off to homestead in Alaska, that sort of thing–then your problems are likely to be basic: collecting enough berries to survive, education for the kids, watering the livestock, and so on. Presumably you know a lot more about it than I do, or you wouldn't be interested in doing it. I don't know anything about "basic" problems; *real* problems are what I deal with.

Dropping completely out may very well be the ultimate solution to the problem of how to be good in a bad society; but like most ultimate solutions, it isn't really a solution at all; it's merely eliminating the problem. You don't find a way of being good in the bad society; what you do is just eliminate the society as a problem, simply by leaving it. As well as moving away in space–to Alaska or Australia or wherever the hell it is you think you're going–you are also dropping out in terms of time–back a hundred years or so into some earlier century or some earlier era, depending on how primitive you're prepared to go. You're not really experiencing modern life at all, much less being good in it.

The secret and the difficulty is to find just the right distance in extrication and just the right degree of virtue once you're there, which is just as much as you can bear and no more, which in turn is hard to find until you've actually gone beyond it and *found* you can't bear it. One wants to be far enough to be out of reach, near enough to be able to go in if one has to, and just the right distance to have some faint sense it's all still going on. In other words: not Australia or Alaska. Like Odysseus, one wants to hear the sirens' song, or at least know they're still singing, but be lashed to the mast for virtue's sake.

Some Thoughts about Unhappiness

THE EXTRICATED life's great at helping you avoid the evils of involvement—temptation, compromise, do-gooding, and the righteousness of busyness, dilemmas, excessive mercy-f**king, and so on—but it just isn't worth a damn at helping you avoid the perils of extrication itself. Too bad, too—be a lot better if it were the other way around.

The perils of extrication all hold hands: acedia, melancholy, boredom, loneliness, and so on. What they all do is make you feel lousy, and it's just awfully hard to feel you're being good—even though you're all extricated and not doing anything wrong—when you feel lousy.

It is one of Life's most unfair Cruel Truths that happiness is some kind of more or less major component of virtue. It even seems to me sometimes (some particularly wretched times) that happiness may be almost the *ultimate* virtue—in that it's the hardest one to attain and (especially) to maintain. They always say happiness is a bluebird in your own back yard, but the way my house is set, I can't tell which of all the lawn I have to mow *is* the back yard, and we don't seem to have bluebirds in my part of Connecticut anyway.

Sometimes you can fake, say, equanimity; or you can even try to fake cheerfulness (pretty unconvincing, you'll have to do better than that); but only an idiot would even attempt to fake happiness. The worst of it is that the idiots seem to *get* more happiness than the rest of us, who so much more deserve it, not to speak of how much more we need it. After a while you begin to think unhappiness is a kind of sin because you get to feeling so guilty about it, especially what it's doing to others, you moping around the house all miserable and blue for no good reason. Guilt, as we know, is a fairly good sign you're not doing good, but bad; and feeling guilty about feeling unhappy makes you feel even worse.

The worst symptom of unhappiness, I'm convinced, also acts in some excruciatingly unfair way as its major cause: I refer to the dreadful, bewildering, crippling feeling of not being able to do anything. You usually can't even *make* yourself do anything; but even if you do, it comes out awful. But then suddenly one day you do something without even making yourself do it and the unhappiness passes and you are able to do things again. But how, before that, do you do something when you're not able to do anything? That question, which seems absolutely absurd when you're out of the depression, seems absolutely unanswerable when you're in it. Sloth and melancholy stick so close to one another, reader, that you can never tell which comes in the door first.

One Sunday morning I was staring at myself dismally in the bathroom mirror. I turned on the radio and there was this minister who was really pretty good: his point was that we make our own fates, a thing I sometimes believe, sometimes not, usually depending on how my fate's going. Then the minister started to tell about this man: he was a simple old man, a workman, but he got to be a sort of celebrity because of his wit and wisdom and whatnot. I gather he was sort of like that longshoreman philosopher who was such a favorite of Dwight Eisenhower's. Anyway, this old man, according to the minister, was on one of those late-night talk shows, like Jack Paar or Johnny Carson, I guess, and he got everybody laughing and in a good mood. And then suddenly Johnny Paar got serious, and he said to the old man, "Sir," he said, "sir, I've known a lot of the famous men and women of my time, had a lot of them on this show. Most of them were successful and talented and good-looking and rich and had everything anyone could want. But *you*, sir, you are the *happiest* man I've ever known. How do you manage to be so happy anyway?"

"Well," said the old man (the minister trying to imitate his voice), "it's like this, Johnny. When I wake up each morning I look at myself in the mirror"—you should have seen how wide my eyes popped open in the mirror when he said *that*—"I look in that mirror, and I say to myself, there's either of two ways you can be today: happy or unhappy"—a pause—"and *I'm* no fool!"

Well, that made a great impression on me, as you can imagine. Who'd be foolish enough to choose to be unhappy? *I* sometimes am, I know; I think I've got some kind of wretched adolescent idea that it's somehow romantic to be unhappy. I thought to myself: from now on I take a leaf from the book of that wise old man; each morning I'm going to decide to be happy.

But then I thought: I think I'll wait until tomorrow morning to begin; I'm just not up to it today.

Melancholy, sadness, sweet *tristesse*—are they really as bad for us as everyone makes out? The blues can be very spiritual. The world's greatest achievements in art—the highest tragedy, the poignant sonata, Keats's poetry, Dostoevski's novels—are like celebrations of anguish, aren't they?

Surely the desire for unhappiness *is* there in some of us, at least some of the time. When it hits, we should perhaps put Verdi's *Requiem* or some other sad-assed music on the stereo, get out a bottle of booze, and just relax and enjoy our unhappiness.

For some of us, the falsification of self required by a decision to "be" happy is just too great. It's just too great a sacrifice of too important a part of our self. It's not our style, it wouldn't be worth it, it wouldn't work anyway, it's not *us.* We can only make ourselves *more* miserable trying to be happy.

"Never Inquire What's Going on in Constantinople"

THESE DISTRESSING paradoxes about happiness and the extricated life are expounded brilliantly in the conclusion of Voltaire's *Candide.* After a million miserable adventures Candide and his party find themselves in Constantinople. The naïve Candide and his faithful slave Cacambo have been cheated out of most of the fabulous fortune in diamonds they brought back from the country of the Incas, but they have enough left to buy back out of slavery Candide's great love, Cunégonde, once beautiful but now dreadfully ugly, and her companion, known as The Old Woman. Pangloss, the optimist ("all is for the best in this best of all possible worlds"), is with them, and so is Martin, the cynic-stoic-realist.

"In the neighborhood," we are told, "was a little farm; The Old Woman suggested that Candide should buy it, until some better fate befell the group." Then, says Voltaire:

> It would be natural to suppose that when, after so many disasters, Candide was married to his mistress, and living with the philosopher Pangloss, the philosopher Martin, the prudent Cacambo, and The Old Woman . . . he would lead the most pleasant life imaginable.

But no. Here is their situation:

> Candide was so cheated by the Jews that he had nothing left but his little farm.
>
> Cunégonde, growing uglier every day, became shrewish and unendurable.
>
> The Old Woman was ailing and even more bad-tempered than Cunégonde.
>
> Cacambo, who worked in the garden and then went to Constantinople to sell vegetables, was over-worked and cursed his fate.
>
> Pangloss was in despair because he did not shine in some German university.
>
> As for Martin, he was firmly convinced that people are equally uncomfortable everywhere; he accepted things patiently.

What they do to pass the time is argue: "Candide, Martin, and Pangloss sometimes argued about metaphysics and morals."

Apparently the place is a salt-water farm, everyone's dream, for what they argue about is what they see going by outside their windows:

> From the windows of the farm they often watched the ships going by, filled with effendis, pashas, and cadis, who were being exiled to Lemnos, to Mitylene, and Erzerum. They saw other

cadis, other pashas, and other effendis coming back to take the place of the exiles and be exiled in their turn.

How they would have enjoyed television, these three men! Imagine the up-close view they'd get of the pashas, cadis, and effendis coming and going into and out of power. No one nowadays would say that Byzantine politics is limited to Constantinople.

"When they were not arguing, the boredom was so excessive that one day The Old Woman dared to ask them a question." Here is the question, a philosophical dilemma constructed of material from their own life histories:

> I should like to know which is worse, to be raped a hundred times by Negro pirates, to have a buttock cut off, to run the gauntlet among the Bulgarians, to be whipped and flogged in an *auto-da-fé*, to be dissected, to row in a galley, in short to endure all the miseries through which we have passed—or to remain here doing nothing?

"'Tis a great question," says Candide, and he's right; it's perhaps *the* great question: Is it better to be run to death in the rat race or to be bored to death out of it? Martin's answer, the stoic's "answer" to this question, is a reconciliation but not a solution: Martin "concluded that man was born to live in the convulsions of distress or in the lethargy of boredom."

Finally they decide to get expert, outside opinion. They go to see a very famous Dervish in the neighborhood, a man who was supposed to be the best philosopher in Turkey. Pangloss asks him "why so strange an animal as man was ever created."

"What has it to do with you?" says the Dervish. "Is it your business?"

And when Pangloss asks him what they should do about all the evil there is in the world, the Dervish really sets him straight:

> "Hold your tongue," said the Dervish.
>
> "I flattered myself," said Pangloss, "that I should discuss with you effects and causes, this best of all possible worlds, the origin of evil, the nature of the soul, and pre-established harmony."
>
> At these words the Dervish slammed the door in their faces.

Voltaire never pauses to relish his effects: *Candide* is a tract, not a novel. Without even a paragraph he resumes:

> During that conversation the news went around that at Constantinople two viziers and the mufti had been strangled and several of their friends impaled. This catastrophe made a prodigious noise everywhere for several hours.

That last sentence seems incredibly apt as a description of our reaction to today's "catastrophes": there is "a prodigious noise" made about them "everywhere" and it lasts "for several hours."

But now comes the well-known ending of the book. As the three walk home they come across an old man "who was taking the air under a bower of orange-trees at his door." Pangloss asks him if he knows the name of the mufti who had just been strangled.

> "I do not know," replied the old man. "I have never known the name of any mufti or of any vizier. I am entirely ignorant of the occurrence you mention. I presume that in general those who meddle with public affairs sometimes perish miserably and that they deserve it, but I never inquire what is going on in Constantinople. I content myself with sending there for sale the produce of the garden I cultivate."

Then he takes Pangloss, Martin, and Candide inside his house. There his two daughters and his two sons present them with "several kinds of sherbet which they had made themselves." Imagine: homemade sherbet! Several *kinds* of it, which they had made themselves! All of them—the father, and I guess the mother and the two sons and the two daughters—had gotten together and made homemade sherbet. I suppose they did it regularly. And without a freezer. They also had "caymac flavored with candied citron peel, oranges, lemons, limes, pineapple, dates, pistachios, and"—and this is what I really can't get over—"and Mocha coffee which had not been mixed with the bad coffee of Batavia and the Isles." I have no idea what "the bad coffee from Batavia and the Isles" is, but the point is that there are these simple-seeming farm folk who are really fussy, discriminating people who have the time and energy and desire and skill really to *do things right!*

Candide naturally enough, is fantastically impressed:

> "You must have a vast and magnificent estate?" said Candide
> to the Turk.
> "I have only twenty acres," replied the Turk. "I cultivate them
> with my children, and work keeps at bay three great evils: bore-
> dom, vice, and need."

Twenty acres! It is the exact amount of land I have, on salt water,
halfway between Boston and Constantinople-on-the-Hudson. If only
I could get caught up on all the chores and maintenance and start
cultivating them and make an end to boredom, vice, and need!

Candide apparently felt the same way, for in his final discussion
with Pangloss and Martin he cites the old farmer's now-famous dictum as being what they should do: "We must cultivate our own garden." Candide might well have repeated the old man's other dictum:
"Never inquire what's going on in Constantinople." Never even *inquire.* Tend your garden and don't pay any attention to what's going
on out there.

CHAPTER FIVE

An Intricate Ethics

Toward a Fashionable Morality

TAINE SAID that Addison made virtue fashionable, and I'd sure like to know how he did it. Have you ever *read* Addison!? I had to read *The Spectator Papers* or *The Sir Roger de Coverley Papers* or whatever they were called, in high school or somewhere, and hated them. Addison and Steele put out this one-page newspaper, daily for the most part, around 1700 I think, and each issue, or most issues, would have a vignette about this English country squire, Sir Roger, square but good. He sometimes visits sinning swinging London and makes the urbanites ashamed of themselves—his simple dignified rural virtue is contrasted with their lewdness or extravagance or whatever. Or sometimes Sir Roger just stays out at his country place being gentle and generous to the neighbors and having his servants uniformly belove him for his unfailing courtesy and kindness. The extricated life with a vengeance. Very dull stuff.

So I started reading around, trying to find out what people thought was so great about these sketches, and that's when I came across what Taine (you know, Hippolyte Taine, the great French critic, 1828–93) said about Addison, which under the circumstances seems to me perfectly extraordinary:

> It is no small thing to make morality fashionable. Addison did it, and it remained in fashion. Formerly, honest men were not polished, and polished men were not honest; piety was fanatical, and urbanity depraved. . . . [But] Addison reconciled virtue with elegance. . . .

No *small* thing to make morality fashionable!? *I'll* say, as my mother used to say. But especially it's no small thing when you use as your example of virtue someone like Sir Roger, who's not just unfashionable, but excruciatingly dull and out-of-it.

The only morality that could be found fashionable these days – and the only morality worth having, actually – is a principled morality. You get to act on the basis of your own personal principles. (It works even if you don't have any; you'll see in a minute.) As such, it may seem to some people a miraculous reworking of a very old idea, but actually it represents a big breakthrough in the morality business, leaving the competition way behind.

It is, for instance, far more grown-up and with-it than any of the morality systems that operate on a "rewards" basis. The central tenet of all rewards-based morality systems is "you act good so as to get something good." Essentially this is an ethic that derives from conning children: "If you don't scream, you'll get some ice cream." Children very soon learn that the actual facts of life are that you're *more* likely to get ice cream if you *do* scream, but the idea of the ethic seems to persist anyway. A lot of fairly nice, very stupid people go all through life, right to their very *grave*, still expecting to get the parental pay-off for being good. Christianity is one offshoot rewards morality system: our heavenly father will give you your reward in a glorious afterlife. This offshoot has lasted a long time, presumably because no one has ever been able to come back and say whether you do finally get the reward or it's just one last gyp. The Work Ethic has been another long-lasting offshoot rewards morality system. "Work hard and you'll get your reward on earth" might make some sense if the work people did were good, which it usually isn't, and if you got as much reward for working hard at ditch-digging as you do for working hard at investment-banking, which you don't. People are too savvy for rewards-based morality systems these days.

For the most part these days, most people go along on some sort of socially "conforming" basis of morality – the most recent and worst morality system of all. You "conform" to a "norm." You do what everyone else is doing, not so much in an attempt to be good – you know what most people are doing isn't good – but just so as not to be *different*. You do what the other lawyers do; you and your wife do what the other couples at the country club do. "Everyone else is doing it," the central contemporary moral tenet, provides no guidance whatsoever for doing what's right; it provides only an excuse (and a feeble one at that) for doing something wrong. Paradoxically, when it comes to ethics, you don't have to conform to be fashionable.

Also outmoded are those morality systems where you act on an "obedience to authority" basis, according to which you act good not in the expectation of being rewarded, but just in the hope of avoiding punishment. In its highest form, which still isn't very high, this system may somehow persuade you to "believe" in authority, to feel that "obeying orders" is some sort of a virtue, to respect the "integrity" of the laws of the land, to assert the necessity of some sort of "social order," and other such baloney.

This leads us to some somewhat more mature systems where you act according to some idea of a "social contract" or a "moral imperative." Here you act good in the hope and expectation others will, as if you'd struck some sort of bargain. You don't harm others so that they won't harm you. Or you act good so as to set everyone else an example.

Here we're up against that wretched "categorical imperative" of Kant's, his famous principle-to-end-all-principles that you should "Act only on that maxim whereby thou canst at the same time will that it should become a universal law." What ridiculousness! That's the kind of rubbish they told you in grade school: you'd ask if you could go home early that day, say; and they'd say, "What if *everybody* did that?" What *rubbish*! Everybody *doesn't* do that, and what if they do, that's their business, or the school's, and has nothing to do with *you*. It's as stupid as having to eat all your breakfast cereal because of the poor starving kids in China—how are *they* going to get it?— *especially* if you eat it!? And everyone knows American kids are overweight, so if they all *didn't* eat their cereal maybe America would have a cereal surplus and the Chinese kids would be *better* off. Eat your cereal if you feel like it, if you're hungry; don't eat it if you don't want it. Tell your mother that's what I said. You do what you yourself think is best for you yourself and don't try to make any universal principle for all mankind out of it. "We like to occupy our thoughts with the universe, which carries on very well without us," says Montaigne. "We worry over mankind—and not over Michel, who touches us more closely."

With a principled morality you don't *establish* principles. The only principles you follow are your own. You don't want to be guided by someone else's principles, so don't expect him to be guided by yours. Your behavior is just a sample of yourself, not an example for anyone.

"No law can be sacred to me," says Emerson, "but that of my own nature." And when later in "Self-reliance" he says, "Be it known unto you that henceforward I obey no law less than the eternal law," you have the feeling that by "eternal" he really means "internal." It is yourself only that you obey, and you obey no one who orders you to disobey yourself.

❦

How to Develop "Principles" When You Have None

A PRINCIPLED MORALITY would seem necessarily to assume that a person actually had some moral principles; otherwise what would he base his principled morality *on?* But few people today have any rigid ideas of what's definitely right and definitely wrong.

A person used to get his principles from internalizing his society's values, but we live in a society where giant forces like Urbanization, Bureaucratization, and Industrialization (the appalling UBI Forces) have eroded the power of the traditional value-providers—Family, Religion, Education, Workplace, Social Class, Community, and so on. Since moral principles cannot now be obtained from the value-vacuumed society, they have to come from the self. And if a man seems to be without principles, they must not just be *sought* in the self, but *wrought* in the self.

What we'd start with, if a person had nothing better, is his feelings—his feelings about what he likes and what he doesn't like. Everyone has *feelings*, for heaven's sake—otherwise we'd all be moral vegetables. Our procedure will be to codify the feelings a bit, into a pattern of preferences and scruples; then develop this pattern into a network of principles that will eventually appear as a principled morality.

A good deal of the method will be cultivating the knack of *talking* morally. Montaigne's great line, previously cited, "I'd rather commit

adultery than tell a lie," is a perfect example of what I'm referring
to. It has exactly the right rhetoric. What he does is make a feeling
into a principle, but still keeps it personal. He has this scruple and
this preference: he doesn't like telling a lie, somehow it doesn't feel
right to him; he'd rather commit adultery, which doesn't feel so bad
to him, maybe even good, who knows. This becomes his "principle,"
but it is a *personal* principle as he states it. He doesn't say, "It is better
to commit adultery than to tell a lie," just says, *"I'd rather."* And the
thing that's *really* good about the line, besides all this, is that while
it sounds high-minded and very moral and all, it's also individualistic
and original-sounding and *also* (the line is a real coup) it is clever
and comic (his drinking buddies must have rolled on the floor when
he first came out with it), *and* of course it makes Montaigne seem a
swinging fellow, game for anything if there's anything going, not
out-of-it, not out-of-it at all, and yet still seeming super-moral. It is
pure genius, that line.

Great as the line is, though, it's Montaigne's line. You have to
learn to draw your own lines. Whatever is distasteful to you – women
smoking while cooking, say, or wearing culottes – you get in the habit
of speaking of it as "incorrect." Going to night clubs – if you hate the
noise and the smoke of them – can seem to you "quite improper."
"Why, I'd rather sneak into an old-fashioned bordello than be seen
in one of your modern discotheques" is how you could put it. Or, if
you don't seem able to dance the free-form way they do now, take
the position that "all dancing beginning with the Twist" seems to
you "so overexplicit sexually as to cause great harm to the society at
large." As such, you want no part of it. Urged by a girl to dance
yourself, you express shock: "I'd sooner see you writhe stark naked
on the floor than abandon myself to such lewd gyrations fully
clothed."

So much of a principled morality is just this matter of finding the
right tone to express preferences and scruples. If something makes
you nervous or uncomfortable, you work it up to become a point of
principle.

If you've got it anywhere in your background, no matter how far
back – or you can maybe get it from some nineteenth-century English novel reading – you can enhance your moral line marvelously
by an arbitrarily exhumed or artificially preserved regard for a whole

set of outmoded "proprieties." "We've got to think of the proprieties, you know," you can say to someone who wants to take you off for a dreadful weekend at her house in the country. Or: "We must consider how this is going to reflect on your reputation"—as if anyone had a reputation anymore. Elaborate your reluctances. Try to remember some of those foolish things your mother used to tell you. Work up any little naggling guilts you have: don't do anything that makes you feel in the least guilty; make not doing whatever it is a matter of scruple.

Whatever you do, then, is moral, because it will be *principled* behavior. It's not just a matter of having a reason or a justification for whatever you do—although you should always be able to work one up if challenged. Rather it is that you must be acting according to a general principle you believe in, or at the very least, appear to be so acting. Principles are even useful in justifying *un*reasonable behavior. The key thing is to make them *your* general principles, to create your own idiosyncratic, individualistic set of them. Your "style," as developed, becomes your ethics.

That's the great thing about this system of developing a system of ethics from your feelings: it is made for you; it all starts from the basis that what you like to do is right and that what you don't like to do is wrong. No more qualms about others perhaps "finding out"! No more misgivings about "what people will think"! Your scruples and your principles, being not internalized but internal to begin with, being so to speak your own private matter, are subject to internal arbitration and debate—not to mention suspension. You can avoid doing all the things that make you uncomfortable. You can go ahead and do what you think just, or best, or good, or even fun, and still have no scruples about it. You can even *say* that, when you do it, if anyone tries to call you on it: "Oh, I have no scruples about doing that," you can say.

With a good, elaborate, distinctive set of things you certainly will or positively will not do, you will seem very independent and inner-directed in this day and age. The more contradictory they are, the better, as we shall see. Your principles will seem very much your own—as they in fact are. And no one ever need know that these lofty moral principles you live by began life as a poor paltry bag of preferences and scruples and before that were nothing more than ordinary finicky feelings of the sort everyone has. Let me quote Montaigne again. This time he is telling why he quit what he called "the servitude of the courts":

> The best qualities I have would be useless in this age. My easy manners would be considered weakness and cowardice, my faith and conscience, superstition and finickiness.

In Montaigne's case people thought his conscience was finickiness. Well, you do it the other way around: you get people to think your finickiness is your conscience. And in this age that's seen the Superego die, it probably actually is.

❧

What Virtue Actually Is, and How Exactly to Achieve It

To THE extent that our principled morality begins in simple "feelings," it seems to resemble the Hemingway dictum we began with: that what's good or bad depends on what makes you *feel* good or bad afterward. Hemingway's statement implies the existence of an elaborate personal code of conduct based on true knowledge of one's own true feelings—a concept of right and wrong potential in each man's emotions. But this feelings-afterward thesis makes an end out of what should only be a beginning, because it doesn't assert the necessity of developing this consciousness, doesn't provide for its elaboration into a principled morality that would help a person determine *beforehand* what would make him feel good or bad afterward.

In Emerson's essay "Character," one reads:

> Impure men consider life as it is reflected in opinion, events, and persons. They cannot see the action, until it is done. Yet its moral element pre-existed in the actor, and its quality as right or wrong, it was easy to predict.

Do you see what Emerson's words add to Hemingway's? It is the idea of being able to *predict* the rightness or wrongness of an act. It is not just that the moral element of an action *pre-exists*, however; the rightness or wrongness pre-exists *in the actor*. Pre-existent, therefore, in a person trying to decide whether a contemplated action is right or wrong *for him* is the knowledge of whether it will feel to him "good" or "bad" afterward.

In considering any action, it's not just a matter of what you want or don't want at the moment. A sense of self, of who you are, past and future as well as present, you yesterday and tomorrow as well as today—a sense of the *continuity* of identity—should govern the action taken. I don't mean that it need inhibit your desires or your wants or feelings, just that you will take your guidance from deeper, longer-lasting feelings that relate more directly to your ongoing identity. The greater one's sense of identity, the more likely he is to be kept from acts that are "wrong"—and remember, I'm saying no act is right *or* wrong *except* in regard to the individual self. Only that which violates the mature sense of self is wrong.

Someone clever once said, "Dirt is merely misplaced matter"; and someone else even cleverer added, "And immorality is merely misplaced behavior." No action is moral or immoral, no act is "right" or "wrong," *in and of itself*. The moral element of an action exists in the actor—there's no use looking anywhere else *for* it. Each act takes its virtue or lack of it from the circumstances that it occurs in, and these circumstances are in each and every case *individual* circumstances, and individual circumstances depend on an *individual*. Making money in business, losing money in business; running an organization well, or secretly subverting its effectiveness—all such actions are virtuous or not-virtuous through the circumstantiality in which they occur, which is a circumstantiality entirely dependent on the individual taking the action. "Good and bad," says Emerson, in "Self-reliance" this time, "are but names very readily transferable to that or this; the only right is what is after my constitution; the only wrong is what is against it."

What is important is not the virtue of an act, or many acts; but the virtue of the individual. Who cares whether an *act* is virtuous? I care whether a *person* is a *good* person. *Acts* don't go to heaven or hell; and, much more important, they don't suffer from having the bad feeling they've done something wrong, nor do they enjoy the good feeling they've done something right for a change. Acts don't feel bad *or* good, afterward *or* beforehand.

What's of concern in working up an intricate ethics this way is not any "goodness" or "badness" of an action, but the extent of individuality that the act represents, the extent to which it reflects your true nature. If what you do represents your own thinking, your manner, your "style"—and especially if it *enhances* your self, your individuality—then it's almost certainly "good." It is when you "miss" your style in an action that it "feels" bad to you and hence *is* bad.

In a bad society—bad in our case not just because it is a touch corrupt and vice-ridden, but more consequently because it is homogeneous, anonymous, depersonalized, and standardized—in such a society, virtue naturally and inevitably resides in individuality.

Individuality *is* virtue. Virtue *is* individuality. If there were another way to say it, I would.

This may always have been true, or it may not. Past societies (perhaps because they were able to think better of themselves than we conceivably can) have often stressed conforming to conventional morality as being virtue. But conforming is the very opposite of individuality, which emphasizes developing what is different and distinctive. The sad fact now is that individuality must be doubly prized because it is so rare and difficult to achieve. The chronic contemporary emotional syndrome is said to be "identity loss." Perhaps in an attempt to be fashionable, many have gone on a characterological fad diet and now find themselves "empty" and "hollow"—entirely without a sense of self.

Individuality (and its accompanying twin, Virtue) will become available, even so, utilizing nothing more than a person's behavior. As feelings were developed into principles, so can behavior be developed into identity. And just as a person must have feelings or be accounted a vegetable, so too must he have behavior. Everyone has *behavior*, for heaven's sake; it's simply what you *do!* In order to establish individuality, we are going to take simple basic behavior and first consider it as a *kind* of behavior—that is, categorize *how* one acts, *how* one speaks, how one does more or less anything—and then by a process of habituation and selective role-playing, these behavior-patterns are internalized. You "become" your behavior; you "are" what you do and say and think. Thus will be created a rich and elaborate sense of identity, an intricate and intriguing inner-directed self, all of whose actions will be taken according to a unique ethical individuality—"ethical" just because individuality *is* virtue.

❧

Of Masks, and Beerbohm's "Happy Hypocrite"

HOW BEHAVIOR can become identity is illustrated by a fable of Max Beerbohm's called *The Happy Hypocrite* that someone once gave me the gist of. I haven't looked it up, because I liked it the way I heard it:

Seems there's this dissolute fellow and he's fallen in with an even more dissolute and evil and depraved lady, and he's getting so he looks just awful. Then one night he sees a beautiful innocent young girl at the theater or somewhere and he falls in love with her; so he puts on this mask, the face of an innocent and beautiful young man, and he woos the young girl and wins her and they are very much in love and move away from the evil urban center out into the virtuous countryside and they are very happy and young and beautiful and in love together for years and years. But then, *then* the evil depraved lady he'd abandoned tracks them down, and she's determined to un-mask him and show what a dissolute sinner he is. But when she does, when she rips off the mask, there of course underneath is the face of the mask—for he's *become* young and innocent and beautiful and in love and all.

I imagine the story was meant as a kind of answer to Oscar Wilde's *The Picture of Dorian Gray*, where the beautiful young man lives a *dissolute* life and all the signs of the depravity show on the portrait rather than the person. But actually both stories make the same point, one just the other way around from the other: your personal appearance may or may not change to show it, but you *become* the way you act.

At a certain point in life's costume party—say about half an hour or so after midnight—you should be willing to take off the costume, or at least parts of it, and be able to remove the mask without everyone recoiling in horror. Depending on whether you subscribe to the Dorian Gray theory or the Happy Hypocrite theory of how these things happen, you've either altered your self so that it resembles the mask, or gradually altered the mask so that it reflects the changes in you underneath. It's as natural as a snake shedding its skin, if that seems natural to you.

Of the "Line," and F. Scott Fitzgerald in 1929

A PERFECT EXAMPLE of how to do what I'm talking about is working on what used to be called your "line." Are you old enough to remember the line? I don't know where the word comes from, used the way I mean; my *Webster's Collegiate* lists no fewer than thirty-two basic uses of the word "line" (with lots of submeanings), yet not one comes close to what I'm talking about. God knows a collegiate dictionary *should* have it, for the line is a very collegiate thing, or it certainly used to be.

The line I'm talking about was kind of a psychological line of approach, a verbal line of attack. What one did was develop a certain line of gab, a certain style one came on with, that was peculiarly one's own, in theory at least, although entirely artificial and invented, and to some extent recognized as such. Maybe the original metaphor's from fishing: you'd "feed" a girl a line, the idea being to catch or hook her—you know what I mean, *land* her. Or perhaps it came from "stringing" someone "along"—as if on a line.

You'd test out different lines on the girls; the ones that seemed to work you'd stick with, discarding the ones that didn't. You'd pick up aspects of some successful older guy's line, trying to make them work with your own. "Giving a girl a line" meant you were trying to make her without revealing much of yourself (as if you had much self to reveal in those days). Your line was a tentative, experimental pseudo-self.

The absolute falsity of a line never seemed to matter much: in fact, the deliberate deceit was rather intriguing and sexy, like masks at a costume ball. The line had many opportunities for irony of a very romantic kind: what you were "pretending" to be could be what you felt the real "you" in fact *was*. The line could function as a very strong "come-on," a way of coming on very strong. But then, by letting the mask fall slightly askew, one could reveal one's line as having been a kind of "put-on," a putting on of a manner that fakes an extraordinary interest in the other person. The line was full of self-mockery and mockery of the other and mockery of the whole idea of romance between you—yet it invited that romance, under sexily false pretenses. It was a sort of contractual con: both parties agreeing to mutual suspension of reality in order to get the job done. Its falsity was very functional.

Admittedly the line was thus primarily a way of manipulating one's relations with the opposite sex—but then what isn't? Surely it's true that what forms one's adult personality—far more, say, than early toilet training, no matter what the Freudians say—is what one found experimentally in late adolescence worked with the girls.

Used often enough, one's line will gradually become part of one's real personality. And simply because it is so fluid and flexible and phony a part of one's self, one's line can be the first experimental thrust, the sharp, carving, leading edge in any reshaping of the self.

For this reason, I think you'll be interested in the line F. Scott Fitzgerald was using at country club dances in Montgomery, Alabama, in 1929, when he was thirty-three years old. We have this report from Sara Mayfield's *Exiles from Paradise*, a gossipy book, the bias of which, like Nancy Milford's *Zelda*, is to defend Zelda by attacking Scott:

> On Saturday evenings, he came to the dances at the club sometimes with Zelda, sometimes with his secretary. He was an incurable flirt; but he was now past the age for it; his style was *vieux jeu*, and his breath smelt of Sen-Sen. No matter how long he had known a girl or how many times he had danced with her earlier in the evening, when he broke on her he would tilt his head back, look down at her intently and open his gambit with that ancient chestnut, "And where have *you* been all my life?"
>
> "Waiting for you to get a new line or stop fishing," one of Zelda's friends finally retorted.

But that did not change his standard procedure. With his usual capacity for self-deception, he attributed his waning charm not to his behavior and his threadbare clichés but to the fact that he had not published a book in six years and people were forgetting him.

What was Fitzgerald up to, do you think? Of course, with all that Sen-Sen on his breath, he may have been too drunk to know what he was doing. Or he may never have used this line at all, or maybe only once as a joke—and Sara Mayfield just made it all up, or most of it. But assume for a moment the account is true, and that he did do just what she says he did—what could have been the reasons?

To begin with, of course, it probably was a joke. "Where have *you* been all my life?"—it's *so* old a line, so much a cliché even then, that it is like a parody of a line, a mockery of the whole *idea* of handing a girl a line. This would go without saying if Sara Mayfield weren't such an idiot. Fitzgerald has to make a joking, careful approach in the situation he's in. He is thirty-three years old, and far from being "past the age for it," as Sara Mayfield says, that's maybe just the age when the urge for flirting *begins*. But he's in Zelda's hometown, with her in and out of a mental home there, and all her old friends are at the dance. He doesn't want to seem to be making any kind of a pass a young girl could take seriously—unless she wants to, of course. There's caution, too, in the way he uses exactly the same line on every girl, singling no one out specially. He offers up his feeble gambit the same way the serve is offered to the lady in well-mannered mixed doubles, as a conventional way of putting the ball in play—but with just a little twist on it too.

What could they have made of it, those sappy Alabama, southern-belle young matrons, when he said the exact same thing to each of them, over and over, dance after dance, week after week, at that wretched provincial country club? What guts it must have taken Fitzgerald to go on doing it! For if it was a joke, it was a very special and rueful kind of joke: it mocks not just himself, but also the girl *and* the idea of something happening between them. The phony romanticism of the line, as he uses it, passes beyond simple bitterness about the situation to the bitterest kind of irony.

What must have made the line "And where have *you* been all my life?" so effective the first time it was ever used (when? by whom? I hope he made out with it; he certainly deserved to) is that it implies that something has been missing all your life and here's this beautiful stranger who has just made you realize what it was—*her.* Now, none of these Alabama matrons at the dance is the beautiful stranger who's been the something missing all Fitzgerald's life, and Fitzgerald knows it. What he's doing, it seems to me, is in equivalence asking the girl to try to see in *him* a stranger, a new Scott Fitzgerald, and *not* to recognize the old one.

In Fitzgerald's case, the old one is the young one. As everyone knows, there are two phases to Scott Fitzgerald's life: Phase One is the youthful triumph (with the suggestion of tragedy ahead somewhere), and Phase Two is the tragedy of his later life (with the suggestion of triumph beyond it). He's using this tired old line (consciously or unconsciously doesn't matter, probably some of each) to move from Phase One (young success) to Phase Two (aging failure). He's trying on this new mask at the dance, seeing how it works with the girls, shedding his shiny old skin for a forlorn new one. What he's doing is readying his character to play his destined role, for the catastrophe he was ultimately to make of his life was ultimately to be his triumph.

❦

Of Eccentricity, and Emerson's Aunt Mary

"WHO SO would be a man," says Emerson, "must be a nonconformist." And he adds that there's freedom in individualistic behavior, once you have the reputation for it. "Always scorn appearances," he says, "and you always may." It isn't only that others get accustomed to your disregard for appearances, but that "the force of character is cumulative," as he says; your habit of individualistic behavior is self-reinforcing. After a while, too, people don't just *accept* your "different" behavior; they rather come to *expect* it.

"What's your Aunt Mary been doing lately?" some friend might ask Emerson. "Got any new stories about her?"

"No," says Emerson. "She hasn't really been herself lately, not doing anything out of the ordinary at all."

"Oh," says the friend, disappointed. "Too bad."

"You did hear the pink ribbons one, didn't you?" asks Emerson, "What she said to Mrs. Thoreau?"

"No," says the friend, brightening. "I certainly didn't. For goodness sake tell me."

This story is told as follows, in a loving memoir Emerson did of his aunt, Mary Moody Emerson:

> When Mrs. Thoreau called on her one day, wearing pink ribbons, she shut her eyes, and so conversed with her for a time. By and by she said, "Mrs. Thoreau, I don't know whether you have observed that my eyes are shut."
>
> "Yes, Madam, I have observed it."
>
> "Perhaps you would like to know the reason?"
>
> "Yes, I should."
>
> "I don't like to see a person of your age guilty of such levity in her dress."

The moral tone here is gorgeous, parallel in manner and method to Montaigne's magnificent, "I'd rather commit adultery than tell a lie." A feeling (against pink ribbons) is turned into a principle (levity in dress is unbecoming beyond a certain age) expressed as a preference ("I don't like to see . . ."). But it's not the sort of thing everyone could get away with saying to Thoreau's mother or anyone else. Aunt Mary gets away with it because she had a character, as Emerson says:

> . . . as could hardly have appeared out of New England; of an age now past, and of which I think no types survive. . . . It is a fruit of Calvinism and New England, and marks the precise time when the power of the old creed yielded to the influence of modern science and humanity.

No need, I suppose, to point out the irony in how each generation through the centuries sees, in the rigid and principle behavior of some representative of the proceeding generation, the "end of an era," due to the influence of "modern" science or the "new" humanism or whatever. We seem to think that values and mores that pertained for centuries have *just* disappeared, "only yesterday."

Anyway, this kind of old-fashioned "character" is cumulative in

that you get to be "*a* character," and then more of the same is expected of you—not just *the* same, but *more* of the same. If you're Mrs.
Thoreau flouting the conventions by wearing pink ribbons at your
age, you're expected to wear maybe *scarlet* ribbons next month. If
you're Aunt Mary speaking your mind, you're expected to speak
more of your mind the next time. People get sick of eccentrics who
don't develop. "Really, Miss Emerson's rudeness is getting to be
quite boring"—Mrs. Thoreau might say—"it's so *expected*." The next
time Mrs. Thoreau calls, Aunt Mary ought perhaps to be effusively
polite: "Oh, those scarlet ribbons are just exactly *right* for you, Mrs.
Thoreau," she might say, which will keep her visitor off balance. But
what's she going to come up with next time? The freedom granted
by "Always scorn appearances and you always may" is sometimes
very nearly canceled out by the obligation assumed by "Always scorn
appearances and you may always have to." It's best to start uncon-
ventionality easy, and work up; otherwise you get into the bind of
the pornographer who's begun his book with the dirtiest scene he
can think of.

Perhaps, after all, it is not your eccentricity but your idiosyncrasy
that I want you to develop. My *Webster's Collegiate* again:

> *Eccentricity* emphasizes divergence from the usual or custom-
> ary; *idiosyncrasy* (properly one's own peculiar temperament or
> bent), the idea of the personal, characteristic, and individual,
> esp. in trait, trick, or habit.

Real individuality, however, the kind in which virtue resides, is not
necessarily distinctive in any immediately recognizable or "trade-
marked" way. "Distinctive" people, people with "flair" and what I
think of as "conspicuous identity"—all the stars of stage, screen, and
tube, and the "celebrities" and "guest artists" and glib talkers and
so on—all of them are not necessarily moral—perhaps the opposite.
One thinks, for instance, of the various "talk show" hosts whose faces
and manners have become so familiar to us through television. Such
people are frozen in their own images, like politicians. They maybe
made a start, then somehow got stuck, infatuated by themselves in
the stage they'd reached, or frozen by overexposure in the media,
prevented from change almost by contract, who knows. Who cares?

Such people, and the real-life "charming" people who resemble them, have such rigid conspicuous identities that they are like what the Elizabethans called "humor" characters on stage—they always come on the same way, and go off the same way. Or they are in life what E. M. Forster called "flat" characters in the novel, characters who remain exactly the same throughout the whole book. To be the hero of your own life story you've got to be a "round" character, with the potential to be altered by the events of the plot, capable of development, of taking some action that will surprise.

But there's also needed some kind of continuity or harmony of idiosyncrasy; some parallel or paradox that relates the man to the mask he's putting on or taking off. When Fitzgerald tries on the persona of the "aging failure," it has a thematic relation to his earlier "young success"; you'd be absurd to attempt the role of a romantic old failure if it had never occurred to anyone that you'd ever do anything in the first place. That would be flat and consistent indeed. But erratic, unrelated, compulsive change in a series of attempts to escape a series of former selfs, as with many restless modern men, is not what's wanted either. What's wanted is a sort of ramshackle accretion or accruement to the self—like the handsomeness achieved by adding porches and wings to a summer place. One wants a continuous deepening and developing of the personality—and this development should always be toward the more elaborate and intricate.

❦

How Life Should Be, as Against How People Should Be

AND so that one will have the time, the freedom, the opportunity to thus develop the self, one's life should be extricated, simplified, and ordered.

Life should be simple, people should be complicated.

People should be complicated, lives should be simple.

If there were another way to say it, I would, for it's my essential point.

We've got it backward nowadays, is the trouble: if our *lives* weren't so complicated, we'd all have the time and mind to develop our *selves* more.

The more complicated the man, the better he's able to bear the simple life. He doesn't need others—or at any rate he doesn't need to use involvement with others as a way of accompanying and occupying himself. He is never at a loss for something to do. Thoreau knew that: he made his life simple and developed his self to become the most complex of men.

The more complex the man and the simpler his life, the greater is likely to be his ethic. It is virtually certain to be that way, for in the complexity of the involved life he is certain to confront temptation. Trying to "get something done" in the midst of quandary, predicament, and dilemma—not to speak of constant change and chaos—he must soon encounter the "need" or "necessity" to overcome his scruples and compromise his principles. His natural "feelings" must constantly give way to the feelings of others. In the involved life you must twist yourself to conform to others and to events; you haven't the freedom to grow as you want, as you *want* to grow.

In the extricated life, in withdrawing, in dropping back, a man gives himself a chance to know himself. He can do what he feels is right: like Montaigne, "resolved to let the world of affairs break its neck rather than twist my faith to serve it." In extrication, there's the chance to order and simplify one's life so as to have the chance to order and elaborate one's self. Not involved with others, one can become involved with self.

❦

Self-Obsession, Considered as a Virtue

SELF-OBSESSION, far from being the evil most think it is, may very well be a modern virtue. If more people were more obsessed with themselves, they'd all have less time to involve themselves in the concerns of others. A nation—even a world—of totally self-obsessed people would be a world at peace, a happy world indeed, everyone free to pursue his own main interest to his heart's content. The Greeks thought maybe the primary virtue was to "know thyself," and how on earth are you ever going to get to know yourself if you're always thinking about something else?

Montaigne was self-obsessed, always picking at himself to see what he could find. Nothing ever interested him half so much as himself. In one essay, after sorting over his vices and virtues, or lack of them, he comes to the conclusion:

> In fine, the only thing I esteem in myself is something no one thinks he lacks: which is good sense.

There has never been anyone who's developed good sense into the high art Montaigne made of it. The supremacy of his achievement is in his realization that good sense "is something no one thinks he lacks." By picking the *one* trait *everyone* thinks he has, Montaigne suddenly and superbly managed to be writing about everyone while assuming, or as he says "attempting" (his *essais*), to write only about himself.

In his essay on Montaigne, Emerson says that when he first read the *Essais*, he thought that Montaigne was writing about him—indeed he fancied he'd written Montaigne's book in some earlier life. But everyone has that feeling, that Montaigne is writing just what he, the reader, always felt himself. That's because what Montaigne wrote was good sense and everyone thinks he has it, only Montaigne got to say it first. As Emerson says in "Self-reliance": "In every work of genius we recognize our own rejected thoughts . . . they come back to us with a certain alienated majesty."

Complacency is seldom a problem with people who are self-obsessed: they get to know themselves too well to think well of themselves. And if they're any good at all at studying themselves, they usually develop a sense of humor too; they more or less have to. Self-obsessed people, for these reasons, and because they don't butt into your affairs, not having the time or interest, are by and large delightful company, as Montaigne must surely have been. If self-obsession is a vice, as most people still say, then Montaigne clearly made it into a virtue.

It may be that that is a good deal of what I'm saying you have to do to be good: you have to make virtues out of your vices. It's not so different from turning your prejudices into your principles. Montaigne's insights are a product of his self-knowledge; his uniqueness and his universality devolve from how particularly he wrote about his own commonality. Of course he says it far better: "I look on my-self as ordinary in every respect, except in the fact I look on myself as ordinary."

How Traits Should Be Elaborated

SELF-OBSESSION makes a person recognize what his qualities are, which is perhaps a necessary first step in the cultivation and development of them. To this extent the Greek dictum "know thyself" is something we can agree with. Otherwise, knowing thyself is not too great, especially if you're not too great yourself. It tends to make an end out of what should only be a beginning. I mean, what's so great, for instance, about a dippy lady who's always getting things wrong giggling when yet another of her mistakes is pointed out to her and saying cheerfully, "Oh, I'm just a *fund* of misinformation." Or some pitiable lush in a bar who just before he knocks over his glass and puts his head down on his arms in the mess mumbles in sudden self-realization, "Oh, I'm just a sloppy drunk, that's all I am." They both *know* themselves, but what's so great about it?

I want to make it clear that I've got nothing against either sloppy drunks or ladies who get things wrong. I just don't think that their "knowing" themselves makes them virtuous. To be virtuous they've got to develop their qualities to a point of interest, and thus make virtues of their vices. A really dippy lady who's always crazily getting things wrong *can* be a delight—remember Jane Ace in "Easy Aces"? Even Camus couldn't make the drunk in *The Fall* completely uninteresting, and as a novelist Camus was a great philosopher. And besides, it's at least better to be sloppy when you're drunk than when you're sober.

Aside from lack-of-sense-of-humor, which is not so much a human quality as the absence of a human quality, there's scarcely a human quality I can think of that can't be made interesting if sufficiently cultivated and developed.

What we have previously said of any given action—that its goodness or badness depends on the level of moral development it reflects—is similar to what we say of traits. No human trait has any intrinsic vice or virtue: its goodness or badness depends on the level of human development it reflects. That is—the trait must be developed, but not simply developed *in degree*. To indicate a stage of virtue achieved, a trait must be developed *toward some point of interest*.

Let's take some sample human qualities more or less at random to show how this works. Let's take, say, frivolity, lechery, honesty, ruthlessness, simplicity, and some others. You remember, of course, that none of these human qualities has any intrinsic vice or virtue; they are good or bad only in proportion to the extent that they are developed, but not *simply* developed. That is to say, it isn't simply being *very* lecherous that makes a man good; there must be something interesting or intriguing about his lechery. If you say to me of someone, "He is a very honest man," my inclination would be to say, "So what?" or even "What a bore." But if you say, "That man has a most complex and perverse sense of honesty," then I am immediately intrigued and attracted. What I'm attracted by is a stage of virtue I assume that man has achieved: he's found some original, individualistic, complicated way to be honest, some way that is presumably entirely his own ("virtue *is* individuality," remember?), presumably somewhat self-defeating ("to be good is to lose," remember?), presumably intricate and elaborate and complex ("people should be complicated," remember?).

Similarly with other human qualities, the kind of question to ask is not at all *what* the qualities are, or even how firmly or compulsively they are established in the individual, but how rich they are in nature. A man is ruthless, yes, even very ruthless; but what I want to know is does his ruthlessness have any real complexity to it? A man is innocent, yes; but is it a knowing kind of innocence? Does his frivolity have any depth? Even simplicity can be developed to a point of interesting complexity—witness Mishkin in Dostoevski's *The Idiot.*

Whatever your traits are, don't correct or change them, and don't simply indulge them. To be good, you should develop them toward some point of interest, elaborate them to some virtuous stage of attractive and intriguing intricacy.

Obligation to Self, as Against Indulgence of Self

NOTWITHSTANDING THE perils, and by and large and on the whole, it is virtually an obligation for you to become more what you are. Harold Nicolson says of Montaigne:

> He taught them [those who were weary of life at court] that every individual possessed a given personality or *maîtresse forme*, which it was his or her duty to examine, to cultivate and to exploit.

The key word in this, at the moment, is *duty*. "Duty" has always struck me as a slightly comic sense of obligation, having to do, as everyone knows, with jokes about "Have you done your duty?" in the bathroom as a child. There are many to whom time spent cultivating their own personality would seem absolutely at odds with their sense of duty. They may feel they have, or "owe," a duty to their parents, to their children, to their brothers and sisters, to their spouses, to their community, to their church, to their nation, to their corporation, to their profession, to the standards of their socio-economic class, to their house and grounds, to their neighbors, to the environment, to the Elks, to all the starving children in the world, to Ohio State or Princeton, to their old college fraternity, to keeping their new automobile in good running order, to being there when the children come home from school, to doing everything humanly possible to keep a jetport from being located in southeastern Connecticut, to the U.S. Marine Corps, and to God knows what—*except* themselves. There probably isn't anything anyone can think of that some idiot doesn't feel a sense of duty toward. But there may really be only one duty—under which all the others can be presumed to subsume—toward the self, toward shaping it, and keeping it in shape.

Now, this is a far different thing from indulging your self. People are always excusing the most inexcusable actions by saying they "owe" it to themselves. Intelligent young people give up scholarships at elegant universities to go live in messy anti-intellectual communes, stoned all day; they forfeit their future on the grounds they owe more of a debt to themselves than they do to the demands of a corrupt society. Middle-aged mothers walk out on their children and run off to art colonies to paint and get laid; they say they "have to" do this as an act of self-fulfillment, just before they slam the door. Husbands abandon families when they're forty-three, because they're bored with them; but they cite some Sherwood Anderson-type baloney about an "obligation" to find a new life for themselves "before it is too late." The loss of aspect of oneself inflicted by these acts can never be recaptured; so many in their search for self-fulfillment turn to self-indulgence and become, quite literally, "lost souls." None of this is remotely what I mean, nor Montaigne either, nor what anyone sensible could ever mean for that matter. Your duty toward your self is toward your life and your self *as it now is. Escaping* your self is in fact *evading* your duty toward your self.

Moral Maturity, as Against "Moderation" and "Consistency"

THERE IS no more fashionable virtue than the ultimate one, a principled morality. No other idea of virtue is even in it, fashionwise—nowhere *close* to in it. Perversions of Christ's teachings to say we should "sacrifice" the self—they're not in it. "Service to others"—that's especially not in it. Even that old Greek idea "moderation in all things, nothing in excess"—even that's not in it. Virtue's individuality and vice versa, they *are* both in it. Nothing else remotely is.

Morality should never be confused with moderation. Moderation is boring. The individuality that virtue requires requires in turn some difference from the normal, perhaps some eccentricity, perhaps even some excessiveness. It requires not perhaps *every*thing in extreme, but at least *some*thing in extreme. Nothing could be duller than "nothing in excess," except perhaps "everything in moderation." And moderate *people* are just the *opposite* of virtuous people. They're the ones who gave old-fashioned virtue such a bad name among interesting people. The middle—whether it is middle class or middleaged or middle whatever—almost by definition, has no individuality.

Just look at the bell curve of normal distribution:

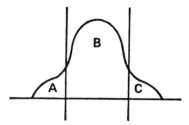

Take any human quality and put it on that bell curve. I don't care *what* it's a distribution of–*any*thing, lechery, long-windedness, any-thing. A and C are unusual and hence interesting. B is ordinary and hence dull. B is the middle and is moderate, mediocre, middling. A and C are excessive, the extremes, the exceptional. In cultivating your *maîtresse forme*, get as much A and C into it as you can; there's enough B already.

Balance is useful and desirable in the cultivation of the interesting self: not the balance of moderation (B), but the balance of alternation and contradiction (A and C). The balance I speak of is not the simple balance of stability. More at the extremes of character, at A and C, develops interest, suspense, tension in the persona.

It's cultivating contradictions in the self that achieves this inter-esting tension of opposed characteristics. Montaigne again, briefly:

> I contain in some fashion every contradiction, as the occasion provides. Bashful, indolent, chaste, lustful, talkative, silent, clumsy, fastidious, witty, stupid, morose, gay, false, true, wise, foolish, liberal, greedy, prodigal: I see myself somewhat all of this as I turn myself around–and so will everyone if he does the like.

This is the same Montaigne who a moment or so ago was telling us how he was just like everyone else because he had only one single trait that everybody thinks he has, good sense. Now he's proving how contradictory he can be by contradicting himself. It's another indi-cation of his greatness, I guess. As Emerson says, "A foolish consis-tency is the hobgoblin of little minds."

So, inconsistency and contradiction are the final embellishments to your handsome intricate ethics. There will be a principle for every contradiction, of course, just as there is a principle that determines everything you do—especially in the shady areas where explanations are so often demanded. We've seen that just as there's scarcely any act that's good or bad in itself, so there's scarcely a human quality that's good or bad. What's good or bad is the use made of the talents given—the extent to which one cultivates and exploits them. The more elaborately and intricately your traits are developed, and especially the more they are counterpoised in suspenseful contradiction, then the more intriguing your concocted, cultivated persona and the more handsome your elaborate intricate ethics. You will be individualistic, and hence virtuous.

You will also seem substantially less coherent to yourself. But that's a small matter, and perhaps can actually be something of a help to you. For the intricacies and inconsistencies and contradictions you encounter when searching for your *maîtresse forme,* the secret design in your own nature—these are what make self-obsession not perhaps fascinating, but at least bearable.

The cultivation of the self can become not just an obsession, or even just an occupation or a duty, but finally something of an art. And what one seeks in art one should create in one's self: the balanced contradiction, the paradoxes and ironies that cut two ways to reveal the truth, the foreshadowing surprisingly fulfilled, the suspended tension within the harmony, the higher equilibrium that's achieved through counterpoised extremes. Let's have Emerson for the next-to-last time: "You shall be consistent in whatever variety of actions; of one will, the actions will be harmonious, however unlike they seem."

❦

Metaphors of Virtue

THE IMAGE I think of for an intricate ethics, the metaphor that somehow insists itself on me, is of an elaborate and handsome wrought-iron fence. It is old-fashioned and elegant. It is rigid and strong like the firmly held principles that comprise it. The ironwork is hand-wrought as the ethics are self-wrought. It has loopholes galore, loopholes that seem to be decorative but are useful too, as loopholes usually are. Thus there's a sense of freedom and openness from within, but the fence looks imposing from the outside. It is elaborate but functional, protective but interesting. Its design is unique—eccentric and idiosyncratic and entirely individual. Sometimes its idiosyncrasies seem entirely random; sometimes a pattern in them seems to appear. Or perhaps it's just that the pattern is *so intricate* that although you're sure there's some pattern there you can't quite make out just what it is. Like anything intriguing, it is both attractive and hard to figure out.

And in my quest for metaphors for your virtue, I keep thinking back to Ben Franklin's great story of the speckled ax, about the man who wanted the whole axhead shiny like the edge, but when the smith made him turn the grindstone, he found that was too hard to do, so decided he liked a speckled ax best. A speckled, motley morality like that is the best we can expect of ourselves—burnished in some places, pitted and stained in others—a spotty morality. Again, the mottling *seems* to have a pattern, but one can't quite make out what it is. It has what Gerard Manley Hopkins calls:

>   *Pied Beauty*
>   Glory be to God for dappled things—
>   For skies of couple-colour as a brindled cow;
>   For rose-moles all in stipple upon trout that swim;
>   Fresh-firecoal chestnut-falls; finches' wings;
>   Landscape plotted and pieced—fold, fallow and plough;
>   And all trades, their gear and tackle and trim.
>   All things counter, original, spare, strange;
>   Whatever is fickle, freckled (who knows how?)
>   With swift, slow; sweet, sour; adazzle, dim;
>   He fathers-forth whose beauty is past change:
>   Praise him.

"All things counter, original, spare, strange . . . swift, slow; sweet, sour; adazzle, dim"—it sounds a bit like Montaigne cataloguing his contradictions, doesn't it? And so it is: for an intricately and elusively patterned character like Montaigne's is the human equivalent of the pied beauty of Nature. That a man freckle and fleck himself this way must please God no less than if He'd wrought it up Himself.

Is Virtue dull? One of the reasons men have gone whoring after

Vice through the centuries, it seems to me, is that Virtue has been presented as plain to look at and dull to be with. Virtue has always *seemed* dull, not just seemed dull to be virtuous yourself, but seemed dull to all the people who have to be with you. No offense, but I'd rather have, say, a witty malicious man in my house than a righteous dull one any day of the week—Monday, Tuesday, Wednesday, and so on. A malicious person is far "better"—better to be with, better to know—you *feel* that, so make a principle of your feeling. If you've got some misconception of Virtue as being "moderation" or "self-sacrifice," then stay away from me—your Virtue is almost bound to be dull. The word "dull" anyway has several opposites, hasn't it? If Virtue were to be all shiny and bright, to gleam all over, with halos and like that, it would be sort of embarrassing; but Percival was the last one, so far as I know, who had *gleaming* as any kind of major problem. But Virtue won't gleam *or* be dull in that sense. Virtue sparkles spottily, with the pied beauty of Franklin's speckled axhead, but with an *edge* that is "sharp," another opposite of dull. "Your goodness must have some edge to it,—else it is none," Emerson says, and a wonderful use of "edge" it is too. I assume he meant it both in the sense of having some sharpness and bite, some effective cutting edge, and in the sense of having bounds and limits to your goodness that contain it within your self and your life rather than extending it to all mankind.

But the real irony in the centuries' halfhearted quest for Virtue is that Virtue isn't dull; it's that other opposite of dull, *interesting*. I don't want for a minute to seem to be suggesting that Vice isn't interesting. You don't get *me* saying that; Vice can be *very* interesting. But it is *a* vice to *be* dull. Similarly, while it may or may not be interesting to be virtuous, it is indubitably virtuous to be interesting. That's why Virtue isn't dull. That's why the cultivation of the self is the *sine qua non*, the without-it-you're-not-in-it, of being good.

Let me try to pull together some of the threads of this tatterdemalion, unconscionably long-winded argument. If the *self* is to be examined, cultivated, exploited, made intricate and interesting this way, then the *life* must be extricated, ordered, and simplified. There is no time *for* and there is no point *in* any other involvement. Life should be simple, we've said; people should be complicated. Now we see that the one requires the other. Life should be simple *so that* people can be complicated. "Never [even] inquire what's going on in Constantinople," said Voltaire, *so that* (he implied) you can "cultivate your own garden." "Let us," said Montaigne, "disentangle ourselves from the clutch of things which hold us elsewhere and keep us from ourselves" *so that* we can "cultivate our own authenticity" and not neglect our primary duty, which is to develop our own "*maîtresse forme.*" Virtue is in the self, there's no use looking for it anywhere else–especially not these days.

Montaigne would assure you that it's not so bad living in–or on the outskirts of–a society that's not just corrupt but corrupting. He gives this reason:

> . . . ill luck is good for something. It is not bad to be born in a depraved age: you will get a reputation for virtue at a bargain price.

But there are other advantages too. First, of course, it means you can get to have a really swinging time if and when you need or want to. The vice is there, *available*–not just fleshly pleasures you just dream about or yearn for, but *there*–and you can actually choose to have them or choose not to have them. This fact, that the choice is yours, is related to the second, and (*of course!*) far greater, advantage to living in a depraved age. In such a time you get to make your own virtue. In being "good" you don't have to conform to some puritanical society's idea of what's good behavior–which, chances are, wouldn't be a way of life you'd like very much. In fact, you don't have to conform to *anything*; in fact just the opposite. An ethics created in a value vacuum is an act of spontaneous generation, done entirely from within, made up entirely from whole cloth, as they say, *all by self,* a child's delight. For your handsome, intricate, self-wrought *maîtresse forme* and the intricate ethics that devolve from it–for your individual self that *is* your virtue–you get all the credit and glory yourself. To be good in the bad society is the ultimate in individuality, and hence the ultimate in virtue.

Virtue *should* be fashionable, God knows; but I still don't see how Addison managed to *make* it so.

L. RUST HILLS has been the fiction editor of *Esquire* for nearly thirty years. He makes his home in Stonington, Connecticut, and Key West, Florida. He has published articles and essays, taught writing and literature, and furthered the careers of writers too numerous to mention.

HOW TO DO THINGS RIGHT has been set in a digitized version of Walbaum. Designed by the German typefounder Justus Erich Walbaum in the early nineteenth century, it shows the characteristics of the "modern" typefaces that originated with Bodoni and Baskerville and were subsequently introduced to France by Didot. Like its cousins, Walbaum is notable for its refined serifs, its upright stresses, and its classical contrasts between thicks and thins. With its slightly more open feeling and wider letters, Walbaum is more elegant than its peers, its contours softened by the sensitivity of the craftsman who cut it.

The book has been printed and bound by Haddon Craftsmen, Scranton, Pennsylvania.